RADIANT AWAKENING

Humanity's Transformational Journey

Ruth Eichler, MSW
&
Lesley Carmack, MS

Radiant Awakening Publishing
Three Rivers, Michigan

Originally published by Inkwell Productions
First Edition January 2014

Revised edition published by Radiant Awakening Publishing
October 2017

ISBN: 978-0-9992617-0-5

Book and cover design by Julie Taylor.

Printed in the United States of America

Endorsements

This luminous work is a journey into the frontiers of spiritual, scientific and personal quest. To read it is to awaken into the mystery of our origin, the revelation of soul-crafted living and the potential future of those who take seriously the rise of the Sacred Feminine. The book itself is a Mystery School offering training and inspiration for seekers who would prepare themselves to be making a difference in both inner and outer worlds." — **Jean Houston, Ph.D., a widely recognized leader of the Human Potential movement and author of many books including *The Possible Human* and *the Wizard of Us*.**

Radiant Awakening joyously unveils the wisdom and power of the Sacred Feminine and her guiding role in the process of Collective Ascension now occurring worldwide. It affirms the sacredness of all life by offering profound insights into the nature of an emerging global consciousness guiding humanity's evolution. The synthetic ideas and principles contained in this masterful treatise will be of value to seekers and practitioners of all spiritual orientations. Highly recommended to all individuals and groups of servers creating a new worldview of heart-mind synergy and interdependence. — **Karl Maret, MD, President of Dove Health Alliance**

This is a landmark book – close to being perfect. It is a genuine education, and everyone should read it. — **Elmer Green, Ph.D., Professor Emeritus, author and cofounder of the Menninger Voluntary Control Program, ISSSEEM, AAPB and the Council Grove Conference.**

An extremely important aspect of health and vitality includes consideration of the growth of the soul and spiritual alignment through the journey of life. This book, written by two experts in transpersonal psychology, is an encyclopedic treatise, which allows the reader to both understand several important concepts as well as formulate a compass in which to personalize individual growth in this crucial aspect of health that has impact on both a personal and global level. This book is essential reading for every individual who wishes to lead a deeply meaningful life. — **Leonard Wisneski, MD, FACP, Chairman, Integrative Healthcare Policy Consortium, Faculty of The University of Colorado, Georgetown University, George Washington University**

Both Ruth Eichler and Lesley Carmack have brought together a lifetime of personal experiences, cutting edge science, stories from the lives of real people and broken through the barriers of this three-dimensional consciousness into the radiant realm of the soul. Each one of us will find aspects of our own treasured awakening in this book. — **Gladys Taylor McGarey, M.D., co-founder of the American Holistic Medical Foundation and is internationally known for her pioneering work in holistic medicine, natural birthing and the physician-patient partnership.**

We dedicate this book to all fellow travelers
on the spiraling wheel of ascension.

Acknowledgements

We would like to acknowledge all of our kind friends, courageous clients, wise mentors, patient teachers, and loved ones who have seeded this book through their example and presence in our lives.

We especially thank our husbands, Jim Carmack and Vic Eichler, who supported us all along the way.

Table of Contents

Introduction

Acceleration

Humanity is in a time of great acceleration of consciousness, sometimes called ascension. Many people feel this quickening. Even though we are in the midst of this rapid change, most human beings — even those very aware and sensitive to energies — can only experience glimpses of what this acceleration means for humanity as a whole. Ordinary life proceeds: we wake up and brush our teeth, walk the dog, and make breakfast. Yet on the subtle level we might "get" something that we can't yet quite name or identify.

Acceleration is not an event, even though some believed that December 21, 2012 would herald either the end of the world or enlightenment for all. Instead, we are offered the opportunity to allow our highest natures to take up residence within ourselves, for humanity is only now at a level of consciousness to enter into and participate with this eternal potential. More and more people have the capacity to see beyond the blinders of cultural and historical conditioning. We can choose to live intentionally from a more integrated, higher state of consciousness. This new awareness coupled with deepened, inner, heartfelt emotional experiences help us realize that we are the creators of our own destinies and that we assist in the co-creation of the future.

We are on the verge of a new level of expression on this earth as we break free from old patterns and align with new possibilities that were previously seen as impossible even though this might not appear to be the case when reading the news. This time of rapid shifting is a collective, evolutionary impulse and not just a quest for individual liberation. Millions yearn for release from the constraints of materialism and the illusion of separation, even though many others fight to keep the old paradigm in place. Insights rapidly impress us with ways to join together to embody and express higher states of love, wisdom, and power that assist evolution rather than self-protection or aggrandizement. We suddenly know that Life depends upon it! This is a time of unprecedented change.

Clarissa Pinkola Estes, author of the best-selling book, *Women Who Run with the Wolves*, countless other stories and leader of many seminars, offers this sage advice:

> "We are needed, that is all we can know. And though we meet resistance, we more so will meet great souls who will hail us, love us and guide us, and we will know them when they appear. … Struggling souls catch light from other souls who are fully lit and willing to show it." [1]

Phoenix

We have used the phoenix on our cover, as the phoenix bird has been a symbol of renewal, rebirth and immortality since ancient times in many different cultures on several continents. The phoenix is an expression of the spiritual emergence that is occurring in humanity at this time. It flames forth as the glorification of spirit being made mortal. According to some traditions, Spirit enters into the condition of Being in order to experience and understand itself.

In Asian cultures the phoenix is considered to be a feminine counterpart to the dragon, hinting at our premise that the Sacred Feminine is an integral part of the ascension process. The higher, fiery Christ consciousness emerges and enlightens the form. The mysteries are then revealed through realization.

Ruth received a vision that included the Black Madonna and a phoenix, which became a background story for a dance that occurred for several years. In this dance, called the Phoenix Dance, dancers prepared for an afternoon and evening. At 3 a.m., the dancers were called forth with the sound of bagpipes. They danced to the sound of drums and other instruments until dawn, releasing old patterns for themselves and for the planet. At dawn, through special ceremony, the dancers burned up the old, celebrated the new and then danced ecstatically.

In most of the myths, the phoenix bird returned to the nest of its birth every 500 years — a rare event portending great happenings. She sits on a nest and is consumed by fire that has been ignited by the sun. The old form of the phoenix becomes a pile of ashes, just as our consciousness moves from one level to another, dying to one way of being so that the next level can be known. One is consumed in the fire of love and rises in the expression of the divine. From these ashes arises a beautiful new phoenix that graces the next era. So it is with us as we enter this unprecedented time, and we become the phoenix as we ignite others by living our truth. In various myths the cry of the phoenix is said to be a beautiful song. We hope that the phoenix's beautiful song penetrates the pages of this book, inspiring all of us to the journey of rebirth.

Phoenix
Are you willing to be sponged out, erased,
Canceled, made nothing?
Are you willing to be made nothing?

Dipped into oblivion?
If not, you will never really change.
The phoenix renews her youth
Only when she is burnt, burnt alive, burnt down
To hot and flocculent ash.
Then the small stirring of a new bird in the nest
With strands of down like floating ash
Shows that she is renewing her youth like the eagle,
Immortal Bird.

~ D. H. Lawrence.[2]

Different "Voices" in This Book

Each of us have had experiences that we can share as stories related to the various themes of this book. Ruth also had many pages of writing that correspond with our message. We have chosen to include excerpts from these stories and writings, as they represent different "voices" from the general narrative.

What we are calling Ruth's "Sacred Beloved" messages are a series of teachings or guidance that Ruth received especially in the middle of the night. This series of conversations spread over a number of years but was mostly concentrated in a six-month period of time. She would awaken, sometimes hearing the sound of a doorbell or a phone ringing without anyone being there. She would then sit in a chair and "listen" to and write down whatever guidance was given through inner hearing or inner knowing. She chose to call the "speakers" the Sacred Beloved because of the loving presence they expressed, and she was "told" that this was a group of beings, not a singular guide. She would often ask questions, and they would lovingly respond. These "conversations" have a different tone from her other writing, so we are including selections from some of these pages when they are relevant to the material in the book.

We similarly include passages from "Ruth's Writes," as they represent the human experience of learning about and incorporating some of the messages of this book. These excerpts will simply have Ruth's name at the end. No one suddenly goes from A to Z in understanding or embodying certain truths, and these writes speak to that process. Ruth has been writing with Caroline Whiting's facilitation for many years in a special method described in Linda Trichter Metcalf and Tobin Simon's book, *Writing the Mind Alive: The Proprioceptive Method for Finding Your Authentic Voice.* Each session begins with a lighted candle, a bell, blank paper and pen, and Baroque music. This method involves writing and exploring what one "hears" during the Write with undivided attention. One listens to the unfolding of one's inner unconscious and spiritual life. Once "heard," the life is changed.

Since birth Lesley's personal and spiritual life has included inner teachers from the non-physical world that have given teachings, offered guidance, and directed her in the healing of others in the outer world. These inner dialogues have not been recorded on paper but rather inscribed in her awareness. We, therefore, do not have the same number of writings for Lesley, although we have included some of her life stories that have her name at the end of each. However, her voice is embedded in all of our text throughout the book.

In choosing what to include in this book we followed the guidance we have been given. We do not know the entire picture or all the answers, and we remain curious and open to purpose even beyond what our minds can presently know. As we began the writing of this book, Lesley received this poetic guidance from the inner world:

> "As you depart for a long journey, notice what is needed in your basket. Trust the Self; the way of skill and

knowledge is given the boatman. Stand tall in the boat to see the way. Listen for the song within that meets the song without. The ancestors, of whom you are a part but no longer recall, have placed that song there. Do not seek to remember; do not revere the past. Sing peacefully what has been given you, and then enter the boat without turning and find the wind."

We stand with you, the reader, and find the wind that moves our collective sailboat.

The Sacred Feminine

With the acceleration of consciousness has come an awareness of the Sacred Feminine in her many forms. Images of the Divine in feminine form ranging from Our Lady of Guadalupe from Mexico and the Americas to Kwan Yin from Asia have deepened their appearances in consciousness. Books have been written about the rebalancing of the masculine and feminine ways of being in the world. Along with these shifts in perspective is the sense that the sacred is not something "out there" but is immanent to all life and that we are all intimately connected. We will further discuss the Sacred Feminine, how it is manifesting and how it is related to the process of acceleration and ascension in this book. We will more deeply explore the Black Madonna and Sophia, two of the many different archetypes or manifestations of the Sacred Feminine and how they relate to this time of increased consciousness.

The invitation to participate in this momentous planetary change — both the possibility for a rapid increase of consciousness and the rising of the Sacred Feminine as a context for it — occurred before birth and is ours to acknowledge, integrate and embody.

It is our hope this book sheds some light on these new possibilities, even though we do not pretend to have all the answers.

Some of the "answers" probably remain forever beyond the scope of what the human mind can grasp.

Like many of you, we felt the stirrings long ago and have listened intently for clues and cues as to how to move through these calls to this impulse. We have been impressed by images of the Sacred Feminine and have been called to many interesting experiences, not having a complete understanding at the time of the larger meaning that only gradually emerges. We share small parts of our own story throughout the book, not because our story is unique but because we believe it may be true for many of our readers as well. Our understanding has come from unraveling our experiences and appreciating the guidance and wisdom that have been offered to us along the way.

> *"The essence of motherhood is not restricted to women who have given birth; it is a principle inherent in both women and men. It is an attitude of the mind. It is love - and that love is the very breath of life.... For those in whom motherhood has awakened, love and compassion towards everyone is as much part of their being as breathing."* — Ammachi [3]

Sophia Emerging
Ruth Eichler

Sophia calls. She moves and breathes in Lesley's and my inspiration to write. She has called me for years, though I didn't always know that. It was She who was tapping at the door, whispering through the eaves when I was inspired to hire a photographer many years ago to take professional photos, later made into slides, of many versions of the

Divine Feminine. I didn't realize Sophia was embedded in all of them.

It is said that She was here before the earth was created. It was She who graces the Sistine Chapel, held by God who reaches His finger to Adam. As the goddess of wisdom, She somehow didn't feel the same as the juicy, heart-filled Black Madonna. The Black Madonna has often been portrayed so mournfully, crying tears for humanity's woes. Sophia seemed somewhat able to live above the fray. Together they are whole.

What would Sophia want expressed in the book that Lesley and I are writing? I'm curious on many levels: what will Sophia reveal to us next?

A Second Edition for Radiant Awakening

In the intervening time since the first edition was published, we have continued to ask, "What is emerging?" just as you also probably have. How do we respond to these times of crisis and "radiant awakening" with presence and engage ever more deeply in the vitality of living? Joseph Campbell would have told us that if we follow our bliss we would be on a track that has always been there, just waiting for us. Many wise teachers have "What we think we create, what we feel we attract, and what we imagine we become." Doors open at the right time with the right people and experiences. With deep gratitude, such has been our experience.

We share our understandings and journeys, not as belief systems but as transformative experiences that lead to the realization that all is sacred. We often speak through story telling that includes swimming with dolphins, building a peace chamber, dancing in ceremonial trance states, meeting and receiving initiations with great teachers such as the Dalai Lama, Mother

Meera, and Ammachi. We have sought the Black Madonna and Isis in foreign lands and interacted with nonphysical beings from the angelic and other realms.

Ours is a combination of the hero's journey and surrendering to an unfolding discovery of all that is, both within and without such as is the feminine journey. Deeply listening to the nudges of intuitive insight, we set out not for just meaning and experience of being alive as Joseph Campbell suggested but to birth a new Radiant Awakening within us. We do not wish to prescribe a way for others to follow, but rather to share possibilities and motivation to interpret the mysteries through ever-arising lenses of promise. We share our experiences in the hopes that they have resonance and inspiration for your own life. Together we join in a transformational journey that involves creating, attracting, imagining and becoming.

ENDNOTES

1. Clarissa Pinkola Estes from her article, "You Were Made for This" posted at www.wanttoknow.info/youweremadeforthis

2. This poem is cited on many different websites. The first Google search for this poem brings up Wikipedia, which says that *The Phoenix*, a pacifist quarterly originally dedicated their journal to D. H. Lawrence who wrote "The Phoenix" poem in 1932.

3. Ammachi's address upon receiving the 2002 Ghandi-King award in Geneva, Switzerland. Her address is listed for sale at www.store.theammashop.org and is written on many other websites.

Chapter 1
The Ascension Process

When an old culture is dying, the new culture is created by those people who are not afraid to be insecure. — Rudolph Bahro

The Meaning of Ascension

Ascension implies experiencing a higher level of consciousness than is generally available to the ordinary human mind. We might imagine the Russian nesting dolls and begin from the perspective of the tiniest doll in the middle of all of them. From that perspective, reality is limited to the space inside the next larger doll. If we were able to move from the perspective of each doll into each bigger doll's view, we would eventually have a much greater perspective of reality by the time we were looking out of the largest doll's eyes. So it is with human perspectives of consciousness.

We are all born with a divine fire in us. Our efforts should be to give wings to this fire and fill the world with the glow of its goodness. — Abdul Kalam, former president of India

We might say that the smaller dolls are "asleep" to the higher realities that exist beyond their awareness and that higher consciousness is becoming more and more "awake" to greater realities including the possibility of union with the Divine. Of course, we are still human, and the limitations of the human mind may prevent our understanding of ultimate cosmic consciousness while in this form. Nevertheless, we can continue to expand our awareness into higher realms. Rumi eloquently exhorts us to not go back to sleep in a favorite poem, of which the first two lines are, "The breezes at dawn have secrets to tell. Don't go back to sleep! [1]

The I AM presence — that eternal flame of our Being — does not change. What changes is our perspective and from which aspect of our being we are identified. We are generally attached to our bodies, emotions and mind, and we must realize that we are none of that. Ken Wilber in his book, *Grace and Grit,* reminds us that:

> "Your primordial mind is unborn and undying. It was not born with this body, and it will not die with this body. Recognize your own mind as eternal, one with spirit." [2]

In this book, we will sometimes interchange the word ascension with acceleration; each is a process, although the word acceleration implies that the rising of consciousness is occurring at ever increasing speeds.

Times of Acceleration

We are in times of enormous, unprecedented change on this planet. One kind of acceleration is simply the speed of change as can be seen in technological innovations that come and go so quickly that the latest device is out of date within a year or so. However, in this book, we use the word acceleration to mean rapid shifts in consciousness. Millions of people pray for peace and for the wellbeing of others out of love and compassion rather than fear. The old clashes with the new. The people in nations ruled by dictators rise and demand freedom, even though the old guard quickly tries to smash the revolutions that began through tweets and texts.

Much has been written about what has been called the "ascension process," meaning that humanity is at a stage of evolution in which far more human beings than ever before are experiencing states of consciousness only available to a few enlightened beings or as occasional mystical and peak experiences by some. Therefore, these states of consciousness are now becoming potentially accessible to the "average, ordinary" person as our lenses to "see" are expanded. We now have the opportunity to see wholeness in others by meeting them in and through our own sense of wholeness. As we rediscover our own sacredness, the world changes in response.

> *The pulse of the future is greater than the tug of the past.* — Pir Vilayat Inayat Khan

With greater and greater complexity and diversity on this planet, there is greater potential for more refined expression. There is more opportunity to come into contact with wisdom from many different cultures and paradigms. The Dzogchen stream of Buddhism believes that we can become enlightened in one lifetime. Perhaps that lifetime is now if we choose it.

Of course, just learning and drawing from the many diverse traditions available to us does not alone create ascension, nor does the world become a utopian paradise. Instead we develop new capacities of feeling, sensing and thinking that allow new possibilities of living in cooperation with each other and of co-participating with spirit. Ascension requires that we attune our "antennas" to deep universal wisdom principles and become more aware of the consequences of our choices. Our attention to what we intend matters. What we put our attention on generates more of the same. Ascension, like the view of the hawk, can be high and wide and can hold a worldview in which all beings and all life is sacred.

In the past great teachers such as Jesus and Buddha were surrounded by disciples who could only observe and report their experiences at a level of consciousness that was available to them at that time. Therefore, a more complete understanding of their teachings was limited by the constraints of the reporters. Those few who have walked the earth before as enlightened beings served as living examples, but they did not have a collaborative collective of others to participate in the teachings at the level at which they were demonstrated.

In indigenous tribes, the shamans and medicine people cultivated very specific and special skills that are believed to allow them access to the subtle worlds, skills that were not accessible to most in their communities. One story or myth says that only the shaman of the tribe could see ships that first arrived on the shores of the Americas, as they were accustomed to "seeing" and reading patterns that were unavailable to others. According to this story, the people not trained as shamans in the tribe did not see something that was outside of their knowledge base or paradigm.

The knowledge and skills that the shamans possessed were often obtained through great personal sacrifice and years of training. Eons of shamanic practice have created a field of energy and information that is now much more accessible to humankind. It is no longer necessary to be the son or daughter of a shaman in order to access this wisdom. Some people tap into this field intuitively, and the Internet makes much information available that used to be secret. Many tribes have now agreed to share their formerly closely guarded ways of living in the non-ordinary realities to those who sincerely seek that wisdom, even though some members of these tribes disagree. Much of this knowledge is now available to all who would turn their inquiry and attention to it even though just receiving the data certainly does not make a shaman or wise being. Not only are practices and training required, but also one has to learn how to embody these principles with integrity.

On an individual level, the first person that ran the four-minute mile did what people thought was impossible, yet once that had occurred, many others began to break through the old barrier. The possible human is now viewed on living room televisions and even more frequently on YouTube. It extends our capacity to believe and know what is possible. Whether it is a three-year-old conducting an orchestra or a ninety-year-old man lifting weights, our psyche is opened to greater possibility. The edge is constantly moving to incorporate expanded potential. Whereas we used to talk about the Possible Human (as Jean Houston so eloquently titled a book), we now are becoming the Possible Collective. What was once only available to the very few is now possible for the many. Laurel Keys shares our appreciation for those who came before us in a line from her prayer:

> "I accept this Gift with gratitude for all those who have carried and held the Light and Truth through the ages, that I may now have this privilege of understanding, freedom and joy." [3]

Yet no one said it would be easy. Humanity has habituated to fear, and resistance to the unknown and change often are responses to fear. For some, fears and questions arise at the thought of ascension. Will I turn into a blob if I am one with

Source? Will I lose my unique identity? What will it really mean for my life? Who will I be?

In order for transformation to truly occur, fear must be faced rather than ignored or prematurely transcended. Ignoring fear leaves us bereft of objective discernment about what needs to be paid attention to and what can be managed in another way. Premature transcendence occurs when someone mentally hangs onto spiritual beliefs and pretends or denies that they have human fears and foibles. In her beautiful *Co-Creation Code Deck* of cards, Rowena Pattee Kryder advises:

> "Cease trying to become fearless or to get away from, or defend yourself from fear. It is time to enter into it, face it and stare it down into dissolution. ... You now have the inner strength and love and power to transform the very root of fear in your psyche. Allow! Allow!" [4]

Love and imagination can transform fear, for fear is essentially love held back for any reason. What isn't love eventually returns to ash. We will present many options in this book that hopefully assist us in ascending with more grace and ease, in spite of fears.

> *When you have a profound awakening that you are part of a cosmic process that is going somewhere, you find yourself falling more deeply in love with what is possible than you are with what has already happened.* — Andrew Cohen [5]

The Process of Ascension

We are learning to live into the opportunity of heightened awareness and quickening vibrational fields. From this view we become aware that, though we each have our own gifts, we are like cells in one body, a unified system, each cell with differentiated roles and yet one with the whole. We are bringing the differentiated, magnificent, and un-watered down expression into the Whole. Because we are aware of the Big View and of the Whole, we are like a liver cell that is not competitive with a kidney cell. We work together for the good of the Whole.

This Shift, meaning shift in consciousness, that is occurring allows the individual cells of the body of humanity and the Earth to realize the Oneness of the entire system. This results in motivation to move in an interdependent way that is resonant with the highest vibration of the Whole. The single heartbeat directs the overarching expression of the parts through resonance. This acceleration means that we are extending into a more inclusive view, thus re-identifying as Wholeness rather than as a part. The worldwide web via the Internet and social media expands our capacity to believe and know what is possible.

On a more personal level, Deepak Chopra shares some of the clues that one has ascended to a higher level of consciousness, which he calls enlightenment:

> "The first symptom is that you stop worrying. Things don't bother you anymore. You become light-hearted and full of joy. The second symptom is that you encounter more and more meaningful coincidences in your life, more and more synchronicities. And this accelerates to the point where you actually experience the miraculous." [6]

Acceleration does not require everyone on the planet to ascend; nor do we believe that this transformation will occur overnight. Each individual does not have to demonstrate extensive growth in all spheres or to be totally enlightened. Ken Wilber speaks about the tipping point in which only 10 percent of the population is needed to influence the entire society. As more people continue to integrate and assimilate, the whole will move forward. Many diverse parts moving forward create an updraft that carries others who share the impulse. It is like the sounding of a bell that some hear consciously, and some respond to unconsciously by being receptive to the field. There are no chosen ones. We choose to respond or not to respond to the call. It is available to everyone who hears the sound. The Shift occurs as a critical mass realigns with the note.

Each individual's attitudes and actions impacts the whole, and Clarissa Pinkola Estes reminds us of the importance of the small things that, when all added together, shift the critical mass. We don't even have to know what our individual contribution makes. She says:

> "Ours is not the task of fixing the entire world all at once, but of stretching out to mend the part of the world that is within our reach. Any small, calm thing that one soul can do to help another soul, to assist some portion of this poor suffering world, will help immensely." [7]

Barbara Marx Hubbard, long a passionate advocate of co-creation and the shifting of consciousness, includes an article by Jack Canfield, in her book about 2012. He says:

> "We are at a time in human history when all of us need to step up and have the courage to create the life we envision, that in our heart of hearts we know is possible. We all need to tap into our deepest essence, discover our true-life purpose; transcend our fears, limiting beliefs and self-doubts; and live lives of passionate self-expression. When that happens, we will truly create heaven on earth." [8]

Partnership with the Great Ones

Different traditions have spoken about extraordinarily advanced beings, some who walked the planet and some who remained in non-physical realms. These Great Ones have variously been called "The Hierarchy," "Cosmic Ascended Masters," or "The Great Initiates." Jesus and the Buddha exemplify such ones who came into physical form. In the past, these masters, teachers, highly evolved beings and streams of light stepped down the enormous power of the Divine so that humanity could receive this great dispensation without being over-activated or perhaps even destroyed. Humanity has now evolved to a state where it can receive these energies directly without the intermediary role of the Great Ones. These blessed ones are still readily accessible and available and can be intimate partners in the next Great Adventure.

This is different from receiving "channeled" information from somewhere else and then bringing it to our lives and the world. Instead, we are enlivened by the loving, co-participation. It's almost like being in a sensory deprivation chamber in which the person lies in water that is exactly the same temperature as the body, and even though one is aware of being a separate consciousness, the distinction of an edge is present but not experienced as "other." Body and environment are experienced as one unit. So it is with the intimate warm, loving interaction with these beloved ones.

Paula Underwood, an Iroquois Indian, teacher and storyteller, reported that her father said, "What is impossible for one is possible for many." He spoke of a rope that bound a whole people together with unified purpose and said that an individual in an isolated context could never have devised it. "Only the presence of many hands could assure such a purpose," [9] he said. We might today use the words "group synergy." The new paradigm honors partnering rather than winning.

The heightened energies entering humanity during this time appear to come into groups of people. When experienced as a group impulse, the energies can be shared, interpreted, assimilated, integrated and redistributed. Some individuals and even systems may be destabilized, but the entire field can compensate and realign with a sufficient amount of vitality. No single individual mind can interpret the complexity in an appropriately expansive way. Only the group field can hold with enough coherence and refinement to re-stabilize in a new way.

Vibration

> *Really only one thing exists, and that is the breath of God in a state of movement creating the vibration of matter.*
> — Joseph Rael

Since ancient times, sages from many different traditions have spoken of a vital, vibratory force that animates matter. In China, it is called *ch'i* or *qi*; in Japan — *ki;* in India — *prana* or Shakti. The ancient Egyptians called it *ka* while the ancient Greeks named it *pneuma*. They all knew about vibratory energy associated with breath and with the cycles and seasons of the earth. They acknowledged that it constantly flows and continuously impacts matter at molecular, atomic and sub-atomic levels. In the Western world, we are becoming more conscious of our connection to a deeper, vaster aspect of our being through awareness of subtle energies. We can revitalize ourselves by intentionally calling forth these increased frequencies and learning to manage and direct them intentionally.

The Sufi master, Hazrat Inayat Khan, often spoke of the vibratory nature of existence, as in the following quotation:

"All things and beings in the universe are connected with each other—visibly or invisibly—and through vibrations a communication is established between them on all the planes of existence. ... In the innermost plane they all become one." [10]

The ascension process implies that the vibratory rate of humanity is accelerating. The capacity to adapt to and thrive with increased vibratory rates within our being is implicit in humanity's acceleration of consciousness, for consciousness itself vibrates at varying frequencies. Thoughts and emotions vibrate at differing rates of speed and interact with both matter and energy. Human intention thus activates subtle energy vibrations, and so intention is one of the ways in which we actively participate in the universe — consciously or unconsciously. Vitalizing our lives with sound and light enhances our ability to heal and build a sturdier "vehicle" for the higher vibrations that mark this time of ascension

Most scientists and mystics today would agree that all of creation is vibratory in nature and that matter is not as solid as once thought. There is only one unified field, everything vibrating within it and interconnected, from the air that we breathe to the seemingly solid chair upon which we sit. Einstein showed us that energy is indestructible and that matter speeded up becomes energy and visa versa when slowed down. The physicist, Heinz Pagels, said that the visible world is the invisible organization of energy.

> *The finest vibrations are imperceptible even to the soul. The soul itself is formed of these vibrations; it is their activity that makes it conscious.* — Hazrat Inayat Khan [11]

> *God's breath is the power, the energy of*
> *matter in movement. Because of this on-*
> *off-on-off pulsation, we become matter.*
> — Joseph Rael [12]

Mystics such as Joseph Rael, a Native American visionary and shaman, have long known of our intimate connection with the vibratory nature of all creation. In his book, *Being and Vibration,* he reports that his people knew they were "a vibration that had come from the Infinite Void...and were made of appearing and disappearing light that came from the inhalation and exhalation of God's breath." [13]

Our five senses can only pick up a tiny part of the spectrum of vibrational frequency. For example, our eyes can only perceive color in a very small region of the electromagnetic spectrum labeled "visible light." We can see the colors of red through violet but not ultraviolet or infrared which have wavelengths not seen with ordinary eyes. We also cannot visually perceive gamma rays, x-rays, microwaves or radio waves. Unless we are gifted with clairvoyance, clairaudience or other psychic powers, most of us do not experience with our five senses the energies that are transmitted from healers, human thoughts that permeate space, nor the plethora of electromagnetic frequencies emitted from cell phones and many electronic devices, to name a few. Yet many of these vibrations can be scientifically measured. Vibrations of the human energy field can now be recorded and photographed by various devices such as EKG, EMG, EEG, MRI, and X-rays. Using the Superconducting Quantum Interface Device (SQUID) that detects ultra-sensitive magnetic field around the body, Dr. John Zimmerman at the University of Colorado has measured significant increases of magnetic fields that are emitted from the hands of healers who are intentionally sending energy to another. [14]

James Oshman, Ph.D., author and energy researcher tells us that:

> "The most exciting property of the living matrix is the ability of the entire network to generate and conduct vibrations. Modern biophysical research is revealing a wide range of properties that enable the body to use sound, light, electricity, magnetic fields, heat and other forms of vibration as signals for integrating and coordinating diverse physiological activities, including those involved in tissue repair." [15]

Physicists such as Fabiola Gianotti, who was one of *Time Magazine's* 2012 "Persons of the Year," will continue to push the boundaries of our understanding of the Universe. She, along with other researchers at the European Organization for Nuclear Research, better known as CERN, have discovered the Higgs boson, a particle that gives other fundamental particles their mass. This particle has been touted in the media as the "God particle." One researcher simply called it the "genetic code of the universe," which has been elusively pursued by scientists for over fifty years. Gianotti leads a team of 3,000 researchers from around the world for this project, but she is not called "project manager" or any other such title. She, and the other team leaders are simply called "spokespeople."[16] The Sacred Feminine is making itself known in our language and ways of seeing the world.

Becoming New
Ruth Eichler

And all things shall be made new. Sometimes my little self questions all of this — perhaps I'm deluded. And yet in every new paradigm there are those who see glimmers before mainstream does. I think of the book, Galileo's

Daughter, in which Galileo recognized the reasonableness of the earth rotating around the sun, and some others began to sense the correctness of his vision of the new paradigm. Yet many others, including the institutional Church, strongly resisted the new paradigm and even punished Galileo for daring to espouse a new view.

New Birth
Ruth Eichler

After my first Sun/Moon Dance: I feel almost wobbly, like a butterfly that has just barely crawled out of the cocoon. I need to rest here in silence. I also had the image of a small baby that needs to be sheltered in rose petals. I feel brand new. It is a peaceful, but also newborn feeling. Something soft hums inside. Tears are close to the surface.

The Edge of the Light
Ruth Eichler

Mary Morrisey says, "Go to the edge of the light you see." It reminds me of another quote that rocketed off of a page many years ago and instilled itself into my brain. That one said, "God never shines the light to the end of the path, but there's always enough light to take the next step." I need to remember the promise in both of these quotations. I know I'm in the midst of a huge transition but don't quite know what it is or how to bring it about.

Once again, the challenge and solution seem to be right in front of my face, and I can't quite grasp it. I know my identification with work has been pervasive throughout my life, and even knowing this, I still can't seem to figure out a graceful way to slow down. I'm not sure what the fear is.

I want to shift, though, without having to be incapacitated in some way in order to get the lesson.

I spent two months looking at the ceiling in 1982 with a herniated disc until I got the message and committed to leaving the public school system as a teacher by going half-time over the next two years while building my new practice. Astrologically, the signs are as radical as they were in 1982, and I still don't have the new life in tow.

Perhaps that's the problem — the shift is not about the little self deciding and towing the life to a new shore. This is about the little self becoming subservient to a Higher Will. The little self can only go to the edge of the light it sees.

Spiraling Up
Ruth Eichler

By unity I mean that place where there is no "we" or "they." Is that still a concept for me rather than a felt reality? I'm quite sure that unity doesn't mean lack of individuation— though at some level we probably do merge back into one big light or where the droplet of ocean water is one with the ocean again. What I do know, though — at least for now, is that I trust and desire to spiral up, to turn over my personality level stuff, including the addiction to busy-ness.

Oh, the Mysteries of Life
Ruth Eichler

The Zero Point Field, as articulated by Greg Braden and others in quantum physics refers to the oneness of all life. The image that keeps recurring for me is one piece of woven fabric with every molecule of every thread embedded with light. Tweak one part of the piece of fabric and every part of the fabric shimmers with ight. A Blue Morpho butterfly breathing in Costa Rica affects my breath.

The Light of Christ Consciousness
Sacred Beloved

"A new to the earth plane energetic is being brought in at this time. This is the Christ consciousness so often discussed. This brilliant frequency is already infusing your stratosphere and the grids that have been put in place. The grids had to be in formation first in order for the Christ light vibration to be held. Some individuals are now accessing light from this grid, infusing their own being. You may ask that you be infused with this light — in joy, safety and harmony. Feel that you are held in the Light of Christ."

The Gathering Basket
Sacred Beloved

"Sit for a moment for this gathering, this collection of joyful impulses. You have heard the words repeatedly the last few days, 'In Christ all things are made new.' Only allow so much to enter this atmosphere at a time, or it burns. We want illuminata (this is not a typo — it's what I heard) instead. Illumine your cells. Bathe them in the light of Christ. All things are made new. You do not need to understand all that is transpiring. You can say, 'I welcome the light of Christ.' Even if this light being received is the Christ light, you are welcome to call upon your beloved Kwan Yin or Our Lady to help disseminate this light. You may now take your gathering basket and disseminate this light to others and to the earth through prayer and through your being. May these mandalas of Christ fill your basket of being with joy, fragrance and delight. May you rise a new being in Christ."

Smiles and Joy from the Christ Light
Sacred Beloved

"You are partaking of the Christ light that you are invoking for others. Remember that the very act of evoking this ancient yet new light/energy helps bring it further into this dimension. All who are evoking this Christ light are calling it forward. Those who have been saying the Great Invocation for decades have helped simply by saying the words, "May Christ return to earth." This energetic is imbued with joy. One cannot but touch the hem of the garment of anyone imbued with the profound love and light without feeling joy."

Equilibration from the Divine
Sacred Beloved

"You are beginning to experience the power of equilibration that comes when the divine love seeps into the lower three vehicles (body, emotions and mind). We also experience awe and joy in the presence of this light. The fullness of this light is only now being made fully manifest in our world. This light is not just the light that Jesus emanated while upon earth or indeed even upon his death, although his resurrection did call upon a similar light. The Christ light now coming into form has been created, born anew from an explosion at the far corners of the universe. The power and glory of this new light extends beyond anything yet known in the universe. The power of the creator is upon us. Instantaneous miracles are at hand, and all things are made new. Yet some people will not withstand seeing the new paradigm. The people who are not open to the new experience of the Christ light will be buffeted in the wind. Pray for their wholeness because indeed you are all part of one hologram."

Christ Light and Cellular Mandalas
Sacred Beloved

"Partake of this light as you would an exquisite meal, ingesting the light and allowing the light to permeate every cell, every molecule. Indeed the radiance of this light makes all things new in its presence. These mandalas are in essence tiny holograms of the Christed being. This is what is meant by 'Rise a new being in Christ.' The little mandala holograms are poly-dimensional and contain the sound of the spheres as well. Listen with cellular ears and you shall hear this symphony of joy. Christ descends on earth to all that will partake. A separation is taking place between the old and the new. Groups praying and meditating help cohere this light into their own beings so that the energy is more fully functioning rather than a being a latent force. Prayer and meditation awaken this light which is now available everywhere."

ENDNOTES
Chapter 1: The Ascension Process

1.   Coleman Barks, *The Essential Rumi.*

2.   Ken Wilbur, *Grace and Grit: Spirituality and Healing in the Life and Death of Treya Killam Wilber*, (Shambala Publications, Inc., 1993, p. 401).

3.   Laurel Keyes worked with a group of women called the Fransisters, and they developed a lovely prayer called "*The Fransister Daily Communion.*"

4.   Rowena Pattee Kryder, *Co-Creation Code Deck,* (Crestone, Colorado: Golden Point Productions, 2003, Card No. 52).

5.   Andrew Cohen, "In Love with the Possible," www.andrewcohen.com.

6.	Deepak Chopra, *Synchrodestiny: Harnessing the Infinite Power of Coincidence to Create Miracles,* (Rider, 2005).

7.	This quotation comes from an article Clarissa Pinkola Estes posted on www.wanttoknow.info/youweremadeforthis.

8.	Jack Canfield's article "Self-Actualization, Life Purpose and the Evolutionary Shift" in Barbara Marx Hubbard, *Birth 2012 and Beyond: Humanity's Great Shift to the Age of Conscious Evolution* (Shift Books, 2012, p. 190).

9.	Paula Underwood, *The Walking People: A Native American Oral History,* (San Anselmo, CA: A Tribe of Two Press, 1993, p. 817).

10.	Hazrat Inayat Khan, *The Mysticism of Sound and Music: The Sufi Teaching of Hazrat Inayat Khan*, (Boston and London: Shambhala, 1991, pp. 126 and 129).

11.	Ibid., pp. 120-121.

12.	Joseph Rael, *Sound: Native Teaching + Visionary Art,* (San Francisco & Tulsa: Council Oak Books, 2009, p. 2).

13.	Joseph Rael, *Being and Vibration.* (Tulsa: Council Oak Books, 1993, p. 23).

14.	This research is cited in www.scribd.com.

15.	James Oshman, *Energy Medicine in Therapeutic and Human Performance.* (NY: Butterworth Heineman, 2003, p. 281).

16.	*Time,* December 31, 2012/January 7, 2013.

Chapter 2

The Sacred Feminine: An Integral Part of the Ascension Process

> *If there is to be a future, it will wear the crown of feminine design*
> — Sri Aurobindo.

Sacred Feminine and Divine Feminine

The Sacred Feminine permeates us with love and wisdom, encouraging us to live in the present moment. She honors the language of the heart as well as the reason of the mind and is imbued in everything.

There is no limit to Source or to Love, which are both the same radiating force. The more that we relate to and know that we are one with Source, the more we can create a new world, for love without condition is our essential nature.

If we are open, we can remember this truth and choose love rather than fear. Unconditionally accessible to everyone, whether or not they are aware of this Presence, the Sacred Feminine is as close as one's breath offering a reciprocal exchange that acts as both catalyst and support in our daily lives.

What is the difference between the "Divine Feminine" and the "Sacred Feminine"? For us, the Divine Feminine refers to specific deities. The Sacred Feminine refers to that essence of the divine that permeates everything from the atoms in our bodies to the far-flung stars across the cosmos.

As one of the definitions of "divine" means "being a deity," the words "Divine Feminine" often connote to the mind feminine deities such as Kwan Yin, Tara, Pele, Kali, the Virgin Mary and hundreds of others. We will later discuss some of these manifestations of the feminine aspects of God.

The word "sacred," deriving from the Latin "*sacrare*," means holy. Sacred, also meaning "entitled to reverence and respect" or "perceived as divine," includes deities such as the ones above and extends beyond them. The Sacred Feminine implies that which is holy in everything, including all feminine qualities expressed in their highest manifestation, whether in the form of a of a feminine goddess or a quality such as receptivity. By its very nature, "Sacred" means that a higher vibratory field is available with greater magnetic appeal and field of influence.

The Sacred Feminine opens our ability to recognize that the divine is an intelligent consciousness and a life force that exists within all life independent of gender. It is immanently accessible to each one of us because it is indwelling rather than something external only available through a few "chosen" beings or scriptures.

With awareness of the Sacred Feminine, we open to the qualities of nurturance, compassion, unconditional love, inclusiveness, beauty, and intuition. We can let go of our need to know. We affirm the creation aspect of the Sacred Feminine — that ability to bring forth new life, to birth new consciousness into the world. We cherish all of earth's beings, whether they fly, swim, crawl or walk on two, four or more legs — to express it as indigenous peoples often do. We affirm life, its mystery, beauty, bounty and at times its terribleness.

The Sacred Feminine is becoming unveiled, and these qualities are an integral part of the ascension process. It is through the Sacred Feminine that the unity of all beings is revealed and that we feel in our hearts, minds and bellies great compassion, love, creativity and wisdom.

The Sacred Feminine Is an Integral Part of the Ascension Process

The Sacred Feminine is essential for the ascension process. She holds the archetypal patterns that are becoming actualized. She holds the impulse through which new patterns are emerging, liberating us from old, outworn ways of being. In the East, the Feminine has long been associated with birth, transformation and rebirth, the nurturing and sustaining influence in the universe.

The living presence of the feminine as the Divine opens us to the sacred in all things, allowing the possibility of transfiguration. We are becoming conscious of the sacred that is embodied in all matter. As we open to light and love, we are infused with the light of higher consciousness, which transforms form, and we begin to realize that we are Light and Love. In order to realize Light, we have to have an experience of it. The mysteries are then revealed to us through the creation process occurring within and around us every moment. Thus, as we embody love and are permeated with light, the Divine is revealed to us, and our form becomes an expression of love itself. Therefore, the Sacred Feminine provides the container, integral to the ascension process. The Sacred Feminine is both illumined substance and also a process inherent in transformation. As Creatrix, we are birthing individuated expressions of Source, of Creator.

This gestation period that we are collectively moving through now is impressed in the psyche and the form nature of humanity. We then become more transparent to each other with nothing hidden, for only the authentic self shines through.

While the Sacred Feminine is an integral part of the Ascension process, paradoxically she also expresses an awakening impulse that descends from the etheric into physicality. This impulse activates the divine that already is hidden in body, mind and spirit — in consciousness itself.

Qualities of the Sacred Feminine That Especially Relate to Ascension

Drawing in and Magnetizing

The feminine draws in and magnetizes. Humanity yearns for intimacy and connection with the divine, especially at this time of ascension. The yearning calls forth the divine impulse, thus deepening our evolutionary emergence into a higher order. Everything is available; it just has to be invoked or called forth. As we draw into deep inner silence, we become more aware of what resides in our hearts, including the longing. Magnetizing awareness of Spirit into our being assists in gathering aspects of us into a coherent whole. Our central core is strengthened, and we become more sensitive to our connection and oneness with each other. Ascension requires this larger, more global view.

Humanity has yearned for a greater light, and this invocation has called forth the higher consciousness that is emerging. In the past, this longing was often expressed as reaching toward the unobtainable Sacred Feminine through devotion to something "out there." Today the Sacred Feminine can be drawn in and embodied.

Receptivity

As we become receptive to our own Presence, matter itself is animated. Having longed for the Light, now receptivity, an aspect of the Sacred Feminine, creates the container to receive Divine Light or higher consciousness. It makes space, allowing Humanity to be impressed with the incoming fiery impulse. As we yield and receive, we are quickened just as a flower receiving sunlight is catalyzed to unfold its full potential. Our readiness to receive creates a vibrant field, ready for activation. Yet the act of receiving does not equate with passivity because opening and softening require volition. Living within the still point, pregnant with possibility, aligns us with the Soul and the incoming Light.

Often equated with the heart, the feminine is a womb of contemplation and insight through its ability to receive. The capacity of the heart is not only receptive but also has the ability to give rise to action. The heart is also thought to be integrative and transformative, and the feminine underlies all of the processes of nature.

Angela Farmer, a beloved, elder teacher of yoga, often suggests that her students ask the body if it is ready to receive the breath. Openness, softness and receptivity ease or prevent pain caused by resistance. Attachment to unconscious patterns or cherished beliefs, whether in a yoga posture held by an individual or doctrines held by a large group of people, cause pain because of resistance to incoming possibility. The Sacred Feminine Presence allows transformation to occur with little or no pain. The feminine state of receptivity creates an interlude or space, a kind of silence that allows a shift to be experienced without friction and dissonance. That which is not needed falls away.

Your head will say, "Don't go any
further." But your heart will send you
right into the hum, where you will be
swallowed by it. You will stand there
and think, "I am the center of the uni-
verse where everything is sung to life."
— from the novel, *Secret Life of Bees*[1]

Deep Listening

Deep listening is another aspect of receptivity. Without judgment, we listen through mind, body and heart for what is present. Welcoming in all that presents itself creates the space in
which to listen to the deeper essence. We don't have to invent
or deny. We listen to what is inside in order to go beyond. We
don't push ourselves into ascension; we listen to what is arising
and respond from that inner awareness. Listening into silence,
into the cave of the heart, brings us to a place of stillness so that
we can deeply hear.

The heart has the capacity to step down the incoming fiery
impulses, and as we listen, we can more safely receive the new
dispensation. The Sacred Feminine allows a deep, felt experience of what is emerging rather than restricting it to a mental
construct. Eventually we realize that there is nothing to push
anymore because we have become that impulse, ignited by the
One.

Richard Miller, a long time yoga practitioner, teacher and de-
veloper of iRest, makes awareness accessible to so many. He
says:

> "Awareness is like fire. Fire purifies, and awareness pu-
> rifies. Fire doesn't judge. It simply burns away the im-
> purities of what is placed within its presence. ... When
> we rest in and as the fire of awareness, we cease trying

to be different and are open to the unknown, welcoming without goal or intention." [2]

The feminine is sometimes known as the silent witness because in the silence we are directed to our inner knowing. The feminine reveals itself in this precious, spacious opportunity between the in and out breath, in the cave of heart. A sense of goodness, wellbeing and joy emerge when we listen to our heart without pre-conditions. New, effulgent, illumined possibilities arise into our consciousness out of this blessing.

> *Souls of prayer are souls of deep silence — interior and exterior silence.*
> — Mother Teresa

> *Flowers teach us the charm of silence and thus the self-giving which demands nothing in return.* — The Mother, [3]

Silence
Ruth Eichler

I recently forgot to make room for sacred silence while away on a trip. In silence, I return to presence of Pure Being. In the silence, I hear the divine speak to me, "Be still and know that I am God." That message easily becomes overridden by the noise of interesting conversations just as the bird songs and chimes fade in the noise of traffic. I want both silence and interesting conversations, and I want to be fully present to myself so that I can also be present to the other. If I don't remember to claim my silence, inner peace begins to be covered by dust.

Only then can I remain true to my own inner rhythm. Nikos Kazantzakis' quotation again comes to mind: "Find the absolute rhythm and follow it absolutely." When that is true,

I can be falcon, storm or song as the need arises rather than rising slightly out of my body and missing the essence of the moment. I'm glad the river-of-silence reminder comes to assist me in finding and following that deep inner rhythm. That's most likely the river through which the Great Mother speaks.

Resting in the Cave
Ruth Eichler

The snow, Solstice, the late rising and early setting sun, and the bone-chilling cold call for silence and interiority. The cave of the soul calls for rest, dreaming and just being. Hibernating bears must hear this call. Seeds lying dormant under the frozen ground blanketed with snow respond to the need to lie quietly while every cell knows what it is to become once spring rains and warm sunrays have awakened them from the dreamtime. I feel this call, too, though I haven't yet hunkered down into my own cave of the heart. I long for that silence — to hear the prayer of the soul as Mother Teresa called it.

Wholeness/Inclusivity

One of the qualities of the Sacred Feminine is the capacity to embrace wholeness, to know and to be the hologram rather than just the parts. This view allows us to join with the complexities of the quickening, energetic fields of potential in which we are immersed. The quickening is both outside and inside, so we are changing and moving to a higher vibratory rate just as the earth is changing. The Sacred Feminine doesn't leave anything out; all is included. She unites polarities — fierceness with compassion; creation with destruction; light with dark; birth with death.

Complex components are brought into a whole — unity out of diversity — so that the whole is much greater than the parts. This is demonstrated in many ways such as in the examples that follow. Numerous levels of consciousness can express simultaneously and synergistically. We can move from the belief that you are my brother or sister if you think like me to we are all in this together. Many people see the divine in all things — animate and inanimate — trees, rocks, plants, animals, land formations, human beings, the earth, gods and goddesses. Spider Woman appears in numerous Native American cultures, and she attempts to weave the great diversity of life into one integrated whole. The Sacred Feminine creates a spacious context that can hold both the teachings that have come down through the ages along with impulses that come from subtle realms far beyond mental fields. All dimensions are included — those that include time and space and those that are non-local and timeless. This vast wholeness opens to a greater reality than we have previously known.

Modern science has helped us understand that wholeness is a reality, and this conceptual understanding helps us to experientially know and embody it. Beginning with Heisenberg and Einstein, physicists claim that in subatomic physics, the universe can be understood only as a whole that is expressed in patterns of relationship. Werner Heisenberg discovered and described what he called "the observer effect" in which the observer brings about a fundamental change in the thing observed. In other words, the whole is one web in which the application of consciousness to something generates manifestation.

The scientific term "coherence" means joined together harmoniously into a unified, smoothly functioning, whole. A laser is an example of the power that is created by coherence of waveforms. HeartMath researchers believe coherence applies to every possible domain, from the invisible, subatomic quantum level to the Universal. A coherent field implies order, structure, harmony, and alignment within and amongst systems — whether in atoms, organisms, social groups, planets, or galaxies. Thus, every whole has a relationship with and is part of a greater whole, which is part of something greater again. Because of this organizing potential, coherence is aligned with the Sacred Feminine impulse.

These scientific discoveries delightfully correspond with our understanding of the Sacred Feminine, as She is alive and present — not just as personalized images of a female but as what those images represent: a vision of life as a sacred whole in which all life participates in mutual relationship. We have to see ourselves whole first — not just as diverse parts that come together. It depends upon the viewpoint. Sophia originates at the point of wholeness, and when we look through her eyes, there is not "us and them" but a unified whole that contains all of the unique, magnificent parts.

> *When there is no more separation between 'this' and 'that,' it is called the still-point of the Tao. At the still point in the center of the circle one can see the infinite in all things.* — Chuang-tzu

Compassion

> *If you want others to be happy, practice compassion. If you want to be happy, practice compassion.* — The Dalai Lama

Compassion can belong to both masculine and feminine aspects of human beings. Many of the hundreds of goddesses around the world express compassion as one of their primary qualities. For example, the Black Madonna and her counterparts — Our

Lady of Guadalupe, the Virgin Mary, and Isis — are available to all who call upon them, and all suffering and pain can be offered to these divine beings. Likewise, Kwan Yin, one of the most revered deities in China and Korea is known as the Lady of Infinite Mercy. Stories of her say when she was ascending into heaven, she heard the cries of the world and vowed to return to alleviate suffering. The many variations of Tara in various Buddhist traditions speak of the same kind of deep compassion.

Compassion can be differentiated from empathy in that empathy means feeling what others feel, whereas compassion means to co-suffer and goes beyond empathy. Compassion gives rise to an active desire to alleviate another's suffering while empathy may simply mean feeling the other's pain. Although this kind of compassion can look like codependence at one end of the continuum, we are speaking about the end of the continuum in which alleviating another's suffering comes from an altruistic place and does not involve sacrifice of self. When one is relatively integrated as a person, then one can experience compassion and reach out to help another while still being aware of one's own needs. At a less evolved place, reaching out to help at the total expense of one's self can drain the person dry. When one is aligned with a higher power, the river continues to flow and one is enriched.

Most major religions of the world have some variation of the Golden Rule. As renowned Jewish Rabbi Hillel said in the first century, "That which is hateful to you, do not do to your fellow. That is the whole Torah. The rest is the explanation — go and learn." The principle of ahimsa in Hinduism means, "Do no harm." In order to apply the Golden Rule with heart, we must be able to see others and ourselves from a larger perspective. We go beyond doing no harm and are also motivated to lend a helping hand.

Thich Nhat Hanh, a Vietnamese Buddhist monk, has helped many drop their rigid defenses and soften into compassion. He says that if we really imagine what it is like to be the other person who we consider to be the cause of our suffering, we realize that we could be that person. Compassion arises naturally, transformed out of anger. He has rephrased the first precept of Buddhism to fit modern times:

> "Aware of the suffering caused by the destruction of life, I vow to cultivate compassion and learn ways to protect the lives of people, animals, plants and minerals. I am determined not to kill, not to let others kill, and not to condone any act of killing in the world in my thinking and in my way of life." [4]

The Dalai Lama has devoted his life to being an example of compassion and to teaching others of all religions and backgrounds how to help people alleviate their own suffering and that of others. He assures us that compassion is not passive but altruistically acting to help others with both wisdom and loving-kindness. Wisdom helps us understand what is occurring for the other, and loving-kindness requires that we empathically realize our interconnectedness and interdependence with others. [5]

Ascension without this kind of wise and loving compassion born of our recognition that we are part of one fabric would only be grasping for the unattainable. Compassion is an essential component of the ascension process.

Nurturance

As we discover the mystery of the Sacred Feminine, we can experience the nurturing qualities of the Loving Mother. Clarissa Pinkola Estes counsels that the Blessed Mother:

> "...continues to live as a huge, not always invisible but palpably felt, force in our world right now. ... Even in dark times She was there, for she is the quintessential Mother who does not, will not, leave her children behind. ... She is here with us, has always been here with us, will always be with us no matter which 'here' we cross over or into." [6]

Although the premise of Estes' book is that we are entering a time when humanity has the capability of becoming a co-creator with the Divine, we still are human beings who can be comforted by the presence of the Divine Mother. We find safety in her arms, and we especially appreciate this caring presence in times of turbulence. We are not alone in our vulnerability. We also learn that we, too, can embody the Divine Mother and provide protection for the vulnerable, no matter what. The Divine Mother is immanent within each of us.

Intuition

> *The only real valuable thing is intuition.*
> — Einstein

Intuition — that ability to know and sense what is beyond usual mental conscious understanding — has long been considered the realm of the feminine. Over-thinking separates us from our true nature and keeps insight and inspiration at bay. Sophia allows the radical wisdom of the heart to flow into awareness, gifts desperately needed in these times. Rather than polarizing intuition with intellect, what is needed is the union between the positive aspects of logic and intellect and the feminine, receptive qualities of intuition. This reconciliation assists in bringing about the transformation that is being called forth that the world needs.

Beauty

Beauty can help us see the world through new eyes and opens us up to startling moments of delight and awe. Who hasn't caught their breath upon seeing sunlight glistening on water or a rose window of stained glass or the radiant smile of a beloved friend or upon hearing a birdsong, an amazing piece of music, or the melodic rhythm of a poem? Or perhaps the beauty seen in the bark or by witnessing scintillating intelligence such as an Einstein equation, whether or not we understand it.

> *For the world is not painted or adorned,*
> *but is from the beginning beautiful; and*
> *God has not made some beautiful things,*
> *but Beauty is the creator of the universe.*
> — Ralph Waldo Emerson

Whatever we perceive as beautiful opens us into a state of receptivity. We become vulnerable and open, expressing who we really are. Once we know that beauty is in all things, we let down our guard, for beauty is our essential truth. The light of the soul shines through the eyes and our very being.

The "Sweet Mother," who worked side by side with the Hindu mystic, Sri Aurobindo, loved flowers, communed with them, and daily gave them to members of the ashram. She said that flowers are open and receptive to everything that surrounds them whether sunlight, wind, or other aspects of nature. Flowers also have a spontaneous, expansive influence on everything that surrounds them. They radiate joy and beauty. When asked if flowers contained a sense of beauty, she answered that the vital element found in organic life creates the sense of beauty. She also said that if we can consciously move to a level of awareness that flowers do unconsciously that we would experience a spontaneous awareness of beauty and feel the unadulterated joy of being. [7]

Any experience of beauty can be a method of transmission of joy and delight, an opening to higher states of consciousness and a sacred feminine way of communicating.

Piero Ferrucci, a Psychosynthesis writer and teacher, reminds us of another essential gift of beauty:

> "Beauty plays a central role in our decision to *be here*. The more we can perceive beauty in our surroundings, and also inside us, the more we will feel at home and glad to exist." [8]

Though we can be awestruck while seeing something incredibly beautiful by ourselves, beauty is often enhanced when shared with one or more persons. After conducting many interviews with people about beauty before writing his book, Ferrucci found that relationships often provide fertile soil for the aesthetic experience to arise. The Great Mother must smile as we come to this recognition.

The Navajo people believe that as a grand cosmic concert, the universe is filled with peace, harmony and beauty, which they call "hozho." When disharmony has occurred and "hozho" has been disrupted, they participate in a beautiful healing ritual called the Beauty Way Ceremony. Out of this ceremony comes the Beauty Way Dance, now made available to others as one of the Dances of Universal Peace. The words are:

> I walk with beauty before me. I walk with beauty behind me I walk with beauty above me. I walk with beauty below me. I walk with beauty all around me. As I walk the beauty way. My thoughts are beautiful,

> Ho! My words are beautiful, Ho! My actions are beauti-
> ful, Ho! As I walk my life the beauty way. [9]

Ruth's mother used to smile rapturously and express delight
any time she was surrounded by flowers whether they were
wild Queen Anne's lace from the meadow, pansies from the
garden, or an amaryllis opening its magnificent petals. When
Alzheimer's disease had ravaged her mind, we knew that she
was no longer herself when Ruth's father brought fresh daffodils from the garden and her mother didn't even notice. Only
her inner beauty remained though in some distant realm.

Many Manifestations

> *The greatest gift that we may offer to*
> *one another is the gift of ourselves, in*
> *wholeness, completeness and truth.*
> — Greg Braden

Throughout the ages, many faces of God and Goddess have
graced every culture and religion in the world. Manifestations
of the Divine Masculine and Divine Feminine have variously
been perceived as teachers, prophets, saviors, companions, and
taskmasters or as deities without physical form. All have left
their mark upon the human psyche, some only for a period of
time in which that manifestation was predominant and some
beyond that time. Isis, for example transcended the epoch
in Egyptian history in which she was revered, as she is still
honored by some people today. All of these expressions of the
divine are part of the Divine Whole — beyond time and space.
The Divine Feminine allows us to see all of these manifestations as aspects of the One. She is the circle that holds yin and
yang, each part containing aspects of the other.

Unlike Sophia whose presence generally is experienced without a specific image of her Being, the many representations

of the Divine Feminine are often depicted in art — statues, figurines, paintings, drawings, and carvings. In this way, the Divine Feminine becomes more personal and accessible, as she looks more like we humans do — at least in imagery — and yet with transcendent qualities.

These goddesses range from the pristine goodness of Mary, Mother of Jesus, to the fierce destroyer goddesses such as the Egyptian Sekmet, the Hindu Kali, and the dakinis of Buddhism.

Each of them — sweet or fierce — assists in our birth, comforts us in the sorrows and joys of life, and participates in our death. Some are most known for their comfort and solace; others for their ability to heal; others for their fierce slashing away of obstacles to the truth. In any case, these many manifestations from every part of the world and every time period reflect the religion, culture and historical time in which they did or do flourish. And, if we look at their mystical qualities beyond the trappings of a particular tradition, they all carry profound love in their essence.

> *Think of this great fount of archetypes as a stream of energy that assumes whatever forms our consciousness can understand.* — Layne Redmond [10]

Perhaps we can gain a recognition that these energies live within us from looking at the myriad aspects of the Divine Feminine. We no longer need the devotional expression that continues to keep these qualities external to us. We can now embody the goddess within us and realize "I am That."

Some traditions, such as certain lineages of Buddhism, have long had a practice in which one uses sacred art — tankas — with the image of a divine being as a way to begin to identify with its qualities and to imbue them into one's own being. These

Beings represent levels and states of divine expression that are either unfamiliar to us or are not yet not fully developed within us. As we meditate with them and relate to their energy and substance, they reveal qualities that we can embody. Glenn H. Mullin, Buddhist writer, teacher and translator of classical Tibetan literature says:

> "Buddhists credit spiritual art work with having the ability to both embody and transmit spiritual energies. After a sacred piece is completed, it is consecrated by means of ritual and meditation. This process calls spiritual energy into the image, much like nectar is poured into a vase. The image becomes what the Tibetans call a ten, ... now a vessel holding transformative spiritual energies." [11]

Whether or not we use practices such as the above, the time is now to reclaim these qualities and to live them through our hearts. The impulse of the Divine Feminine makes available to us all the qualities of the heart: safety, vulnerability, courage and creative expression. More and more of humanity is coming into a greater expression of the heart chakra. The qualities of the heart can be identified as Divine Feminine attributes.

Through much of our history, the goddess has been seen as "other" with qualities unattainable to mere mortals, even though she might be seen as a divine comforter or companion. In ancient times when the feminine goddesses prevailed, she was worshipped and adored and was experienced as beyond what humans could fathom.

"The sky and its stars make music to you. The sun and the moon praise you. The gods exalt you. The goddesses sing to you." — Inscription on a wall of the Temple of Hathor, Dendera, Egypt[12]

The world shifted into another age, and for centuries she became more or less veiled. Even in traditions that continued to honor the feminine with visible images of goddesses such as in Buddhism and Hinduism, for example, most of the teachers and lineage holders were male. The relationship with the divine, whether Divine Feminine or Divine Masculine, remained more like a parent-child relationship with perfection beyond the reach of human beings. In these times of acceleration, we have achieved a level of maturity to be able to re-engage in a co-creative relationship with the Divine, and the Sacred Feminine is paving the way.

Sacred Feminine Is Becoming More Visible

Another world is not only possible; she is on her way! On a quiet day, if you listen carefully, you can hear her breathing. — Arundhati Roy

The Sacred Feminine is becoming increasingly unveiled in our time. Dozens and dozens of books — both fiction and nonfiction — have been written about the many faces of the Divine Feminine in recent years. Goddesses and feminine manifestations said to be divine from every culture and time have appeared in print, movies, dreams, inner images and outward signs. From the Black Madonna to Mary Magdalene to Isis to Mary to Spider Woman to Brigid — to name only a very few — images and experiences of the Divine Feminine have begun to permeate the culture and our lives. Many have spoken of her presence, and we have experienced unexpected, sometimes silent nudges and revelations. Central to this awakening is a caring and loving concern for humanity and the earth and a heartfelt quality of spirituality.

Sue Monk Kidd's book, *The Secret Life of Bees,* a novel about a girl learning that Mary lives in the heart, became a bestseller and a movie. This is only one example of the proliferation of stories that speak to the longing for a feminine expression of the Divine. Many books about Mary Magdalene have been published, such as Margaret Starbird's *The Woman with the Alabaster Jar,* all revealing that she is not the woman that has been portrayed by the Catholic Church and others down through the ages. These books speak of the forgotten feminine with the hopes not only of redeeming a woman's life but also of restoring balance and harmony to the world. Andrew Harvey has written several books that honor and breathe life into the stories of Divine Feminine goddesses and teachers from several religions. These are only a tiny representation of the books, stories, and movies bringing Her into view.

> *Listen to me, Lily. I'm going to tell you something I always want you to remember. Our Lady is not some magical being out there somewhere, like a fairy godmother. She's not the statue in the parlor. She's something inside of you.* From the novel, *The Secret Life of Bees* [13]

Over the last several decades, hundreds of visitations or appearances of a Divine Feminine Being, especially Mary, have been reported on several continents. For several decades, Mary, sometimes called "Queen of Peace," has presented herself and given instructions to the world through six local youths (now adults) in Medjugorie, Bosnia-Hercegovina. The messages are staggeringly simple: open your hearts and seek reconciliation with others, love everyone, and pray to Spirit from your loving heart. Thousands of pilgrims have visited Medjugorie since the first visitation from Mary in 1981.

The peasant, Juan Diego, experienced a vision of Mary in 1531, and her shrine is in Mexico City. Besides roses falling from his cape, the image of Our Lady of Guadalupe was imprinted on the inside of his cape and for nearly 500 years, millions of visitors — now over 20 million per year — have made their way, most on their knees, to this shrine.

In Lourdes, France, Bernadette Soubirous experienced many apparitions of Mary in 1858, and many thousands of people have reported healings after visiting this shrine that remains a popular pilgrimage place, visited by over 6 million people each year. These are just a few examples of the many places where such experiences have been reported, all of which have been accompanied by numerous stories of miraculous healings.

Unusual events have also occurred in various places around the globe ranging from images of the Virgin Mary appearing in unexpected places to many reports of statues of Mary weeping, reportedly sometimes tears of myrrh. Miraculous healings have also occurred at these sites. These reports have been aired on BBC, CBS, and other stations and in many newspapers. However, it is not her appearance that is important, for she is always here and always has been, even if veiled. Such phenomena create a greater openness to possibility rather than being just an end in and of themselves. They help open awareness of what the unseen world impresses upon us. The softening and expansion of our hearts creates greater spaciousness within us. We become more aware of the sacred, and these internal changes are more important than external phenomena.

Clarissa Pinkola Estes urges us to consider these appearances as follows:

> "What made some minds on earth think that a Mother of such magnitude would only appear just every now and then? What crabbed, narrow, deadly thought would deign that a devoted and loving mother would be stingy with her visitations to give guidance and knowings to her beloved sons and daughters? ... No loving mother follows such a dictum." [14]

On other fronts, scholars such as Maria Gambutus have studied ancient goddesses in recent decades, giving us a greater historical perspective of the Divine Feminine. Many people report dreams of a Divine Being in a feminine form coming to them. As just one example, a woman named Tataya Mato shared many of her drawings, dreams and inspirations with the famed analyst, Marion Woodman, which later appeared as a book, *The Black Madonna Within*. [15] Gradually, the Sacred Feminine is becoming known again, though often hidden in most Western cultures for many past generations. Whether reports of present day phenomena, scientific discoveries, new explorations of the meaning of the Divine Feminine, or stories from ancient cultures, our vast access to instantaneous information from around the globe makes the revelation and unveiling of the Sacred Feminine even more accessible to the collective.

We see the rise of the Sacred Feminine in increasing awareness and movement toward community in which collaboration and cooperation predominate rather than competition and dominance. Community gardens are increasingly sprouting into reality across the country, the produce of which is often available to everyone. This spirit of cooperation and interdependence, both qualities of the Sacred Feminine, shine forth in a multitude of books such as the one edited by Angeles Arrien,

Working Together: Producing Synergy by Honoring Diversity or the one by Juanita Brown, David Isaacs and the World Café Community, *The World Cafe: Shaping Our Futures Through Conversations That Matter.* Countless YouTube videos and websites promote sustainability, inspiring innovations that call upon people to work together. We now have the opportunity for the "survival of the fittest" mind-set to be revolutionized by "we are all in this together, and together we will find the solutions needed."

The *Course in Miracles* defines a miracle as simply a shift in perception. Transformation occurs when we open to infinite opportunity, and the real miracle is when we re-identify with the Self and a larger possibility, thus shifting our perspective, rather than just looking through the eyes of the "small, personality self." Thus a healing occurs in mind, body and spirit, sometimes as a peak experience and often as a sustained way of being. In either case, a miracle has occurred, and a miracle is occurring with the Sacred Feminine. Her time has come.

She's Always Been Here
Ruth Eichler

I recall the Japanese story about the Zen master who pours tea into the cup of a student until the cup overflows. The master says that the man isn't empty enough to receive the teachings. In what way have I needed to be emptied? This new learning is not of the head kind. This is more experiencing or knowing at a cellular and heart level. The Black Madonna is like that. She crept up on me or into me. Or perhaps She was always there—it just took a long time for me to discover her.

She made appearances in my consciousness on various occasions. Once Our Lady of Guadalupe in Mexico impressed herself upon my inner world when I visited her church in 1980. Pilgrims walked for blocks on their knees to see Her. I vividly remember seeing the outdoor shrine, which tells the story of the man named Juan who had the initial vision of Her. On that same trip, I visited a humble, simple little convent in Mexico City. I sat on a wooden bench at a plain table eating fish that these simple nuns had prepared for me and the man who accompanied me as translator. Even though I'm not a Catholic, tears streamed down my face when I entered their tiny chapel, not realizing then that I had been in the company of Our Lady herself.

A Visit to Mother Meera: a Story of Discovery

> *How long the road is but for all the time the journey has already taken how you have needed every second of it in order to learn what the road passed by.*
> — Dag Hammarskjold [16]

Our journey to deepen and understand the mysteries of the Sacred Feminine together began in 1996 with a serendipitous set of circumstances that was not orchestrated by our conscious minds. The story that follows was the beginning of our friendship and shared soul journeys. While these are personal stories, we believe they are resonant with millions of people who have found their own way to the Sacred Feminine.

Ruth: My heart caught on fire when I read a story in 1990 about Mother Meera, a woman born in India who was reported to be a manifestation of the Divine. At that time Mother Meera occasionally came to North America, and I vowed to put everything aside to visit her the next time she came to America. However, after settling in Germany, Mother Meera no longer ventured out of that country. Though I continued to feel the impulse, the compelling desire mostly slipped into the unconscious. Then one day in early 1996 I saw an astrology client who said that she had just returned from visiting Mother Meera in Germany, and the flames soared again.

A short time later at the Council Grove Conference, an annual gathering of kindred spirits, I invited anyone who might be interested in visiting Mother Meera to gather at a table during a break. Lesley wandered by and joined the small group of women, only because it was the least crowded table. Though she didn't want to interfere with the dialogue and had never heard of Mother Meera, the transmission that came into her heart caused her to join in the conversation.

Lesley: Unlike Ruth's response of putting aside everything in order to have this experience, I decided that a number of "tests" or synchronicities would have to occur if she was to commit to this pilgrimage. The airfare would have to be provided by frequent flyer miles that would overlap with the dates that Ruth had chosen. The costs would have to be within a tight budget constraint, and the rental car would have to be not only afford-able, but the driver would have to have an international drivers' license. I also called a friend, Judy Homer Wisneski, know-ing that this would be an important transition in her evolution, something I didn't see for myself. Judy agreed to go with the same spirit of surrendering to the impulse that Ruth had felt. Somehow all of these things fell into place, and I found myself on an airplane flying to Germany.

Ruth: I called our daughter, Kris, who had attended her junior year of university in Germany to see if she would like to go with us on this trip. She eagerly agreed, perhaps seeing the trip as a Mother-daughter adventure. I called Mother Meera's ashram to make reservations, as the number of people permitted at the darshans (the times of being in her presence and receiving her blessings) was strictly limited. Uncharacteristically someone answered the phone and said, yes, the dates were available, and the flight tickets were easily arranged. Kris became our driver, navigator, and translator. In fact, Frau Russman, owner of the B&B where we stayed, only spoke with Kris because she was the only one of us who spoke German.

Both: Sitting in darshan with Mother Meera activated us and subtly opened our hearts. This influence facilitated our being immersed in the essence of the sacred throughout the trip. Surprisingly, the four of us received another taste of the Divine Feminine in just being together. We sat together for several days over five-hour breakfasts telling our stories and experiences, laughing and crying together. These stories carried greater depth and scope than everyday conversation. We began each morning's conversation by drawing a card, calling upon wisdom in a state of openness and being guided by these synchronous insights.

These conversations were not cathartic but created a resolution of old ways of knowing and opened the way for greater insights that inspired each of us. We created sacred space without structure or agenda and extended the edge of our belief systems through sharing stories that carried a deeper spiritual context within our lives. We listened deeply to each other, dialoguing from a place of equality and mutual respect, as we softly revealed our souls. The depth of presence allowed the gentle release of old assumptions and limitations. These conversations were also animated and joyful in spite of a few sorrowful tales. No one was the leader as we organically and spontaneously moved into a "circle" process, known by various names, that is born of a deep, sacred feminine impulse.

Looking back, we see that the Divine Feminine was guiding us into direct experience of her most basic principles: inclusivity, sacred space and process, spontaneity, deep truth, and authenticity brought into the present moment. Our stories wove a tapestry of diverse experiences and insights into one woven whole, each woman's experiences now part of the fabric of our collective experience. Through serendipity born of time while waiting for the darshans, we experienced the Divine Feminine authentically revealing herself in unexpected, delightful ways. Though we came from four different parts of the country and brought different life experiences and assumptions, we shared a deep respect for the adventure that unfolded for each of us.

Ruth: The second totally unexpected experience regarding the Divine Feminine occurred during the week when we were waiting for the second set of four darshans. People from outside Europe coming to receive these special blessings were allowed to attend each evening, Friday through Monday, two weekends in a row. In the intervening time, Kris and I visited a family she had previously known in Germany while Lesley and Judy remained in the town. When Kris and I returned, Lesley insisted that we visit a museum that was beside a cathedral. She guided us to a vault in the basement of the museum where many sacred objects were displayed, and many people were milling in and out of this space. Suddenly, everyone left the room except for Lesley and me, and she guided me to stand directly in front of a cross that contained a reliquary of Mary, Mother of Jesus. As I faced this object, I was suddenly overwhelmed by a vision of a large lighted being standing behind me, leaning over my head. She said, "I will be with you forever," and I then collapsed onto a bench in tears, moved to the core of my being.

Perhaps it's important to mention that I never personally identified with the Roman Catholic Church or had a devotional relationship with Mary, at least not in this lifetime. We were attracted to that energy field, even if we could not read the German explanations. We were drawn by the Divine Feminine to be in the right place at the right time, and we were open and receptive to whatever experiences arose.

Lesley: Before I left for Germany I had a dream about descending down a spiral staircase into a basement area. When I inquired about where I was, the words I received were "in the catacombs." Once I was actually in Germany and literally began descending the stairs in this museum during the midweek when Kris and Ruth were gone, I became aware that these were the stairs in the dream and so began to pay attention to all of the subtle nuances that might arise in this space. I milled around with acute antenna drawn to a cylinder in the center of the room containing something, but not speaking German, I had no idea what it was. Curious, my heart, third eye and crown chakras became very activated. Tears poured down my face, and I was aware that a blessing was occurring for me in a more direct way than participating with Mother Meera in the darshans. Judy joined me, and we stood together in this aura of nourishing and stabilizing presence. Judy's husband had recently died, and in this sacred presence, she felt a deep release of the sadness and received comfort and reassurance.

When we left the museum, we quietly sat on a bench in the sunshine and listened to the church bells ringing which helped create an inner stillness. We later found out that the notation over the box in the museum described a relic from the Divine Mother. We were aware that we were in a heightened, altered state and so decided to get a bite of food to ground us. We seated ourselves in a Chinese restaurant and ordered some plum wine and before it was served to us, we remarked that the paintings on the wall were in shades of white and ivory and wondered how such detail could be provided without color. It was only after we had eaten part of our meal that we noticed that the images on the wall were in fact colorful — flying cranes with orange beaks and black bodies and Oriental women in vividly colored and detailed costumes. We had received a transmission in the museum that activated a heightened state of awareness that transcended color. We decided to include Ruth and Kris when they returned without telling them anything, allowing for their own discovery if that occurred.

Who Is She? Unfolding Awareness of the Divine Feminine

> *Have patience with everything unresolved in your heart and to try to love the questions themselves as if they were locked rooms or books written in a very foreign language. Live the questions now. Perhaps then, someday far in the future, you will gradually, without even noticing it, live your way into the answer.* – Rainer Maria Rilke [17]

Ruth: Sometime after the Mother Meera trip, the desire deepened to understand what the Divine Feminine really meant. I began collecting images of goddesses and revered spiritual feminine deities from around the world: many versions of Tara from the Buddhist tradition, many images of Kwan Yin from various Asian countries, Black Madonna from Europe and America, Our Lady of Guadalupe from Mexico, and expressions from several Native American traditions such as Changing Woman, White Buffalo Calf Woman and Spider Woman to name a few. Images danced through my life from ancient times such as various Celtic goddesses, the Egyptian Isis, and further into antiquity with Venus of Willendorf and her many comrades scattered throughout the world. I had such passion for these images that I hired a professional photographer to make slides of these many images so that they could be shared with others.

Later, when Lesley and her husband, Jim, were the program chairs of the Council Grove Conference, they invited me to be part of a panel presentation on the Divine Feminine. Even armed with all of those images that so inspired me, I still had many internal questions about what and who the Divine Feminine really is: Are these images really of one being or energy, or are they different from each other? Are they universal archetypes? Is She the Creator? If light connects everything in the Universe, is this light the Divine Feminine? How is our present day understanding of the Divine Feminine different from in past ages when she was revered? Who is Sophia? What is the difference between the words, "Goddess" and "Divine Feminine?" Do Hindus and Buddhists who have incorporated both female and male deities have a greater understanding of the Divine Feminine than those of us in the West who didn't grow up with those images?

Many questions arose regarding masculine and feminine such as: At what planes of consciousness do feminine and masculine qualities disappear and are no longer relevant? Is this impulse really androgynous? What does the Jungian concept of the marriage of masculine and feminine mean in this context?

I wondered about the Earth and her connection with the Divine Feminine: Is Gaia the same as the Earth? What is the meaning of World Soul (anima mundi)? Is this the same as the Great Mother?

I have lived the questions as the poet Rilke suggested. The journey has taken me to many experiences and projects that in retrospect all contain Her call. This book is just one more manifestation of this deep resonance with the Divine Feminine.

Grieving with Mary Inside
Ruth Eichler

Mary and humor provide the antidote, the medicine. They perhaps can help us retain perspective in a hot, un-air-conditioned Kansas farmhouse with sweat and dirt caked in the outer crevices of skin as my siblings and I clean out 62 years' worth of our parents' belongings. As I feel into this Kansas trip only two months after my father's death, another wave of grief begins to surface, a grief that has been dormant the last few weeks. I can be present to that, too, with Mary living inside.

Lessons from Bali's Mt. Agung
Ruth Eichler

What would it be like to have a profound belief from child-hood onward that the place where the gods and ancestor spirits reside — heaven to our culture — is a known, visible place? The Mother temple of all Balinese temples, Besekih, resides at the foot of the mountain rather than higher up. People do not climb on the mountain because it is so sacred.

Perhaps that image keeps coming to me because The Great Mother is gradually coming into my consciousness in the same way as a more or less steady state. I would like all of my life to be in the kaja direction — toward Her. I went to France and found the Black Madonna as a poor woman passing through a coffee shop selling newspapers. I met her in Bali as a volcano.

Lesley: I too had a desire to learn more about the Divine Feminine and chose to listen to CDs, read books, and immerse myself in other people's exploration of the Divine Feminine. As it turns out, these were primarily feminists who believed that the Divine Feminine was a counter force to masculine domination or women who were devotionally aligned with the Virgin Mary in the Roman Catholic Church. Early in my life I was very attracted to the Madonna and remember repeating "Holy Mary, Mother God, pray for our sins now until the hour of our death — Amen" over and over again. This image of the Holy Mother with a flaming heart held special focus for me, which was later to become a focus of years of teaching seminars on the heart. These seminars eventually initiated me into the deeper mysteries of the Divine Feminine.

Through teaching meditation, self-regulation practices and intense focus on the field of the heart, I learned that the virgin birth symbolizes our own birth into the light of infinite potential. The heart has been identified as the chalice and is thought to be the place in which the internal and external and the visible and invisible are linked. I discovered at a deeper level that the heart is the home of higher intuition. I applied this learning in my healing practice, which was the focus of my work at that time. The Feminine teaches through direct experience of living her principles. My experience with this came through the focus on the heart that began with the Madonna when I was a child.

Sophia, Goddess of Wisdom

> *There is a mystical ground within Wisdom, an ocean of endless reach without a shore, a vast clarity whose light is a source of quickening life, a profound energy of creation.* — Lee Irwin [18]

For us, Sophia represents the Sacred Feminine, as She contains the entire cosmos and also penetrates every aspect of creation. She is in our bones and blood, just as she is in the stars and galaxies.

Generally she is not portrayed with an image, as is Kwan Yin or Tara or the Black Madonna or the many other goddesses. Sophia transcends and contains all of these many manifestations of the Divine Feminine, for each is an aspect of Sophia, presenting differently in different environments and times. She is beyond time and place, yet imbued in all. She unifies diversity without harming any of the parts. She offers complete peace and presence from seeking and yearning, because She is present in everything right now — beyond duality. She is the "peace that passeth all understanding." Like the Buddhist concept of emptiness, she ineffably contains everything and is an intense and unimaginable Love beyond any conditions. She is a timeless presence, wisdom beyond interpretation or understanding.

Caitlin Matthews says that the current millennium is the millennium of Sophia.[19] Sophia, meaning wisdom in the Greek language, is described and celebrated in the Old Testament and Gnostic gospels and has re-emerged in contemporary times. We are using Sophia's name to mean a Sacred Feminine Being who is beyond custom, tradition, culture, religion, and time, though we can learn something of her presence through old stories from different traditions.

> *Everything you see has its roots in the Unseen world. The forms may change, yet the essence remains the same.*
> — Rumi

King Solomon was devoted to Sophia, as can be seen from this passage from the Wisdom of Solomon, a biblical book printed separately from the Old and New Testament:

"Her radiance that streams from everlasting light is unceasing. She penetrates and permeates all spirits, all

63

> things for She is the breath of the power of God, a spot-less mirror of divine activity. Herself unchanging, she makes all things new. Age after age she enters into holy souls and makes them friends of God." [20]

From Proverbs 8:23-19 in the Old Testament:

> "I was set up from eternity, and of old, before the earth was made ... When he prepared the heavens I was there. ... When he balanced the foundations of the earth, I was with him."

Isis is also often depicted like Sophia or even as Sophia. At the base of one of the black stone statues of Isis, we find this inscription: "I am everything that was, everything that is, that will be, and no mortal has yet dared to lift my veil."

The Gnostic Christians also believed that Sophia preceded creation, and they added that She suffered as the world fell out of Paradise and that She assists in the redemption of the world. Throughout the ages, She has been called Holy Mother Spirit, Mother of Humanity, Soul of the World, Holy Spirit, and Creating Goddess. The Jewish Kabbalah calls her the Shekinah, the feminine presence of God.

Earth-centered traditions have called her Mother Earth, finding her spirit in all living things — animals, plants, and minerals. She unites all of life in a sacred whole.

Mahayana Buddhism teaches that Prajnaparamita, the Mother of all Buddhas, symbol of wisdom, reveals the Buddha mind or the awakened mind as the potential mind for all beings. As she transmits the energy of awakening to all conscious beings, Prajnaparamita births freedom from limitation by catalyzing consecrated hearts and clear minds.

Rudolph Steiner, an Austrian mystic, philosopher and social change agent who died in 1925, continues to be a force of influence today through schools and societies he inspired. He said that Sophia is the being who directly enlightens all beings.

Sophia is alive and well, though She has been seen through many lenses throughout history. She continues to shape our lives in modern times as we open to the Great Mystery and to heart-centered wisdom. Joseph Campbell in *The Power of Myth* referred to our time as the "age of the Holy Spirit who speaks directly to the individual." Sophia is equated with the Holy Spirit.[21] She is revealed and known from within, through a caring and listening heart. She calls forth an integrative, relational, egalitarian response, uniting heart and mind. She assists us in shifting from an egoic perspective to one of Wisdom.

At this time, Her call is not bound by culture, tradition or language but is instead a global call for the awakening of humanity, for the good of all, not the few. Lee Irwin counsels:

> "We do not need teachers of Wisdom; what we need is a shared context within which the processes of inspiration can be fostered. ... Wisdom does not give us 'answers' — She teaches us through the gifts of our own potential, reveals a resolution based on the integrity by which we live, by the honesty and truthfulness between our thoughts, words, deeds, and promises." [22]

Sophia Speaks
Sacred Beloved

You ask what it means that I was here before the Word. I imbue all that is, and I preceded language. Yet language was created so that the human, conscious mind could grapple with meaning. As you exhale into the void, there I am, pregnant with essence and being. Words are unnecessary.

One has to rest into the silence, into being-ness to begin to sense my Presence. I am that divine spark that courses in your veins. I am in your biology, and I am no less in the stars and the space between the stars. I am the spider weaving the world into creation visible to those sitting quietly in the mossy cave.

You ask what it means that I am Holy Spirit. I am the divine essence present throughout the Universe. Like the story of Jesus, I descend like a dove to all who are open to the heavens, repeating again and again, "You are my beloved daughter (or son), and I am well pleased." Whereas you have been taught in various ways that consciousness ascends up the spine as in kundalini, my essence of Spirit descends like the dove into your awareness and into your heart.

Black Madonna

We have been impacted by the fierce love of "dark" deities from several traditions and have benefited from practices that evoke their presence. For example, the Buddhist Mahakala or the Hindu Kali and Durga can assist us in confronting and eliminating disempowering beliefs about ourselves. They show us that dark and light are part of one unified whole.

In the West and in Eastern Europe the Dark Goddess has generally been known as the Black Madonna, and she has so deeply etched her presence into Lesley's and Ruth's souls that we wanted to speak more about her.

In the West, we have generally polarized light and dark. Mary, the Madonna, especially venerated in the Catholic Church, has been seen as the pure and untarnished Virgin and our doorway to Jesus and God. She could be called upon her as an intermediary to pray for special favors or to remove our sins and to be present with us at death.

Certainly she has been a comfort to millions, just as she is to those who come in pilgrimage to the sites of her present-day visitations. Yet somehow she hasn't been allowed full expression of her Being, just as the goddesses Persephone and Inanna were not complete women until they descended into the darkness in order to find wholeness. Light and dark are interdependent in life, both aspects of the One. Helen Luke, a Jungian therapist, author and founder of Apple Farm, tells us:

> "If one can bring up the dark things and give them equal status with the light, while at the same time the light descends into the dark, then earth is raised to heaven, and heaven descends to earth, and the holy marriage may be consummated not only in *pleroma* — (the divine realms) — but here and now." [23]

Luke continues by referring to the Chinese symbol of yin and yang, a circle with one part dark and one light with a tiny circle of the opposite in each half:

> "The seed of the light is seen in the dark, the seed of the dark in the light, and all the scraps and fragments, so meaningless in isolation, so incoherent in the light of unshadowed reason, are revealed as the significant threads of a great pattern, with which the ego must never identify but of which it is an essential part." [24]

The Black Madonna in her darkness, holds all as sacred. Nothing need be repressed. Consciousness and unconsciousness; grief, sorrow and joy; suffering and non-suffering; birth and death; and perfection and imperfection — all are accepted as part of the divine whole. Her infinite capacity to hold all things helps us face the dark and unknown and begin new patterns of living. We then can freely choose how we live.

She is robust rather than fragile, and she invites us to remember our divinity. She invites us to move beyond polarization and to hold paradox and ambiguity with grace. She unflinchingly walks with us as guardian of the night when we are facing the dark night of the soul. She encourages us to enter the fear, to face it, so that the fear does not own us. She is ever present. Courageously facing our shadow provides the gateway to transformation.

> *August tells Lily, "When you start pull-ing back into doubt and small living, she's the one inside saying, 'Get up from there and live like the glorious girl you are.' She's the power inside you, you understand?* From the novel, *Secret Life of Bees,* [25]

She is often associated with a cave, deep and dark within the earth. On the one hand, this cave symbolizes her ability to walk with us as we liberate our own shadow or aspects of ourselves that we have hidden even from our own awareness out of shame. Jungian analyst, Marion Woodman, says that what has been in the unconscious is a psychological reality that has simply been underground for too long.[26] We believe that somehow we are not enough and hide those perceptions in the cave of our own belly. On the other hand, the cave can symbolize the velvety blackness that holds us with comfort and support. Though dark, the cave simultaneously emanates soft luminescence and its walls breathe with sound, allowing us to become one with her, one unified vibration. We don't have to live in a convent or a Himalayan cave today, not when the cave lives within.

The Black Madonna embodies compassion, often fierce compassion, just as do her Asian sisters, Kwan Yin, the various Taras, or her Mexican counterpart, Our Lady of Guadalupe, and many others from around the world. This undying love, regardless of how we see ourselves, gives us the courage to face not only our fears and feelings of inadequacy but also to embrace our divinity. She summons up our unconscious feelings and judgments that can now be resolved and healed in her spacious acceptance. Thus we are liberated, for she reminds us that we are already whole and filled with magnificent light.

The Black Madonna, deep and strong, does not flinch at death but loves us through and across all thresholds and worlds. She embraces us in times of sorrow, encouraging us to be with the grief in order to come out on the other side without hidden capsules of tears in our bellies and hearts.

After the death of a dear friend, Ruth received this guidance during a session with the Sacred Beloved, which could easily have been the Black Madonna.

Donna's Death
Sacred Beloved

Ruth: Beloved friends, my heart hurts, and my body feels like shredded wheat since Donna's death. I am crying. Are these tears of grief or gratitude that you are here?

Sacred Beloved: Beloved One, we are clearing the channels so that you can feel our love.

Ruth: As I feel your love, grief rises. Tears come.

Sacred Beloved: Let us hold you now. Let the tears flow. Let go of understanding. Let the river flow, washing free the grief that has been held in tissues, muscle and blood. Yes, let it flow. Allow the heart to cradle you. Enter now the cave of the heart. It is here that we fully join you. The entry to this cave is through your own heart that is processing, holding, and transmuting grief from your body. The cells of the body are releasing so the grief can flow to the heart like many tributaries to the ocean. And now walk with us into a much vaster cave of the heart — the loved Dark Mother who holds us all. Yes, even us. We who dance in the light can join you in this womb, this cave. Feel the presence of so many illuminated souls, so many Bodhisattvas, so many who have sung to Tara, Kwan Yin, and thousands of others. They, too, are here in this cave. Listen now. They sing for the dying, for the grieving — soft and tenderly, sometimes not heard amidst the crashing water rushing over craggy cliffs. Yet they are there, tenderly present. Allow this tender sound to penetrate all the cells of your body, assisting the heart. Grief must be transduced before the birth can fully arrive because the physical body and energetic bodies interpenetrate each other.

Lesley's Black Madonna Experience in Switzerland

She Takes Us Where We Need to Be
Lesley Carmack

For a number of years, I worked with Mietek Wirkus, a bio-energy healer from Poland who had immigrated to the United States. He carried the presence of the Divine Feminine energy in his work through his deep devotion to Christ, the Virgin Mary, and the Black Madonna. This devotion was so intrinsic in his energy field that people who came for healing felt this deep love of the Christos that he carried. At one point I was having dinner with Mietek and Margaret, his wife, at a Polish restaurant, and I was deeply moved by a picture of the "Polish Black Madonna," Our Lady of Czestochowa. Mietek was delighted at how my heart opened upon seeing her. He told me that the portrait had an amazing documented history of miraculous events associated with it. The painting had been said to protect towns under siege on several occasions. In 1430 warring factions overran the monastery and attempted to steal the sacred icon when one of the looters slashed the painting with his sword. Before he could strike a second time, he fell to the floor writhing and died. Mietek explained that for centuries miraculous events such as spontaneous healings were reported to occur to those who made a pilgrimage to the portrait. That evening I set an intention to visit Poland to meet this sacred teacher.

A few years later a group of us traveled to Europe to attend a series of seminars researching subtle energy healers and practices. During the weekend break one of the partici- pants, Karl Maret, a physician native to Germany, offered to drive me to Poland for mass at the church of Czestochowa. To our surprise when we arrived at the Polish border we were denied entry for some reason concerning passports. Karl knew that there was another Black Madonna in the vi- cinity so we decided to try to get to that mass in Einsiedeln, Switzerland.

Pilgrims who had been prostrating themselves for days along miles of road were entering the huge cathedral when we arrived. We humbly joined the throngs of people and were somehow pushed directly in front of the Black Madonna statue. In that moment, I had an intuition that the "coincidence" of not going to Poland had all been orchestrated.

I soon sadly realized, however, that although this statue was a deeply sacred symbol, it was not the Black Madonna that my heart knew. Following mass I walked through the rolling hills and historical courtyard of the church and was drawn to a woman who was selling watercolor images of angels. Since I don't speak German, I asked Karl to ask the woman, "Where is the real Black Madonna?" Karl and the woman conversed for several minutes, and then the woman began to cry and said, "The Black Madonna was taken up into the high alpine meadows for safe-keeping in earlier times. My family hid the Black Madonna for many generations."

Although at that time I had no idea then of the history of the Black Madonna of Einsiedeln, I have since learned that the lineage of the present Black Madonna statue at Einsiedeln is not the original Blessed Virgin statue given to the hermit priest by Abbess Hildegard of Zurich. It is likely that the present Black Madonna is a statue carved in the fifteenth century and restored in the eighteenth century.

Although the woman in the courtyard did not tell us of the location of the original Madonna, she told us of a number of places to visit in order to gain a deeper intuitive align-ment and receive transmissions in several potent sacred sites in the vicinity of Einsiedeln. Along many alpine paths in the surrounding hills, various chapels and places of worship that looked like small huts carried the energy of the Black Madonna. Many of the current Black Virgin sites in Europe are located atop energy centers that have been used as celebrations of ancient earth rituals for centuries.

In those days of meditation and prayer, one of the many insights that I gained from the Black Madonna was that a relationship with Her is more than a personal one. I see the Black Madonna as the promise of new beginnings and rebirth. We all have the capacity to express that new life opportunity. The Dark Mother represents creation through integration of heaven and earth. From her roots in centuries of earth-focused, feminine goddess traditions that experienced the earth as the mother of all that sustains life, the Black Madonna of Einsiedeln transmits a timelessness of wisdom and a continuation of the evolutionary expression of light in all living substance. The Sacred Feminine brings direct realization of unity, rebirth and return.

The Black Madonna offers a place of refuge and demonstrates constancy of transformation. Unlike the white skinned Virgin Mary, a Madonna that invites purity and transcendence, the Black Madonna invites and holds unconditional love as possibility. From centuries of initiations into the descent into the depths and trials of feminine manifestation, she offers a direct transmission and presence of living out the truth of our possibilities. She is a wise sage that includes Isis, Persephone and all Divine Feminine beings who embody descent into darkness, and She brings forth blessings and transformation from embodied living and rebirth. This theme of death and rebirth is the constant symbol of the Great Mother and the Black Madonna.

The personal quest for the Black Madonna revealed to me that She is a universal, evolutionary impulse also wanting to be known and expressed through medical doctors, scientists, researchers, men and women. In the past, people experienced her through a mystical and devotional context, but now she is available through insight and intuition. We came thereafter to refer to her as the Initiatrix.

The Divine Feminine has frequently been associated with water and its potential for healing, blessing as well as carrying alchemical properties. Sacred sites have often been constructed on top of or along side healing waters, and many sacred traditions have incorporated water into ritual and ceremony as a conduit for spirit. When we were in that Black Madonna energy field those two days, I could see her distinctive energy signature in the water.

Later, we learned about the resonant capacity of water and its ability to be structured and how it holds blessings and information. Through the meditations, we intuited that in the future structuring water would be one of the bridges between the subtle worlds and conscious intention and that it would be scientifically validated. Since that time, Dr. Masaru Emoto and Dr. Bill Tiller have both done work on intention and its effect on water. We knew this would be of global importance. Now we can participate in creating this sacred imprint on water through our intentions.

We learned that the Divine Feminine takes us where we need to be, provides us with what we need to learn and what we need to bring to others in service to her impulse if we listen. For many people, deep devotion provides depth and purpose for their lives. In fact, the profound passion, love and devotion of the people who have come for centuries as pilgrims created such a loving and resonant field in Einsiedeln that allowed a far deeper intuitive transmission when we were there. At this time of acceleration, we have the opportunity to bring together both the unquestioning, mystical heart and the scientifically inquiring mind.

Ruth's Black Madonna Writes from a Visit to France

She Who Is Hidden
Ruth Eichler

As my friends, Deborah, Laya and I wandered down a Montpellier street, we accidentally bumped into one of the churches reputed to have a Black Madonna inside. Where is she? The White Virgin's statue is in a little anteroom at the back of the church. The black one is nowhere to be seen. We decide she must be locked in the basement, as was St. Sarah in Stes. Maries de la Mer. Just as we are ready to leave the church, a short, chubby, gray-haired man with a key in one hand came forward to talk with us in French, or rather, I should say to Deborah and Laya, saying that he was a lay pastor. When Deborah asked him about the Black Virgin, he said that it was heresy and idolatry and that the Black Madonna had been cut up and burned during the Reformation. I was horrified. I'm still sickened and appalled thinking of this massacred Madonna.

As we sat dejectedly talking over lunch, we realized that we would not find the Black Madonna in a church — even if we saw her statue. This trip seems to be about finding her inside of us, in our stories, in the fabric of our lives. Even though the lay pastor said there were some relics related to her at the Jesuit College, none of us felt a spark of enthusiasm for trying to find the college. The Black Madonna is still real to me beyond symbol, metaphor and thought forms. We talked about how the Catholic Church especially has created thought forms for Mary that probably have little to do with the Mother of Jesus who walked the earth.

After lunch and a failed attempt to send email home at an Internet Café, we stopped for a café au lait at an outdoor restaurant. I was still feeling the pain of a cut up and burned Black Madonna, and we all felt sad. Just then, a beautiful, petite woman with an ageless face and dark hair came to our table with a newspaper entitled "Sans Logis" which we later deciphered as "without lodging" or "without home" i.e. homeless. She was asking for alms for her wounded husband who had no legs and for her hungry babies at home. She looked more like a grandmother without gray hair than a young Mother of babies. She deeply connected though eye contact, words, and most of all presence with each of us even with me, the non-French speaker. Usually people we encountered only looked in the eyes of those who spoke French. We all responded to this woman's request for money, and then she left. Deborah immediately said, "That was the Black Madonna." Laya and I excitedly agreed, and tears rolled down my cheeks. A few seconds later, Laya dashed to the street where the woman had gone, but she was nowhere to be seen. She seemingly disappeared into thin air. I was so deeply moved that I could hardly talk and felt outside of time for several hours after this moving experience.

The Many Faces of the Magdalene
Ruth Eichler

Deborah, Laya and I have all become aware that we, like all women, actually carry the archetypes of the Black Madonna within our bodies. We are seeking the still, small voice or the inner listening to bring this great dark feminine shadow into the light. Reclaiming her in her wholeness and restoring her to the daylight of consciousness brings us into balance. We, as a tiny speck of the wholeness of humanity, feel her stirring. All of humanity needs her blood, passion, fierceness, and compassion in order to be restored to wholeness — not just women but men as well. Within the Judeo-Christian heritage, Christ and the Virgin Mary need to come down from the cross and pedestal in full life and wholeness. Many of the thought forms that surround them do not nourish.

Tears come as I feel her who has been hidden come closer into consciousness within my own body and dance of life. I have been waiting for her all my life though I didn't consciously know that until a few years ago. Even then, the veiled one did not instantly remove her veil and allow me to see her with my thinking, articulating mind.

The Dweller at the Threshold
Ruth Eichler

Last week at my writing group, I alluded to the night in France when a strange, most likely drugged man tried to break into our kitchen at Antonelle, the place where we were staying in the south of France. Laya, always the warrior woman, assertively confronted him until he left. We wondered, "What does it mean that a drugged man tried to break into the citadel with a watchful Warrior Magdalene at the tower? Michelle, a very spiritually astute woman in the writing group, commented that, of course, something like that would occur because we were on the threshold, and thresholds always carry potential danger. She reminded us of the ancient temples and initiation rites that always were guarded by the guardian at the gate. Most temples I've seen from other cultures and times have lions, gargoyles, angels or even monsters at the portal. Laya embodied our guardian at the gate.

She who has been hidden does not reveal herself much through the rational, linear mind. Even thoroughly researched books like Margaret Starbird's The Woman with the Alabaster Jar are potent because they embody the writer's deep passion. Apparently Margaret Starbird's life was turned upside down by her research. What threshold continues to welcome we three pilgrims? Are we experiencing the proverbial shift in consciousness? Or, is the Great Mother reworking the cells of our sinew, muscle, blood and bone, permeating our very existence? How do I welcome her even more fully, and how do I bring what is being worked into full consciousness? Writing and story telling have helped, as has meditation. Because this is the feminine story, I am noticing that greater understanding emerges in our collective sharing. Sitting on Laya's watchtower bed the morning after the intruder experience, we deepened our understanding by reading our writings with each other. One person's thought catalyzes another until no one remembers who thought what. This is the way of the feminine.

The Great Mother

> *How hungry the human heart is for an image of a Divine Mother that would, like an umbilical cord, reconnect it to the Womb of Being, restoring the lost sense of trust and containment in a dimension that may be beyond the reach of our intellect, yet is accessible to us through our deepest instincts.* —Andrew Harvey and Anne Baring [27]

From the dawn of human history, the Great Mother has been present to life on this earth. Many people have seen an image of the voluptuous, heavy-breasted figurine of Venus of Willendorf dating from 25,000 — 15,000 B.C. or perhaps the Australian

Aboriginal image of Kunapipi, Mother of All Things, with legs spread wide, giving birth. Fertility goddesses who presided over birth of babies and abundance from the earth existed in most societies. Hathor, an Egyptian goddess, wears a head-dress symbolizing the nurturing horns of a cow, similar to the sacred cows of India. China had its White Dragon Mother, Tibet and India the White Tara, Germany revered Freya, and the West African Yorubans had Oshun. The Greeks called The Great Earth Mother Demeter, and many indigenous peoples of Central and South America still call her Pachamama. In Navajo myths, the Great Mother is called Changing Woman, referring to the idea that the planet periodically sloughs off its old skin and is reborn as fresh as a young bride. In all of these cultures the Great Mother was celebrated as the sacred container of all life. Sexuality and fecundity created abundance and was a power of transformation.

This Great Mother has remained the same throughout all of these cultures, even though seen through very different eyes and often with different interpretations. We are now coming to a more complete view of her presence. Because consciousness is evolving at an accelerated speed, many now have the capacity to experience this Great One as a co-creator. As history pushed on, the goddess became relegated to the past or denigrated as she was when thousands of "witches" were killed in Europe between the 15th and 18th centuries. Andrew Harvey and Anne Baring warn:

> "Those cultures that have no image of the Mother in the godhead are vulnerable to immensely powerful unconscious feelings of fear and anxiety, particularly when the emphasis of their religious teaching is on sin and guilt. The compensation for this fear is an insatiable need for power and control over life." [28]

Most indigenous cultures from around the world call us to return to a profound respect and love for Mother Earth. We have much to learn from them in our return to embracing the Sacred Feminine in all of life and realizing that the Earth is our Mother. A late 19th century Paiute Indian named Wovoka passionately tried to protect Earth Mother by saying:

> "You ask me to plow the ground. Shall I take a knife and tear my Mother's bosom? ... You ask me to cut grass and make hay and sell it and be rich like white men, but how dare I cut my Mother's hair?" [29]

A century later, Deepak Chopra says that when he is in nature:

> "It soothes my hurts as well as when I sat in my Mother's lap in infancy, because the earth really is my Mother, and the green meadow is her lap. You and I are strangers, but the internal rhythms of our bodies listen to the same ocean tides that cradle us in a time beyond memory." [30]

The Role of "Grandmothers" of the Earth

What is it about "Grandmothers" that is intimately involved in this time of acceleration? Hopi prophecy states, "When the grandmothers speak, the earth will heal." The International Council of Thirteen Indigenous Grandmothers has received much attention over the last few years. They have gathered in many locations around the world calling for the healing of the earth and for the next seven generations. Representing Asia, the Arctic Circle, Africa and North, South and Central America, these women formed an alliance in 2004 to speak out to the world in a united way through prayer and education. Believing that the traditional wisdom of the ancestors has the potential to create a more sustainable earth for future generations, they meet every six months, traveling to each other's home places to carry their message to the world.

Our friend, Raymond Ruka, who is described in greater detail in the section on Egypt, eloquently thanks those grandmothers of his own Waitaha tradition in New Zealand in a Facebook post:

> "Thank you all dear Waitaha Grandmothers for holding resolutely the Whispers of the Divine Voices of our Awakening Consciousness. There are many sacred names given to those Voices, for surely whatever the final or true name might be, we are all connected to the universal culture of Humanity and the all encompassing, sacred land that is Papatuanuku, Mother Earth.

He continues by thanking them for fighting to keep the waterways pristine and away from a new breed of "gold-diggers." His gratitude is echoed by our gratitude for all of the grandmothers of the earth who fight to preserve and protect our sacred home.

> *"Earth Mother is a source, not a resource."* — Raymond Ruka

Many other groups of Grandmothers from every color and creed, indigenous and non-indigenous, have also formed in recent years. A Google search lands over three million hits for "grandmothers for the earth." Some of the grandmother circles gather locally; others come together from wide geographical regions. All appear to share a common belief that women elders have a deep responsibility to act on behalf of humanity and the planet to stop the destruction and to unite for peace. The grandmothers bridge past, present and future. In many indigenous cultures, women are not even allowed to become medicine women until after the age of 50. Although many young people open their hearts and souls to Great Spirit, the second half of life often offers more opportunities to live more globally.

The Weeping Camel Documentary
Ruth Eichler

I loved the grandmother whose face was lined by years of sun and wind on the Gobi desert. They filmed her offering splashes of milk and praying to the four directions. Perhaps it's because I am a grandmother and also pray to the four directions that I identify with her. When this Mongolian family goes to a special place in the mountains to receive prayers from orange-clad monks, the grandmother is the one who prepares and takes the special food offerings. Because she is fairly quiet, compared with Ugma, her grandson who in many ways steals the show, it is she I identify with—she and the daughter who sings to the Mother camel.

Gender and Beyond

Ammachi (Mata Amritanandamayi Devi) declared in an address to the Global Peace Initiative of Women and Religious and Spiritual Leaders Conference:

> "Women are the power and the very foundation of our existence in the world. When women lose touch with their real selves, the harmony of the world ceases to exist, and destruction sets in. It is therefore crucial that women everywhere make every effort to rediscover their fundamental nature, for only then can we save this world." [31]

She went on to call for the cooperation and harmony between men and women. She said that if we don't cooperate with and support each other that peace in the world would never be achieved.

Beyond Gender

The Sacred Feminine cannot be defined by gender, for masculine and feminine qualities exist within all of us — male and female. We were born with these polarities, both equal and fundamental aspects of the Divine, yet in the past rarely balanced within a person. Neither gender fulfills its true potential when part of their nature remains submerged in the unconscious. The energies are ours to bring into balance within us. The rising awareness of the Sacred Feminine allows this facet of the Divine to come into harmony with the Sacred Masculine in the collective consciousness so that we may be whole. The Sacred Feminine, with its integrative nature, helps us bring forth the greatest gifts of each.

> *I, you, he, she, we... in the garden of mystic lovers, these are not true distinctions.* — Rumi

We cannot ignore that both genders have been wounded in the past from lack of integration. In patriarchal cultures, men have often been identified with competition, force and domination, suppressing not only the women in their lives but their own tender side and ability to connect and communicate with feeling. Women have also suffered greatly from living in narrowly subscribed roles and have fought valiantly in many parts of the world, especially in the West, to reclaim their power. We owe a lot to the brave women and some men who spent decades winning the vote for women in the United States and to others who have championed equal pay for equal work and for equal rights. It is time to make compost of the past suffering, compost that can now fertilize collaboration and cooperation.

The Sacred Feminine encourages integration of our masculine and feminine qualities within each of us. As we come into wholeness, we are able to hold polarities as rich resources rather than as forces that divide us into factions that wound and limit our vast potential.

Within the analytical tradition of Carl Jung and work of mythologists such as Joseph Campbell, much has been written of the feminine and masculine principles. Jung said that spiritual growth within the individual involved the development and integration of those male and female components in the human psyche. He also spoke about the "inner marriage," meaning the harmonious coming together of these aspects internally. Externally, we often seek a partner who will fulfill what is latent within us. However, when the inner marriage has occurred within ourselves, we no longer have to seek another to complete ourselves, like two halves becoming one whole. Instead, rich, meaningful relationships are now possible between people who are already balanced and whole.

Neurobiology and Masculine and Feminine Qualities

The brain is yet another arena where masculine and feminine seemingly play out separate functions yet seek integration. Much research has been done in the field of neurobiology in the last few years, and the research reveals that the right and left cortex perceives and creates reality in quite different ways. Daniel Siegel, MD, a neurobiology researcher, teacher and author of several books including *The Mindful Brain* and *The Neurobiology of We* gives four "L" words for the way the left brain typically processes: linear, logical, linguistic and literal. Archetypically, these qualities are associated with the masculine. Siegel says that the right brain processes in this mode: holistic (things perceived in their essence or whole), visuospatial (decoding the meaning of words), and non-verbal. In addition, Siegel says the right brain has:

> "A wide range of functions, including the stress response, an integrated map of the whole body, raw, spontaneous emotion, autobiographical memory, dominance for the non-verbal aspects of empathy. The right mode has no problem with ambiguity and is sometimes called 'ana-logic' meaning it perceives a wide spectrum of meaning, not just a digital restricted definition of something." [32]

These right brain modes of processing are generally associated with the feminine.

Jill Bolte Taylor, Ph.D. has a marvelous chapter in her inspiring book, *My Stroke of Insight*, titled *"My Right and Left Minds."* She was a brain scientist who suffered a stroke that severely damaged the left side of her brain and then spent ten years recovering the functions of the left-brain. During that time she became intimately acquainted with the two "characters," as she called the hemispheres of her brain. She credits her "right mind" with being able to live in the present moment with com-passion and non-judgment for all human beings. Innocence and joy were hallmarks of that "character," and the right brain liked to think out of the box. Here is one excerpt about the right hemisphere when it was the only one primarily functioning:

> "Freed from all perception of boundaries, my right mind proclaims, 'I am a part of it all. We are brothers and sisters on this planet. We are here to help make this world a more peaceful and kinder place.' My right mind sees unity among all living entities, and I am hopeful that you are intimately aware of this character within yourself." [33]

As you can see, the qualities of the right brain that she describes are what we ascribe to the Sacred Feminine. Even though she highly values the right side of her brain, Dr. Taylor doesn't marginalize the left side that it took her so long to resurrect. She says that the left-brain takes all of that beauty, energy, information about the present moment and awareness of possibilities accessed with the right brain and "shapes them into something manageable." [34]

We seek integration so that we can bring our whole self to the ascension process. If men more often experience themselves as "left-brained" and women more often access right brain processes (though there are many exceptions), then we are seeking integration within each gender so that we all become all that we can be.

All of these various ways of experiencing masculine and feminine qualities demonstrate that the union or sacred marriage, independent of gender, serves to create a "sturdy" vehicle or personality to more readily and safely access and respond to higher states of consciousness. The inner marriage creates the opportunity for true synergy within the individual and within the collective, thus accelerating the Divine impulse.

Women's Special Role

Whereas men certainly are called into wholeness and can embody the Sacred Feminine just as women can, and many are a vital part of the raising of humanity's consciousness, women do carry a special role in the ascension process. In utero, females are exposed to estrogen, which promotes growth, survival and regeneration of brain cells that especially enhance verbal and emotional processing, listening, and decision-making. Louann Brizendine, M.D explains that female babies are able to recognize more subtle differences in facial expression than male babies in her popular book, *The Female Brain.* [35] Because of the lack of testosterone in utero, their communication centers are more vital. Girls can hear a broader range of emotional tone in the human voice than can boys. Girls as young as one year old are more responsive to the distress of other people, especially those who look sad or hurt. Young girls are twenty times more likely to share and to take turns than boys.

Cultural differences in the expression of male and female roles do exist, although these roles in Western culture have blurred in recent decades. Yet, females generally more often demonstrate nurturing, tenderness, support, collaboration, and compassion. Women have resonance with the qualities of the Sacred Feminine, and many women's hearts are ignited into living out these principles. It is not surprising then that women may be taking a leading role in cultural and spiritual human evolution and the acceleration process at this time.

The Dalai Lama has widely been quoted as saying that the world will be saved by Western women when he spoke at the Vancouver Peace Summit in 2009. Perhaps his comment was inspired because he was on a panel that featured four Nobel Peace Prize Laureates, three of whom were strong Western women. The four Laureates are: the Dalai Lama (1989); Mairead Maguire and Betty Williams, founders of the Northern Ireland Peace Movement (1976); Jody Williams, crusader against land mines (1997). The Dalai Lama responded to the panel moderator's question about priorities in the quest for world peace by saying, "Some people may call me a feminist...But we need more effort to promote basic human values — human compassion, human affection. And in that respect, females have more sensitivity for others' pain and suffering." [36]

Where we are is perhaps the greatest transition point in human history — the most massive shift of perspective human kind has ever known. Women are the pilgrims and the parents of this new world. — Jean Houston

As far as we know, no research yet exists about male and female differences at the various levels of consciousness. Perhaps the differences become less apparent at higher levels of consciousness as greater integration occurs within the being at all levels — from the sacred inner marriage to the balancing of both sides of the brain. We can only speculate that that might be the case.

The Sri Yantra

The Sri Yantra of Creation symbolizes both the masculine and feminine principles we have been discussing and the unity in which everything is held together. This symbol has been used in the Hindu and Buddhist traditions since the earliest Vedic times as a powerful symbol of the physical universe and its source from the non-physical realms. Upward triangles represent Shiva, the masculine principle, and the downward triangles represent Shakti, the feminine principle, both inherent in the creative force that holds them into One. They are surrounded by further geometries representing creation, the creative process and the omnipresence of the transcendental source. It is a beautiful symbol of the Wholeness that is manifesting through Ascension.

ENDNOTES
Chapter 2: Sacred Feminine

1. Sue Monk Kidd, *The Secret Life of Bees,* (NY: Viking Penguin, 2002).

2. Richard Miller, *Yoga Nidra: A Meditative Practice for Deep Relaxation and Healing,* (Boulder, CO: Sounds True, 2005, p. 33).

3. The Mother, *Flowers: Their Spiritual Significance,* (Pondicherry, India: Sri Aurobindo Society, no date listed, back cover).

4. Thich Nhat Hanh, *Living Buddha, Living Christ,* (NY: Riverhead Books, 2007, p. 91).

5. Tenzin Gyatso, the Fourteenth Dalai Lama, *Essence of the Heart Sutra: The Dalai Lamas's Heart of Wisdom Teachings,* (Boston: Wisdom Publications, 2002, p. 52).

6. Clarissa Pinkola Estes, *Untie the Strong Woman,* (Boulder, CO: Sounds True, 2011, pp. 2-4).

7. The Mother, *Flowers: Their Spiritual Significance,* (Pondicherry, India: Sri Aurobindo Society, p. 8).

8. Piero Ferrucci, *Beauty and the Soul: The Extraordinary Power of Everyday Beauty to Heal Your Life,* (NY: Jeremy P. Tarcher/Penguin, 2009, p. 31).

9. *Dances of Universal Peace: Toward One World, Within and Without: Instruction Booklet, Vol 4,* (Peace Works Center for the Dances of Universal Peace, 1990, p. 18).

10. Layne Redmond, *When the Drummers Were Women,* (NY: Three Rivers Press, 1997, p. 9).

11. Glenn H. Mullin, *Female Buddhas: Women of Enlightenment in Tibetan Mystical Art,* (Santa Fe, NM: Clear Light Publishers, p. 25).

12. We visited the Dendera Temple and saw this inscription from the 2nd Century BC on our visit to Egypt.

13. Sue Monk Kidd, *The Secret Life of Bees,* (NY: Viking Penguin, 2002).

14. Clarissa Pinkola Estes, *Untie the Strong Woman,* (Boulder, CO: Sounds True, 2011, p. 184).

15. Tataya Mato, *The Black Madonna Within*, (Peru, IL: Open Court, Dream Catcher division, 1994).

16. Dag Hammarskjold cited in Phil Cousineau, *The Art of Pilgrimage: The Seeker's Guide to Making Travel Sacred,* (San Francisco: Conari Press, 1998, p. 211).

17. An excerpt from Rainer Maria Rilke's poem, Letters to a Young Poet.

18. Lee Irwin, "Wisdom and the Way of Self-Awakening," (www.sevenpillarshouse.org, Fall 2009).

19. Caitlin Matthews, *Sophia: Goddess of Wisdom*, (London: HarperCollins Publishers,1992).

20. *Wisdom of Solomon*, 7: 10-26.

21. Joseph Campbell with Bill Moyers, *The Power of Myth,* (Crown Publishing Group, 1988, p. 199).

22. Lee Irwin, *"Wisdom and the Way of Self-Awakening,"* (www. sevenpillarshouse.org, Fall 2009).

23. Helen Luke, *Such Stuff as Dreams Are Made On*, (NY: a Parabola Book, Bell Tower, 2000, p. 3).

24. Ibid.

25. Sue Monk Kidd, *Secret Life of Bees,* (NY: Viking Penguin, 2002, p. 288).

26. Marion Woodman, *Addiction to Perfection: The Still Unravished Bride,* (Inner City Books, 1982).

27. Andrew Harvey and Anne Baring, *The Divine Feminine: Exploring the Feminine Face of God around the World,* (Berkeley, CA: Conari Press, 1996, p. 11).

28. Ibid.

29. Quoted in *The Wisdom of Native Americans*, ed. By Kent Nerburn, (Novato, CA: New World Library,1999, p. 6).

30. Deepak Chopra, *Quantum Healing: Exploring the Frontiers of Mind/Body Medicine,* (NY: Bantam, 1990)

31. Ammachi (Mata Amritanandamayi Devi) address to the Global Peace Initiative of Women and Religious and Spiritual Leaders Conference at the Palais des Nations, United Nations, Geneva Switzerland, October 7, 2002.

32. Daniel Siegel, *"An Interpersonal Neurobiology Approach to Psychotherapy: Awareness, Mirror Neurons, and Neural Plasticity in the Development of Well-Being"* which was posted on the website, www.iThou.org.

33. Jill Bolte Taylor, *My Stroke of Insight* , (NY: Viking, 2006, pp. 139-141).

34. Ibid., p. 141.

35.   Louann Brizendine, M.D, *The Female Brain,* (NY: Broadway Books, 2006).

36.   This quotation from the Dalai Lama at the Vancouver Peace Summit in 2009 has been widely circulated and is available on various internet sites.

Chapter 3
Egypt: A Story of the Sacred Feminine and Ascension

There is no event manifest in heaven or on earth in which some myth is not also manifest and in which some spiritual principle is not being activated. If you exist at all, you exist within the realm of the Divine. — Normandi Ellis [1]

Though each of us have had many experiences of the unfolding of the Sacred Feminine in our lives, one of the most profound was our two-week trip to Egypt in February 2010 when we went with ten other women. Regardless of the reasons we thought we personally answered "the call" to go to Egypt as a group of twelve women, we all believed the story was much larger than us. Perhaps the following poem describes best what happened for some of us:

I have a feeling that my boat
Has struck, down there in the depths,
Against a great thing.
And nothing happens!
Or has everything happened,
And are we standing now quietly in the new life?
Juan Ramon Jimenez[2]

Mackie Ruka, the Maori Healer, and the Ceremonies for the Great Mother

The story for this particular trip began with a New Zealand Maori shaman/healer named Mac Wiremu Korako Ruka, also called Mackie, who carried the oral tradition of his ancestors from 74 generations, all trained by the grandmothers. He was spokesperson for the indigenous people of New Zealand at the United Nations Conference that took place in Australia in 1993. He also was a consultant on the acclaimed movie, "Whale Rider." In the 1980's the indigenous Maori grandmothers charged Mackie, as a spiritual leader and elder of their people, to conduct ceremony with circles of twelve women. The ceremonies were to honor and raise the consciousness and energies of the Great Mother on seven continents, and he carried this ritual to at least eighteen places around the world. Ceremony would help rebalance the energies that had been present since the beginning of Creation, bringing the feminine into balance and partnership with the masculine. The grandmothers understood that it was now time for the feminine to assume her rightful place.

Carrying on of the Grandmother's Wishes

As Mackie lay dying in 1998, he told his brother, Raymond Ruka (Kahu o te Maunga, son of Waitaha), that one circle had not been completed — the one in Africa at the Great Pyramid of Giza. In the spring of 2009 for the first time, Raymond Ruka attended the Council Grove Conference, a conference that both of us have attended many times. Bernice Hill, a Jungian analyst, who had gone on two of these journeys with Mackie, sat with Raymond and learned about Mackie's dying regret. Bernice, aged 76, was moved to facilitate the completion of this contract, even though she knew it would be a daunting task. She carefully selected older women who were self aware through years of personal and spiritual inner work and who had the potential of working cohesively as a group and of dealing with harsh, external circumstances if need be. She outlined the itinerary and began newsletters and group dialogues, catalyzing the groundwork for this pilgrimage. She asked each of us to begin meditating with a rose quartz, which we would each take to Egypt, and thus we began to be called the Women of the Rose Quartz.

The ages of the group of us women who traveled to Egypt ranged from 60 to 83 with the majority in their 60's — all of grandmother age though not all had grandchildren. Many women of this age are able to make such a pilgrimage because they no longer have such pressing responsibilities for their immediate, biological family and can bring their attention to the larger human family. Generally, they have released their earlier identifications and now have a longer view of time and space and a much wider perspective of who their "relations" are.

We wanted to fulfill the request of the Grandmother seers who had foreseen this trip as a possibility of balancing masculine and feminine energies and of serving the Earth. We also responded to the call to fulfill our personal life contracts. From the beginning we were aware that there would be personal activations as well as our collective interaction with other levels of consciousness that affect future possibilities.

Our mentor and friend, Elmer Green, called us the Silver Women based upon a dream he shared with Bernice, not because we were silver-haired grandmothers but because of our silvery, etheric bodies that would act as conduits for higher consciousness and would help bring this refined, etheric substance to these sacred sites in Egypt. Due to centuries of intentional alignment with Divine Truth, these sacred sites offer special openings to the hearts of the Mother and to humanity. As the earth is ringing at a higher note and humanity is also quickening, together we catalyze each other through reciprocity. His dream concluded with the words, "This heralds the end of the Age of Maya," that is, the end of illusion and the belief that duality is all there is.

What Called Us to this Journey?

Ruth: The call to Egypt began in the spring of 2009 (or perhaps eons ago) when Lesley told me about this trip, and in the midst of life, I forgot about our discussion. Egypt had never been on my list of places that "I-must-go-before-I-die." A couple of months later, however, Lesley again asked me if I was going to go. As she doesn't ask twice if I want to do something, I knew it was very important and began to feel the pull. Lesley then asked Bernice Hill, the organizer of the group of twelve women, if I could be invited. Bernice said, "Yes. The twelfth woman just cancelled." I heard the call, purchased tickets and began meditating through the ethers with these women, having only met three of them prior to the trip. Once I made the plunge, it pulled as strongly as an undertow. The trip felt like a destined experience, one that was chosen long ago by each of us. Of course, I believe we have choice on whether we say, "yes" to these pre-chosen events.

Though I have traveled to many places in the world, I never prepared so long or so deeply as for the trip to Egypt. During the months of preparation — reading, meditating, watching DVD's — it felt as if I were living in an Egyptian mystery, another reality, in spite of being present in my ordinary life. Something about that ancient culture pulled at my heart and soul asking remembrance.

Lesley: I accepted the invitation to journey to Egypt to serve as a player in a story that was written long ago. I knew that a group of us would be doing this, though I didn't know the exact location or even whether this would occur in dreamtime or ordinary reality. I said "yes" because I believed that as a group our presence, along with compassion for the unfolding process of awakening humanity, served as a bridge that lights the etheric web surrounding the planet. Many people have done this and are doing this. Ours was not a "special" task, but a very particular one.

Ruth Meets Raymond Ruka

In November 2009 I met Raymond Ruka through a delightful serendipitous experience. While attending a yoga workshop, a friend who lived in the town where the workshop was held arranged for my husband and me to meet Raymond. He happened to live in that town through twists of fate in his own life. I had no knowledge that he lived anywhere other than New Zealand and was shocked and deeply moved when I was able to meet him.

"Egypt is our ancient home," he quietly stated, "and we all came from Africa in the dawning of humanity on this planet. This journey will re-empower the Divine Feminine in the world." He spoke of the power of yoga to bring union within and without. He spoke of Asia and the East and that in the re-balancing that is needed on the earth, the qualities of East and West, feminine and masculine, can now be brought together.

He then gave me a smooth white stone that the Maori grand-mothers had blessed, a stone that had been blessed by the Dalai Lama, and had traveled to several continents and was in turn blessed by grandmothers on each of these continents. I was to take this stone to Egypt and leave it at the Great Pyramid. He was a little reluctant to give it up, but he knew it must go to Egypt. He told us that he knew when he was at the Council Grove Conference that someone from Council Grove would come to him to get this stone. Not only had I attended this conference where people from all over the world gather for over 20 years, but also I coincidentally was born in the town of Council Grove. Isn't it interesting how synchronicities unfold?

From a matrilineal lineage, Raymond reminded us that the male is totally important, too. It is now a time for relationship — balancing, which includes compromise. He reached over to my husband, Vic, and gave him a small black stone and said, "The men are to totally support the women in these ventures." And they did. As we left, Raymond gave a blessing and called upon the stars in the night to illuminate our journey.

As we prepared to leave for Egypt, Raymond sent this email to all of us women:

> Grandmothers,
>
> As the Circle of Rose Quartz departs these shores of the Red Earth on the 14th of February, I will recall the numerous times that Grandmother voyagers of bygone times left the shores of their ancient lands to seek the beating heart of Earth Mother to lay their sacred prayers of gratitude upon her breast.
>
> My Grandmothers' wish is that you will find her heart and leave beside your prayer an eternal whisper for the daughters of tomorrow who will be called by the

wind-song of the Sacred Feminine that your circle will have left behind.

We will await the circles safe return. In Peace, Raymond (son of Waitaha)

After coming home from Egypt, we received this message from Raymond:

"Do you hear the voices of the mothers and the children? The stones sing! In the river of peace with its pebbles and stones, the raging currents are the voices you hear coming out of Egypt. In peace, your brother Raymond"

What Was the Role of the Maori Grandmothers?

In a note to Bernice prior to our going to Egypt, Raymond said,

"My Grandmothers simply believed that humanity has a greater purpose than what we currently and historically have experienced. For those of us who are prepared to unlock the door to that understanding, we must as a prerequisite prepare ourselves spiritually to enter into that sacred realm, hence the need to lay a foundation of global entry points at sacred sites, which my brother was tasked to do. He completed his mission to the very best of his human abilities. You sisters must complete yours now. The form of it will follow."

Ruth: Knowing that Raymond and the Maori Grandmothers were holding our group that went to Egypt with such depth of awareness, we often felt their presence on our journey. When Vic and I met with Raymond prior to our trip, we meditated in silence for a time, and tears suddenly rolled down my cheeks. It seemed as if there were 1,000 grandmothers crowded into that small room, called into that time and space through Raymond who is so closely connected with the Maori grandmothers. An image emerged of interconnecting circles within an atom, each circle filled with grandmothers from different cultures around the world. They all came together in the dot in the center where all are one.

Both: Our group went to Egypt because Raymond and the Maori grandmothers asked us to go, and we were there to do a task Mackie was not able to complete. No one went because they just wanted to have a vacation or travel to an exotic place. The task was mandated many generations ago, only voiced now. We saw ourselves as the hands and feet of those who were out of form and unable in their time and place to do this assignment. Of course, like most pilgrimages, we were participating in a greater mystery than we could consciously know. We answered the call without having to have complete understanding of its nature but believing we were in collaboration with the grandmothers. They had a vision, and we resonated with it. We believe that the visionary grandmothers placed seeds into our baskets, seeds from the stars and the earth.

What Was the Deeper Purpose?

Lesley: An ancient prophecy says that when the Eagle of North America and the Condor of South America unite, peace will awaken on Earth. Many believe the time is now. In New York on the night before our departure for Egypt and after intentionally asking for dream guidance about our journey, I had a dream in which Lloyd Elm, an Onondaga elder from one of the Iroquois nations, came and gave instruction. A few years earlier, I attended a gathering in which Lloyd, as holder of the eagle symbolizing North America and an indigenous representative from South America as holder of the condor image came together as prophesied, to smoke a peace pipe.

As holder of Eagle Medicine, Lloyd embodied the eagle as could readily be seen when he danced. When he gave teachings, his heightened perspective evidenced his eagle-ness.

Before going to Egypt, I received a dream including the following poem:

> *There was a man called Eagle*
> *I call myself Eagle; I am Eagle.*
> *I am the wind through the Eagle's wings.*
> *I am the wind; I am change.*
> *I am the bringer of all patterns.*
> *I am dynamic electrical impulse.*
> *I am potential beyond imagination.*
> *I am coming.*
> *I AM*

By his demonstration of being an eagle, he provided instruction for how we could most benefit from the Egyptian experience. We were to observe and participate with symbols not only from our current understanding but simultaneously living into the time in which the symbol originated. We were then to incorporate these multi-leveled understandings into our current life on this planet.

After arriving in Egypt, Bernice offered a meditation in which she said that the new birth on this planet was coming and might be thought of as a "tiny green shoot that needed nurturing." When I brought this phrase into meditation, I was given this message:

> This potentiality is so forceful and yet gentle beyond a whisper. Ride this tsunami wave with such surrender that no sigh is heard. Become the feminine, receptive principle that is consort to the change principle so joined through love that there is no space. The depth of fusion

is so complete that there is no edge and is unending. You cannot tiptoe into this change incrementally; fully immersing into participation is the only way. Become the Creatrix.

Both: Perhaps our call to Egypt was written in the akashic records. *Akasha* is a Sanskrit word meaning sky, space, or ether. Theosophy describes the word *"akasha"* as mystical knowledge encoded in the non-physical that is impressed on subtle substance. Existing since the beginning of creation, it is considered to be a holographic matrix of consciousness that is like a Universal filing system. Perhaps we were to enter into these records on this trip, entering multiple layers of substance.

We went with an overall intention of serving the highest good and to be fully present to all of the aspects of consciousness that we could tune into while simultaneously being present to each other, grounded in time and space in Egypt. We entered this experience with readiness to be aware of whatever emerged without trying to pre-determine the outcome. The Pharaohs intentionally dreamed and intuitively witnessed past and future events, watching the pictures without time elapsing. We were to do the same.

Often the study of Egypt and its mysteries has been presented as a rational exploration of theories on why things happened as they did from a material, observable standpoint. Understandably, many theories abound, such as how the pyramids were constructed — whether thousands of slaves and mechanical pulleys were used or whether extraterrestrials facilitated construction or some other explanation. Instead, we were plunged into a direct, conscious, and living participation in the myths and symbols.

The symbols provide doorways to move through to the substance from which the symbols come. Our current consciousness can join, through sound and intention, with this originating substance, allowing us to live out new ways of being. Tibetan Buddhism holds the idea that ancient ways of knowing have been placed in the etheric field of consciousness as well as in sacred sites on the earth, and in the Earth itself. They call these buried pockets of information *"termas."* When the time is ripe, those who are ready to uncover these mysteries do so. The Egyptians were also adept at encoding wisdom and knowledge into the sacred geometries embedded in the pyramids and other sacred sites.

We believe that some of the larger purpose of going to Egypt was to gain a greater understanding of the coming new cycle of time often signaled to begin in 2012, according to the Mayan calendar. Many cultures and traditions have spoken about the great ages of time, including the Yugas in the Hindu tradition, usually based upon the precession of the equinoxes that change an age approximately every 2000 years. Whatever the cosmology, it appears that we are now in the early stages of a new cycle, a "new world." We can choose to open ourselves to a much larger perspective in this new energetic, and we have a great opportunity to align with the new vibration. Although we thought we were completing something that the Grandmothers envisioned, we realized that we were actually participating in a birthing process, being one of the thousands of midwives of the new world.

Not only are the cycles of time also recognized in Egyptian cosmology, but the ancient Egyptians were adept at entering the *akashic* realm. By going to Egypt, we too could more easily participate in an expanded awareness of time cycles and simultaneously into a realm beyond chronological time. Awareness of the stars and planetary movement is embedded in the temples and sacred sites in Egypt. Their myths and stories carry the message of moving cycles of time celebrating birth and death, the rising and setting of the sun, and seasonal floods. The phases of the moon are cut into the bases of columns at various places, including the Luxor Temple.

As more and more people are learning, "as I am, so is the world," we had moving, personal experiences that we believe served the Universal. Our personal transformation offers a tincture to the greater whole, and yet we are not "fixing" anything or making something happen. We are one with the whole, as a cell is one with the whole body. The Egyptians knew about extended, expansive consciousness because they made this a life practice. The Temple of Man at Luxor verifies that they knew about *chakras*, as reported by John Anthony West in his excellent *The Traveler's Key to Ancient Egypt: a Guide to the Sacred Places of Ancient Egypt.* All of the temples in Egypt display sacred geometry and the capacity to be affected by sound.

Candidates for initiation in the ancient Egyptian mystery schools were taught to shift consciousness from one level to another. We tend to think of their training as a kind of testing or "running the gauntlet." Instead they used the experience of extended consciousness to retrieve awareness of the many aspects of existence as well as continuity of consciousness that includes immortality. The theme of life and death, so prevalent in all of ancient Egypt, appears to be part of the mystical teachings that bridge various levels of consciousness. Through principles of correspondence, the Egyptian mystics brought maps of other realms to their teachings. These mystics can still teach us how to be to be living bridges. These altered states, free from the physical body, allowed expansion beyond the limitation of the form to enter into the limitless, divine being and then return to the earth with an intimate knowing of the divine nature that lives within each of us. After we returned from Egypt, Lesley commented, "Tell the secret of Egypt and you will liberate initiation."

Sirius and Egypt

In esoteric circles the third initiation that human beings can experience involves alignment with an individualized, immortal spark of the Creator and an aspect of our being beyond the soul, called the monad. At this time of great acceleration of consciousness, more and more people are coming to the third initiation, something that only a very few reached in past times. "The Tibetan," speaking through many of Alice Ann Bailey books, tells us that the Great White Brotherhood, also called the Blue Lodge or Solar Angels, send impressions from Sirius to our planet Earth. According to these texts, as we align with Sirius, many solar angels (a higher expression of our own souls) are liberated to return to their place of origin, Sirius. That ascension process, that updraft, in turn pulls humanity into a similar evolutionary expression that it has invoked through a yearning and free will, releasing the lower into the higher. Through opening to that energetic stream from Sirius, humanity is lifted to a more refined mode of expression. As the sun shines on a plant, the essence of the flower is released, and it can express its reason for being.

The "Tibetan" reportedly said that our solar system emanated from Sirius, and that Sirius impulses love and is especially important to Earth in this cycle. As more of humanity experiences a synthesis of body, mind and spirit, we become more closely identified with our originating impulse and are also drawn closer to the star Sirius, from which the higher expression of our souls came.

When our group of women entered Egypt, we could feel in the energy field the belief about the connection to Sirius that was held so deeply by the ancients. We not only received an Egyptian history lesson, but our own cellular memory was quickened. The force fields were palpable in Egypt, and our souls were stirred. Lesley believed that going to Egypt would help us to further refine and understand the relationship between the angelic and the human kingdom.

Ruth: Little did I know that images from one of my favorite movies of all time, *The Dark Crystal,* a Jim Henson movie that was released in 1982, would re-surface in an Egyptian pyramid and connect me with Sirius, a star sacred to the ancient Egyptians. I have seen this movie perhaps 80 to 100 times, as I've shown it to almost every class or workshop I've taught or facilitated since it appeared. Jim Henson, the creative genius of the Sesame Street Muppets worked with Frank Oz to create an allegorical story that uncannily depicts the human and world condition. Gentle Mystics chant "Om," express love and teach sacred geometry to the main character. The awful Skeksies greedily shriek and cry in their fear of a prophesy that the world will would end if a missing crystal shard is returned to its place of origin. In the final scene of the movie, the Skeksies and Gentle Mystics merge into giant beings of light. The disparate aspects of a personality are reunited into wholeness, ascending to an entirely new level of consciousness, one that could not be seen or understood from the previously limited view.

The image of these lighted beings burst into my consciousness while in the Pyramid of Chephren, also called Khafre, the day before our group visited the Great Pyramid. We came into a circle to do our usual ceremony in the room with the sarcophagus, and the throngs of tourists walking through the room seemed oblivious to our group. We spontaneously recited from memory various lines of Mackie's prayer, and

Christine invoked a central column of light deep into the earth. I experienced this column of light going all the way up to the star Sirius, so closely allied with these pyramids. Suddenly we became transformed light beings like those at the end of *The Dark Crystal,* and we united into a circle of light. In my vision, each of us held a rose quartz in the left hand. The quartz emanated intense vibrations, which moved into the heart and then went back into the world through the right hand.

The ancient Egyptians worshipped the god Ra, which was also the Sun. At the time of the pharaohs when the pyramids were built, Sirius was the polar Star, some saying the point of origin for the Sun in our solar system. One of the lines in the prayer that Mackie gave the women on the various pilgrimages, and which we used at every sacred site, was: "We seek unity with ourselves and the universe." Although "the universe" might not exactly mean Sirius, it certainly does point to our originating impulse.

Lesley's Experiences of Four Received Teachings

> *First the theory, then the experiment, and lastly realization.* — Alice Ann Bailey

Lesley: Parallel to the group events and sharing in Egypt, I had a separate stream of teachings. While I was present to the environment, people and events around me in Egypt, I was also engaged in an altered state of consciousness. Perhaps in one state, the intellect and physical were more engaged, while the other was more aligned with the intuitive realms. Fortunately I have had experience in each of these states so was able to function simultaneously in each and not create undue dissonance in either.

The assimilation of the substance of the altered states and the subsequent integration was greatly enhanced by dialoguing about the experiences with Ruth and another friend, Karen. Each is a friend of long standing and so they were at ease with my intuitive bent of personality, and each is highly trained at questioning for clarity and integration and in grounding intuitive awareness. Without this process I am sure that the experiences of these teachings would have either been forgotten, discounted as passing fantasy or been marginalized as something unworthy of further understanding. I am most grateful to the loving presence of these two soulful friends. I did not journal the teachings because living in two levels of experience seemed to be all that I could manage at the time. The teachings arrived in four distinct experiences, yet are all connected. We hope that the reader may be able to personally identify with some of these teachings, as these archetypes are as true now as then.

No. 1: New Understandings of Christ's Transfiguration, Crucifixion and Resurrection
Lesley Carmack

The first of four teachings began as physical pain. While dressing to attend a morning meditation, pain shot down my arm like a dagger. I was immediately aware that my attention was multi-layered. It was as if I was in Egypt with my fellow travelers and simultaneously immersed in the Akashic records of the crucifixion of Jesus. I could witness and simultaneously "be" in both places and states of awareness. These intuitive, holographic impressions eventually led to an extension and synthesis of my understanding of the Biblical transfiguration, crucifixion and ascension of Jesus.

Throughout the day, pain from my experience in the intuitive realm brought insights into focalization. As pain stabbed in my side, an image emerged of Christ's blood flowing into the Earth along with the intuitive thought, "Golgotha is now." We act as conduits, like multi-directional antennae, that receive and transmute more refined energies and light coming into the earth and our form nature at this time. We also receive energy and information that emanates from the earth, and we add our human experience and essence to the process. Just as the tree knows how to convert carbon dioxide into oxygen and send it back out, we transmute the vibrational information and impressions that we receive from the etheric field. As we align with and take in these energies, they are re-magnetized through our bodies and chakra systems and then disseminated into the subtle energy of the planetary field.

Transfiguration:

This awareness moved me into an understanding of Jesus' transfiguration. When Jesus took Peter, James and John to the mountaintop prior to the crucifixion, they awoke to see him "as a form dazzling white and brighter than bleached clothing." He was speaking about the coming crucifixion, resurrection and ascension with Moses and Elijah, both long ago deceased.

This demonstration moved his teachings from the strictly manifest world of birth and baptism to the to the more subtle vibrational realms of the far greater possibilities of human experience. He showed the disciples his lighted etheric body and moved out of manifest time and space into the timeless and non-local fields of infinite possibility. From this teaching forward, we can interpret the teachings of Jesus from material life examples as illustrations of expanded, limitless, mythic, archetypical, and eternal life. He not only fulfilled the law and the prophecies of all world teachers but also moved from the Son of Man to the Son of God.

The transfiguration displayed to the disciples the radiance that lies within the material, physical medium of our human bodies. It was a display of the etheric, lighted aura both inside and outside of human form. Subtle energy research has demonstrated that the entire manifested universe, cosmos, solar system, human beings, and the various kingdoms of nature are not only made of physical energy or matter but are also imbued with an underlying subtle energy field, which is the matrix for consciousness. The transfiguration demonstrated the ability to change material form into a more refined and subtle living expression. It also foretold the subtle and more refined expression of Christ's body when he rose from the tomb.

Crucifixion:

The crucifixion was a vivid presentation of the reality that human experience contains suffering. Through the excruciating demonstration of "taking on" human violence and cruelty, Jesus transmuted this suffering and demonstrated the possibility of transcendence to everyone throughout eternity. He promised liberation from suffering and a life full of potential like an overflowing cup. (John 10:10) Jesus tells us, "The kingdom of God is within you." (Luke 17:20-21)

The message of Jesus' ordeal is not solely associated with suffering as a means of redemption for humanity but as a greater teaching through an event as a living parable. The crucifixion was not meant to model appeasement to a higher power through pain and sacrifice. Rather, it was a profound demonstration of embodying the universal purpose of recognizing our worth and responding to the worth of all that is living. The crucifixion forever replaced looking at events out of fear of retribution and punishment or for reward with the ability to choose our response in the present moment and creatively choose goodness. It offered pure and complete forgiveness and total atonement clearing the way for new beginnings. The crucifixion allowed us to experience oneness with the divine rather than the pain of separation. Understanding that there is no separation led to my understanding of the union of spirit and matter.

Resurrection:

Resurrection means to rise up and return to a fully alive state. The view of the crucifixion from the subtle energy vibrational realms allowed me to reinterpret and expand the Biblical version by including my observations from the subtle energy realms. Most Biblical interpretations do not include teachings about the luminous etheric or the subtle energy body. The etheric body surrounds and interpenetrates the physical body and can be seen and measured on subtle levels when vitality is present. When Jesus said on the cross, "Father, into Thy hands I command my spirit" and "It is done," it marked the end of his physical life, but he had such tremendous, all pervading light that even after the crucifixion his etheric form was seen by many for forty days. During the forty days, Christ was able to demonstrate that through continuity of consciousness, his form was not completely dissolved but rather resurrected to a subtler one without a body. He demonstrated that divinity is continuous and liberation from suffering is available to all. The realm of the subtle energy matrix is the map of creation that precedes all manifest form, and his consciousness resides there for eternity.

The Egyptian story of Isis and Osiris:

The story of Osiris and Isis is also a story of death, resurrection and rebirth, a story that precedes and in many metaphorical ways parallels the story of Mary and Jesus. In the Egyptian story, Isis is the heroine because she brings Osiris back to life, demonstrating eternal life. The meta message of these stories is the transformational journey that we are now living.

The death process began for Osiris when he climbed into a coffin and was sent into the turbulent waters, symbolizing the initial entry into the bardo, that state of existence after leaving the body. Isis found the coffin and erected it into a pillar and flew around it in the form of a swallow, symbolizing the vertical alignment into higher realms and attending to the lessons given in the afterlife.

Isis recovered Osiris body that was fragmented into parts, because he was not yet "whole" in his spiritual reunion after death. She recovered all of his body except for his penis that was eaten by a fish. The penis was not needed for physical creation in the higher worlds. However, Isis becomes pregnant because he has continuous creative possibilities in the subtle realms. Like the Black Madonna in Christian traditions, Isis assisted in Osiris rebirth as he was "born again and resurrected." He became the Lord of the underworld, demonstrating that he is conscious both in life and death. Life is everlasting and immortality is possible.

Just as the story of Jesus is a story of eternal life, so is the story of Osiris. They both depict that there is no death — only transition and re-emergence into new form.

Integrating then and now:

In altered states of awareness it is not unusual for the relationship of subject and object to fall away and for a holographic view to be present. This is referred to as "consciousness without object." The experiences I was emerged in Egypt were like simultaneously being both witness and subject. With no "out there object" to impose a historical story on, I was "IN" the experience in a new way. From direct experience I was able to come to new awareness about the teachings of Jesus that did not separate me from the loving presence of the teacher or the teachings. The understandings gained from direct experience bring expanded perspectives and more subtle insights and awareness but do not necessarily omit any other version or create conflict with the more concretized historical understandings.

The process I was immersed in seemed to be an experience happening to all of us now as the veil lifts in these times of great quickening. We have the opportunity to re-identify as agents of the Christed energy. We know today from quantum connectedness that the Universe is not a collection of physical form objects but is an interweaving of all parts that includes the observer. When we know our essential nature to be divine and we re-identify ourselves as Soul, we have the capacity to be vehicles of light, acting as agents for the Christ energy.

Timeless realm:

In addition to the insights into the transfiguration, crucifixion, and resurrection, my experience extended into a galactic event. I experienced and saw intensely brilliant lights that were not only angelic but also were trans-dimensional energies and information. I understood these images to foretell of our increasing awareness of interplanetary beings and consciousness, as potentiating impulses of energies now available. This orientation of extra-planetary awareness was a new experience for me and having it coupled with the images and teaching of the Master Jesus seemed to imply that these images reside in the timeless realms of the Master's teachings.

No. 2: Experiences in Abydos: We Initiate One Another
Lesley Carmack

As we walked through the Seti Temple at Abydos, the first painted image on a wall that I saw was of a temple priestess putting an ankh that was shaped like a cross with a loop at the top — also called the key of life — into the mouth of an initiate. The ankh symbolized the spring from which flowed divine virtues and the elixir of immortality. Therefore, to hold the ankh was to drink from the well of life. The loop at the top perfectly symbolizes having neither a beginning nor an end and stands for the eternal soul that sprang from the spiritual essence of the Egyptian gods. The ankh also symbolizes union of masculine and feminine, life and immortality. When entering the mouth, it may also depict conferring the gift of enlightenment to another. [3]

Hieroglyphs and images depict meaning in a synthetic way, pattern upon pattern of thought, seeding thoughts and opening awareness. I stopped transfixed by this image and found myself out of space and time in the holographic state of awareness of then and now, "remembering" the intention and feeling from that time as a current process, revealing eternal life not to the pharaoh but to all of humanity. I felt as if I could walk as the barefooted priestess and experience her intentions at all levels. If the earlier lesson was about the embodiment of the Christ energy, then this experience with the image on the temple wall means that we can all now serve each other as priests and priestesses, mutually bestowing a shift in consciousness and collaborating in the creation of the new world.

As I watched the painted priestess, now alive through continuity of consciousness, she telepathically transmitted to me just as she had transmitted to the candidates for initiation centuries ago. By placing the ankh that was imbued with divine substance into the mouth of the initiate, the priestess became a conduit for the Mother of the World and the bringer of new life, also as the wife of God.

She assisted the candidate in understanding the bardo, that transitional state after death. The Egyptians believed the passage to the afterlife was a horrifying realm that included a series of gates and caverns guarded by aggressive supernatural creatures. *The Egyptian Book of the Dead* that has also been translated as *The Book of Emerging Forth into the Light* gives maps of the terrifying lower realms. The book tells how to travel across the sky in order to appear before Osiris, god of the afterlife, the underworld and the dead, with a "heart lighter than a feather." The priestess provided rituals that decreased the terror of the underworld upon death and provided spiritual, empowering force. Isis is often the priestess offering the ankh symbolizing eternal life into the mouth of the initiate. Today we initiate one another.

In my experience, the candidate walked while receiving calming transmissions and telepathic instructions from the initiating priestess. The alignment created by walking certain patterns altered the brain and released complex geometric patterns of light. My intuitive understanding is that this process created an altered state of enhanced receptivity, intensifying the transformation from fear to positive expectation. The candidate was able to imagine the experience of passing through the terrifying lower realms without reactivity, thus calming his or her fear of death. Initiates were trained for the afterlife experience, just as the pharaohs had been trained to do. Now we all have the possibility of being initiates and priestesses.

Following the first experience of the crucifixion as transformation, transcendence and resurrection, perhaps this image represents the similar impulse of rebirth and ascension that is occurring now. Barbara Marx Hubbard in her book, *Birth 2012 and Beyond,* describes the birth of "universal humans" as humans not driven by their egoic ways. They put the good of the whole before their own personal good. Universal humans are spiritual, though not necessarily religious. They are creative, and generally they are pioneers. The universal human is one who knows they are connected, as one with all life — with the Divine, with the earth and all life on the earth.

> *We are the people and now is the time.*
> *— Jean Houston*

No. 3: Initiation at Dendera: Light and Sound Activates Higher Potentiality
Lesley Carmack

Still integrating the experience from Abydos, I was hardly prepared for what occurred at this Hathor Temple. As our group walked up the long steps to the temple, our leader Bernice tripped. We only much later learned that her hip had actually broken in the fall, resulting in her being transported back to the United States where she received surgery, after which she fully recovered. Unaware of the seriousness of the event, three of us helped her to a corner of the temple where a man called the "Guardian of the

Temple," who was also a healer, was summoned. This respected elder had served at Dendera for thirty-three years. He assessed her body by waving his hand over her head and then seated her. Karen who has studied various healing modalities, Christina who is a medical doctor and a shaman, and I stayed with her. Bernice insisted we see the temple, so we agreed to take turns sitting with her.

Karen and I started to return to the group and quickly realized we had no idea where our group of women might be in this large complex temple. We asked the healer/priest who had assisted Bernice to show us where we might catch up with them. As he took my arm to guide us, he looked at me and said, "I know you are a healer, and I will show you the way." He began running me, with Karen following, from room to room. As we flew past guarded rooms, the guards would look away or nod signaling me that this person had free reign of the premises.

I was aware that I needed to be discriminating about my level of openness and trust and so tried to notice what I could about this person. First he had acted with expert intuitive skill in reading Bernice's field and had acted kindly to her when she declined further attention from him. Along with what appeared to be respect from other priests and guards in the temple, he felt kind yet authoritative, something I had experienced with other physical teachers with a high level of consciousness. Thirdly he smelled like roses. I completely trust smell, and this was a scent similar to Mietek, my most beloved teacher, and also of Ammachi, with whom I meditate at a distance.

I allowed my consciousness to shift deeper and deeper into the subtle realms and felt gratitude to Karen for her footsteps and deep presence as she ran behind us. This healer/initiator/priest spoke softly and moved with decisive intention. He placed my hands and feet against the images on the walls, pressed my head against the walls, twisted my body to align with various directions and with openings that aligned with star system that were placed in the ceiling, and chanted into my ear. We ran from image to image, room to room and alignment to alignment. On a few occasions he put my head with Karen's, sometimes triangulated with his own forehead. He breathed decisively and purposefully, creating an even greater altered state of consciousness, and he paced my heartbeat with his. I reminded all aspects of myself to "pay attention" in all the ways I have been trained in all lifetimes. I continued to trust the process and at the same time discriminated for any clues of magic with which I might not have resonance or trust, and I found none. He used various shamanic practices and transmission techniques to bring about an experience of self-realization or "remembering."

Before he left I told him that when I had awoken that day I was told in meditation that I would receive a new name today and asked him if he knew what that name was. He said, "You speak it." I could see colors of golden light and angelic presence but could not speak audibly what I "heard" and so asked if he could speak for me. He said, "You are the Christos." I believe that this naming suggests re-identification with this increasing energy potential that we might call Universal Understanding, Christ consciousness or the Maitreya as Buddhists would call it and is available to humanity at this time through the ascension process.

The group field that had been created by the openness and diversity of the "silver" women facilitated the experiences of heightened awareness that I have described as "mine." Although this account sounds personal, it was experienced in a group container that fostered exploration, respect, safety and openness to greater possibility. This collective field allows for each person to become a thread in a tapestry with each person holding a part of the whole. Such synergistic group collaboration is the key to the ascension process, which is an updraft of humanity, not just one of individuals.

Dendera is a huge complex that tells the creation story and depicts the path of unfolding spiritual life as a method of healing, celebration and devotion through feminine principles. In the Egyptian view, these activities are intrinsically interwoven with esoteric processes that link priestesses with knowledge of star beings though rituals of sound and light. Zodiacal and celestial records are encoded into the art on the walls, the ceilings and statuary. The square zodiac on one of the ceilings gives great prominence to Sirius, symbolized by the cow-goddess Sothis. The star Sept, or Sirius, was the symbol of Isis in the heavens and was thought to be the resting place of her soul. Images alluding to the mysteries of sound and light hint at energetic transmissions from other dimensions and perhaps from the goddess Hathor herself as one of the representations of the Divine Feminine. She welcomed the dead into the next life, and she was the goddess of music, dance, and fertility.

The Hathor Temple at Dendera was renowned as a healing center at one time in Egyptian history. Hathor, sometimes known as Isis' sister and sometimes as another version of Isis, is often depicted as a benevolent cow face. In many cultures, including Egyptian, cows represent nurture, birth, dawn, rebirth and new beginnings. Those messages are encoded into the temple itself and are still present in living substance even though the temple is now more or less seen by tourists as a museum. Through its essence, the temple still teaches that healing is a transmission of more expanded life essence rather than renewing diminished capacity to normal. All of our sense organs respond to the intention and transmissions from these images.

I have speculated on the Hathors as similar in their mythology to that of the Solar Angels. The Wisdom Teachings and various scriptures speak about Solar Angels as advanced Beings who came from Sirius to the earth to assist in the individuation, spiritualization and mental processes of humanity. Various sacred texts report their appearance as the time "when gods walked among men." According to Torkom Saraydarian [4] the role of Solar Angels is to inspire spiritual freedom, joy and purity and to open humanity to its relationship with the Universe through creative sound. Though no longer walking the earth, they continue to communicate to humanity through symbolic dreams, telepathy and revelatory sound.

The solar angels sound like the Hathors from whom Tom Kenyon, musician, author and highly respected sound healer, receives telepathic teachings. He reports that they are a group of inter-dimensional, intergalactic beings that originally came by way of Sirius. They connected through the temples of the Goddess Hathor as well as with Tibetan lamas in the formative period of Tibetan Buddhism. They say that they are now an entire civilization that has ascended into non-physical realms. Their intent is to bring to humanity information about the "vibratory nature of the cosmos, the use of sacred geometry as a means to stimulate brain performance, and in the use of sound to activate psycho-spiritual experiences." [5]

No 4: The Great Pyramid: Our Connection with Cosmic Potentiality

Lesley Carmack

Having the opportunity to visit the King's Chamber in the Great Pyramid at pre-dawn hours before the tourists arrived captivated the group long before we left the shores of the United States. Adventures and synchronicities ratcheted up the group's excitement for our final experience before flying back home. Unknown to the group, however, was my deep dread of the experience, as I imagined it to be painfully claustrophobic. During a lengthy hospitalization as a young child, my legs were tied to boards to prevent me from pulling out the IV's, and I was under an oxygen tent to enhance breathing. Having seen images of the narrow passages ascending to the King's Chamber, I was literally "breathless" imagining the scene and was increasingly concerned that I would have to back out on the group rituals and experience.

The night prior to entering the Great Pyramid was one of great turmoil for me because the fear of claustrophobia was compounded by lung congestion. I was deeply concerned that my inability to join the group would detract from the beautiful matrix of group dynamics that had intentionally been created, and yet my physical and emotional bodies were too unstable to move forward. Throughout the night the pressure and congestion in my chest activated by fear and bacteria became overwhelming. I honestly thought I might die. Only because of love for the group, its promise to the process, and Ruth's support was I able to go forward.

I now know that the fear of literally dying is a component of any true initiation experience, though I doubt that even that awareness would have made a difference that night.

Although we had agreed to be in silence once on the bus to the pyramid, I was able to communicate to both Karen and Ruth my need for support in order to move up the entrance way. One of them preceded me as the other followed, and I moved into the chamber feeling as if it were a labyrinth into the greatest imaginable mystery and the unknown.

Once in the King's Chamber, I was overcome by the feeling that I had made it in there alive. I now understand that I was dying to an old self, an old identification. When these kinds of greatly accelerated vibrations enter into the field, they penetrate our bodies, and we experience it physically. Sometimes physical crises indicate the dying of the old form.

As I looked around the chamber, the group members seemed to simultaneously be both my traveling companions and starry beings. It was a strange cross between a celestial peace and the *Star Wars* bar scene. By now I was getting accustomed to being on planes that were not familiar to me, but the King's Chamber appeared to be "off planet." The planes of this planetary system seemed to extend to the consciousness of Universal Being. I could see webs and streams of living light and tiny forms that appeared to be living geometrical shapes. Later Christine said that she had also seen the same images.

I was "reminded" to use the water I had brought into the chamber to create a resonance with the many vibrational systems I was observing because water that has been "structured" with love and prayer can assist in cohering dissonant vibrations. Holy water has been used for this purpose in many traditions for eons. I then was inspired to bless each person individually, using water to create greater coherence in the field of each. Water is a great conduit for teachings that transcend space and time. In that Chamber, our beliefs and assumptions were suspended, and we became vehicles for the accelerated transmission of love and light.

The group then followed the suggestion of one of the group members and lay in a circle on the floor with crystals on their foreheads. Three of us sat in the middle of the circle with the intention of centralizing the flow of intuitive downloads and codes about the future of this planet and its relationship and "agreements" within the larger context of the planetary system. Ruth led the group in toning, as we had done on many prior occasions, the sound moving through all of the dimensions. Just as water coheres the field when "structured," sound transcends the limitations of cognitive thought and provides a conduit for more re-fined and transcendent qualities, linking hearts and minds of the human participants with the subtle worlds.

Before hurrying out of the Great Pyramid at the end of our appointed time, a small group of us also went to the Queen's Chamber. Here the energy was very different and we toned for several minutes in resonance with this tender feeling space.

Following the pyramid experience, we rested and later met to dialogue about our observations and experiences and to share a closing ceremony. We shared intuitive insights ranging from personal to global, and we happily felt that we had "accomplished" our purpose for coming to Egypt though still open to its expanding meaning.

Some believe the Great Pyramid holds the codes or subtle energy maps until they can be directly used again in the ascension of humanity. However, the body must first be able to receive the multi-dimensional messages and then be able to interpret them into deeper meaning. Every initiation is a process of energy transmission from a higher center of energy to a lower center. These transmissions of energy and the magnetic activation charge the recipient with electrical force that influences all aspects of the being and may require lifetimes to integrate and bring into everyday living.

The pyramid is a bridge between levels of physical, subtle and spiritual energies. The building structure itself expresses the golden mean or phi ratio. The shafts in both the Kings and Queens Chambers align earth with galactic constellations, which may have been a reciprocal antenna. These subtle energy forces likely assisted sacred telepathic contact and communication with spiritual and extraterrestrial beings.

It is difficult to separate out the influence of the Great Pyramid from the entirety of the series of insights from our Egyptian experience. Ruth and I took notes after the event and researched such images as the rhombus dodecahedron that is meant to represent multi-dimensional reality. But, the wholeness of the experience continues to reveal itself even now, four years later.

The metaphor of rebirth and renewal is obvious. Initiation is an expansion of consciousness and requires stimulation from outside influences to hasten the evolutionary process. Within the pyramid one can lie down in the coffin-like sarcophagus and surrender to the near death experience while traveling to the inner planes. The Great Pyramid and its sarcophagus is a womb initiation chamber and like the Phoenix represents the promise of resurrection. The hermetic traditions refer to the phoenix as the bringer of light who perishes for its effort. [6] We chose the image of the phoenix for our cover because we believe the light is already within all of us, and we are rising to meet it.

This is the final email I sent the group when we returned:

> May all of us continue to fall into the welcoming arms of "the place and the times" we are entering into with gratitude and joy for this unbelievable time of grace.
>
> May any and all suffering and sacrifice made for the increasing good of this group, its process and evolution be revered in its integrity and resolved with the greatest of ease.
>
> May all hearts everywhere receive the substance of light conveyed in this endeavor and may it bring forth the way of kindness with the gentleness of a feather to all mankind.
>
> May the earth be seeded with the prayers and resonance of the rose quartz ring with the note of purity and intention brought to it from its sacred sister systems of light.
>
> May the aroma of the lotus prevail across the land of the blue planet and join with the greater federation in the starry sky in accordance with the greater plan of infinite potential.

Nut's Vast Sky Birthing a New World
Ruth Eichler

Now home from Egypt for nearly a month, the experience and all of its ramifications continue to occupy lots of psychic space. The unpacking of this momentous journey has come in bits and pieces: writing short pieces about experiences

127

and insights; alphabetizing gods and goddesses and pasting corresponding images on the pages; sorting through emails and conversations from friends and the women who went to Egypt. What looms in consciousness feels as vast as the sky that the goddess Nut drapes over. She is always seen as having tippy toes touching the earth at one horizon and finger tips on the other horizon, her belly filled with stars and arched high above the earth.

Articulating the ineffable challenges me. How does one explain, "I am a star on Nut's belly?" One image offers clues, an image that appeared before going to Egypt and that vividly presented itself again in Egypt and daily since my return. One pyramid pointed downward descends onto another upright pyramid. At first just the apexes touch, and then they quickly glide into each other. I have learned that it is called a star tetrahedron, a very sacred symbol of wholeness and integration. The Jungians might call it the coniunctio or sacred marriage.

More Than Myself
Ruth Eichler

After returning home from Egypt, I frequently felt "more than myself." I felt more largely present than my usual sense of being present. It feels as if more of myself is available to "reside" in my little self or to shine through. I am aware of a vaster Self, not just in concept but also in experience. This vaster Self is not "out there" as a separate but connected reality. Instead, I am one with this greater Self that extends all the way to the stars. The large Pisces fish swallows the little fish. The pyramids have merged into my effulgent heart. I have been deeply catalyzed into a new life by this experience — probably more so than with any other trip to foreign lands. I am curious about what lies in this vast sky of consciousness.

Uncharted Waters
Ruth Eichler

Mackie's brother, Raymond, a dear, powerful spiritual being, now reports to us in his mystical, poetic way that in truth, our job was not to complete but to initiate a whole new beginning. We are in uncharted waters. This is one reason why Lesley's ability to bring forth the wisdom from Beings of extremely high consciousness and vibration is so important. We are not re-interpreting old texts and meaning handed down through the ages, even that from the mystics. We are at a new place in the evolution of con-sciousness on this planet. We are in some ways like a babe being born, one that can assist in the co-creation of the New Earth. These concepts have been spoken in various places and ways for some time, but at least for me they were concepts and not a living reality. They are becoming a living reality as vibrant and alive as all the stars in Nut's belly, as vibrant and alive as all the sparkling energies and messages embedded in stones, trees, and the cells of all living creatures. The particles of Light emanating from ev-erywhere are all part of The One. So, we on the Earth stand together in the unfolding Mystery, present to each other and to the process with love, appreciation and respect. I believe that that was true for all of us going to Egypt. We enter the unknown with an open heart and arms.

ENDNOTES
Chapter 3: Egypt — a Story of the Sacred Feminine and Ascension

1. Normandi Ellis, *Feasts of Light: Celebrations for the Seasons of Life based on the Egyptian Goddess Mysteries*, (Wheaton, IL: Quest Books: 1999, p. x).

2. Juan Ramon Jimenez's poem, *"Oceans"*

3. Kristen Wilkerson, *"History and Meaning of the Ancient Egyptian Ankh Symbol,"* (Religion and Spirituality, August 1, 2009).

4. Torkom Saraydarian, *The Solar Angel,* (TSG Publishing Foundation, Inc., 1992).

5. Tom Kenyon, (tomkenyon.com/who-are-the-hathors, October 2012).

6. Tricia McCannon, *Jesus: The Explosive Story of the 30 Lost Years and the Ancient Mystery Religions,* (Charlottesville, VA: Hampton Roads Publishing Company, Inc., 2010).

Chapter 4
Levels of Consciousness and Initiation

The Buddha was asked, "Are you an angel, a prophet or a god?" He replied, "I am awake."

Ascension: Movement to Higher Consciousness

Many contemporary researchers of consciousness have identified developmental phases that correspond or reflect various levels of consciousness. One cannot experience a sense of oneness with the universe unless one has progressed through the various earlier levels of understanding. Clare Graves, Don Edward Beck, Deepak Chopra, Ken Wilber, and others have mapped stages of consciousness. At the beginning level, people see the world through the lenses of "me against you" or "us against them." We eventually move to a level in which we recognize that not only do we need to treat others as we would want to be treated, but also to a level beyond in which we realize that we are indeed one.

In between are various other levels such as being able to see and understand the other person so that there is willingness and desire to cooperate and collaborate. Mystics such as St. Teresa of Avila have also written about stages of development through their own experience, and she called hers the "seven interior castles." Ancient yogis who wrote the Sutras and the Vedas described landmarks on the way to enlightenment, beginning with the taming of the mind. Mystics of all spiritual traditions have spoken in one way or another of lifting the veils of ignorance and entering more sublime realms. Yet we want to be clear that it is not necessary to strive for these states of consciousness, for that might be the ego's desire for spiritual glorification or what could be called a state of premature transcendence. We can be faithful to the call of the Soul without grasping. When we ask without hidden agenda and with openness to the unknown, wisdom evolves and unfolds.

The ego remains with us, though, and as our friend and mentor, Elmer Green said, "The ego has to be excited enough to participate." Jack Kornfield, the Buddhist teacher, reminds us that spirituality doesn't save the ego from suffering or confusion, as it still has to live in the world.

> *Do not think that enlightenment is going to make you special; it's not. If you feel special in any way, then enlightenment has not occurred.* — Adyashanti

> *You really don't have any idea who you are. If you did, you would be capable of anything.* — Pir Vilayat

The value of maps of consciousness is that they reflect different lenses through which people see the world, and they help us understand the dynamic, evolutionary forces expressing as the ascension process. Spiral Dynamics is one theory of human development that has been popularized by Don Edward Beck, who co-authored *Spiral Dynamics* with Christopher Cowan. Beck also founded the Center for Human Emergence and worked alongside Nelson Mandela and F. W. de Klerk in creating reconciliation strategies in post-apartheid South Africa.

According to the view of Spiral Dynamics, people expand into progressively more complex stages, depending upon life conditions and response to them. Each stage represents a new worldview that encompasses new assumptions, interests, motivations and preferences. Beck believed each new level to be more enlightened than the previous one. Each time we spiral up, we have the benefit of what we have learned from previous struggles as well as new perspectives. The movement up the spiral is not automatic, for sufficient challenges must emerge in the current worldview in order to be motivated to change.

According to Beck, one of the values that motivates behavior in the lower realms of awareness is "do what you must do to stay alive" reflecting instinctive and survivalist values. Over thousands of years, humanity evolved to the fourth stage, which he calls "authoritarian," in which people believe that a code of conduct is based upon external, absolute principles. This level holds the values of law, regulation and discipline as the means to build character and moral fiber. Perhaps 35 percent of the population is at this level today, or at least when the book was published in 1996. He surmised that another 30 percent of people were at the next higher level, which he called "Strategic or Entrepreneurial."

A brief summary of the stages follows:

> **Semi-Stone Age** — natural order and natural law — perhaps .1% of the world's population is currently at this level.
>
> **Tribal** — safety and security; blood bonds — perhaps 10% of the world's population is at this level.

Exploitive — survival of the fittest; conquest of and domination over others — perhaps 15% of the world's population is at this level.

Authoritarian — order, structure, reliability, and existence is ordered under ultimate truth — perhaps 35% of the world's population is at this level.

Strategic/Entrepreneurial — act in your own self-interest playing the game to win, personal autonomy, manipulation of the environment — perhaps 30% of the world's population is at this level, although it is estimated the they exert 50% of the power.

Communitarian — peace and harmony within the inner self and explore with others the caring dimension of community and social cohesion — perhaps 10% of the world's population is at this level.

Integrative/Systemic — live fully and responsibly as what you are and become flexible, spontaneous, creative, innovative, integrated and interdependent — perhaps 1–2 % of the world's population is at this level.

Holistic — the wholeness of existence is experienced through mind and spirit, and the Self is both distinct and a blended part of a larger, compassionate whole, able to see and honor many perspectives — perhaps .1% of the world's population is at this level. [1]

At the end of the twentieth century, Beck estimated that slightly more than10 percent of the population was living at the last three levels with only 0.1 percent at the holistic level. We believe that this percentage is probably much higher today.

The ability to see multiple perspectives of life, including understanding lower stages, generally does not occur until the last two levels of consciousness.

The "holistic" level is what we are calling "ascension." According to Beck, at the holistic stage, the world is a single, dynamic organism with its own collective mind. Holistic, intuitive thinking and cooperative action are to be expected, and collective human intelligence can be used to work on large-scale, planetary problems without sacrificing individuality.

Every human being must grow level by level through the entire spiral of developmental levels of consciousness. Only when one stage has been sufficiently mastered does one move to the next stage of evolution, some progressing rather swiftly and others much more slowly. We don't get to skip anything. Beck and Graves believe that we must feel discomfort in our current state and feel judgment of those below us in order to separate and move into the next level.

The forerunner of Spiral Dynamics was the work of Psychologist Clare W. Graves. In mid-1981 he summarized his discoveries, which are just as appropriate today, in this way:

> "Briefly, what I am proposing is that the psychology of the mature human being is an unfolding, emergent, oscillating, spiraling process, marked by progressive subordination of older, lower-order behavior systems to newer, higher-order systems as an individual's existential problems change. Each successive stage, wave, or level of existence is a state through which people pass on their way to other states of being." [2]

He went on to say that each stage contains its own perceptions, beliefs, and even biochemistry particular to that state. Beliefs about religion, politics, education, and mental illness vary from one level to another.

Earlier, Dr. Graves wrote an article for *The Futurist* magazine titled, "Human Nature Prepares for Momentous Leap." He believed that an impending change in human consciousness would occur that would be difficult and at the same time the most exciting transition that humanity had yet faced. He said, "It is not merely a transition to a new level of existence but the start of a new 'movement' in the symphony of human history." [3]

> *"The human is at a cultural impasse... Radical new forms are needed... Everything depends on a creative resolution of our present antagonisms."*
> — *Thomas Berry*

Dr. Deepak Chopra has authored over fifty books and is called "the poet-prophet of alternative medicine." He has spoken about how the new paradigm change that is occurring is supported by new discoveries in quantum physics and neuroscience. He is quick to point out that these views are consistent with the Vedic seers from ancient times.

He believes that we no longer need to debate about these findings as speculative because science has now validated the long-held beliefs and spiritual experiences of thousands of people. He says the new paradigm holds these beliefs:

> "We live in a participatory universe. The objective world is created by a response of the observer. Time is not an absolute but a learned perception. We are not our bodies, egos or personalities but the Seer who creates and witnesses the changing scenery. The mind is not trapped in the brain or even in the body. Humans are interdependent, pulsing patterns within the Unified

Field. At a certain point, life awareness becomes aware of itself. Awareness becoming aware of itself is 'the second birth.'" [4]

Even with a new paradigm, Chopra admits it's not all easy. He says, "Buddha sitting under the Bodhi tree and Jesus wrestling with demons in the desert are symbolic of the same drama of the soul that you were to repeat." [5]

We can be drawn into the next level because of its beauty, vitality and coherence. The movement toward these last four levels of consciousness is inevitable. Sri Aurobindo, a yogi and teacher from India, The Tibetan scribed by Alice Ann Bailey during the last century and the *Course in Miracles* all agree. The *Course in Miracles* says, "It is a required course. Only the time you take it is voluntary. Free will does not mean that you can establish the curriculum. It only means you can elect what you want to take at a given time." [6]

> *The thing is to stalk your calling in a skilled and supple way, to locate the most tender and live spot and plug into that impulse.* — Annie Dillard

Even though only a relatively small percentage of the population may be truly living in these higher states at the present time, the coherence of these higher fields catalyzes those in the less evolved levels to come into stability and pattern, matching with the higher level. The less coherent energies come into resonance with the higher note. Much has been written about the hundredth monkey phenomenon in which once a critical mass is reached, a rapid shift occurs and all of the monkeys washed their sweet potatoes in the same way. As we put our attention on what is possible rather than what is wrong, change is catalyzed. Attention to intention brings about further acceleration.

*Allow ourselves to transcend that which
we have been taught.* — Greg Braden [7]

In spite of these levels of consciousness, ascension is not necessarily a linear process. Many who have dealt with personal
struggles are now coming into greater integration and maturity
at personal and spiritual levels and are now ascending. The
soul invokes the higher level of consciousness rather than the
personality self willing it or causing it to happen.

Many are shifting rapidly in consciousness, seemingly cata-
pulted into a new level simply because their hearts are being
opened, whether through trauma or an unexpected, heightened
blissful state. Many people have reported this phenomenon
after near-death experiences, and others have jumped into a
more transcendent level through stunning, peak experiences.

However, that person generally will return to the previous level
of consciousness until the lessons of that level are mastered, but
a new perspective has been offered that pulls the growth forward. Life never looks the same again. Because there has been
an acceleration of consciousness and an updraft of humanity in
recent times, it is only now that humanity as a collective is able
to access these higher states of consciousness without teachers,
gurus, and years of deep practice.

Our bodies, minds and emotional states can participate at these
higher vibrational levels now without becoming totally discombobulated. But many people are experiencing dissonance
in the body, emotions and mind because the higher vibrations
stimulate and affect those stuck places that are not yet in resonance with the higher impulse. We are still in the transitional
stage so that few can sustain into living in these states although
more and more glimpses are available.

The enormous influx of energies coming at this time is an unprecedented opportunity for humanity and the earth. In order to sustain with these heightened vibrations, we need to cultivate greater health and wellbeing physically, emotionally, mentally and spiritually. In his book, *One Taste: Daily Reflections on Integral Spirituality,* Ken Wilber says: "When the body/mind is strong and healthy—not ascetically starved and despised — it is all the easier to drop it, transcend it, let it go."

In the past, we most often looked at the world through the eyes of our "small personality self" believing we were separate, often fighting for survival, at least from our perspective. We can still read the daily news and see that this view has not disappeared from the planet and indeed notice some moments of our own belief in separation from others. However, sometimes in small and unnoticed ways and sometimes in global movements, we see a shifting of the view from "us" and "them" to a much more comprehensive and compassionate view of the world.

> *God does not die on the day we cease to believe in a personal deity, but we die on the day when our lives cease to be illumined by the steady radiance of wonder renewed daily, the Source of which is beyond all reason.* — Dag Hammarskjold

We can easily find examples of ways in which we are moving away from "us" and "them" attitudes. One such example comes from the work of David Kennedy, director of the Center for Crime Prevention and Control at John Jay College of Criminal Justice in New York City and author of *Don't Shoot*. He has had remarkable success in helping inner city gangs in seventy major cities in the United States and a few other countries to shift from polarized "us" and "them" perspectives to cooperation.

He first piloted his Operation Ceasefire program in Boston where youth homicide rates were dramatically reduced by as much as 66 percent, a program now called the "Boston Miracle." His program brings gang members into meetings with family members including their mothers, social services representatives, community members they respect, and law enforcement officials. The gang members are treated with respect, and the law enforcement teams aggressively target people who retaliate against the gang members who participate.

Another person who has tirelessly campaigned against gang violence is Aqeela Sherrills, who continues to live in the Watts area of Los Angeles, California. He brokered a peace agreement between the notorious gangs, the Crips and Bloods, who had fought and killed each other for decades, an agreement that still stands today. These two courageous men, Kennedy and Sherrills, are among many who fight valiantly to move us beyond separation and violence. As Rumi said, "There's a field out beyond right and wrong. I'll meet you there."

When Lesley and Ruth traveled to Egypt in February 2010, the Egyptian government required that guides and occasionally armed guards accompany us. Therefore, a "bubble" from which we didn't fully see the repressiveness of the regime in power surrounded us. During the 2011 revolution in Egypt, CNN News said that a "shift in consciousness" had occurred. The overall vision arose from a possibility of freedom for the people in response to inner stirrings that extended beyond sectarian and religious divisions. As with many collective breakthroughs, those with an authoritarian level of consciousness become frightened of the changes and do their best to squelch, at least temporarily, the rise to freedom that threatens to change the status quo.

Wendell Berry, a prolific writer and poet, spent his life sharing his views on sustainability of the planet and the interconnectedness of all life. One of his often-quoted poems shares how our connection with each other and nature is part of a much larger dance of life. The first few lines of this poem called *"Healing"* are below:

> We clasp the hands of those who go before us,
> And the hands of those who come after us;
> We enter the little circle of each other's arms,
> And the larger circle of lovers
> Whose hands are joined in a dance
> And the larger circle of all creatures...

Initiation

The essence of initiation, as described in various esoteric traditions, involves transcending levels of consciousness. In that regard, it is similar to the levels of consciousness described above and relevant to the ascension process. However, whereas the above maps of consciousness include everyone, even the first level of initiation requires a certain level of maturity. As one ascends through levels of initiation, one must master challenges at each level before being able to pass through an energetic "doorway" or passageway to another level.

The initiate experiences the energy of each level and incorporates it harmoniously into his or her life purpose. Initiation involves increasing the vibratory capacity of one's being and in so doing becoming more and more aware of the unity that exists with all sentient beings and with all of life. Each initiation involves a burning away of that which no longer serves. Initiation creates tension and the opportunity to use that tension, along with a quiet, focused mind, to burn away the old. The Phoenix burns and rises from the ashes time and again.

Increased vibrational capacity creates a wider "bandwidth" that allows a more direct relationship with all sentient beings regardless of their level of consciousness. Gradually, the struggles and suffering experienced from a dualistic, separative frame of reference drop away, and greater and greater freedom is experienced. One is able to surrender into the plan of the Great Mystery and in so doing find comfort in the opportunity to serve, to know oneself as divine and to be in contact with the great enlightened beings. Some say it is a progressive entry into the mind of God.

Hazrat Inayat Khan, a Sufi Master, says:

> "Initiation requires courage, steadiness, and patience. It is utmost trust, which is the greatest power in the world. Real initiation is taking a step in an unknown direction, to another level of consciousness, becoming free from all the limitations of life. I, by the light of the soul, realize that the beauty of the heavens and the grandeur of the Earth are the echo of Thy magic flute."

Each initiation is like a movement to a higher classroom with greater awareness of light within that seeks to shine through and into the life. As consciousness expands, the personality expression is elevated into the higher wisdom of the heart-mind, higher self, or soul. This increasing of the "voltage" or vibrational activity of each individual atom in the physical body results in a greater degree of energy and elasticity. Increased refinement in the emotional and mental bodies is created as lower qualities and habits are "shaken loose" by exposure to the higher vibration. Quickening of the fields of energy surrounding the body makes it more similar to the subtle realms.

Initiation implies greater light, coherence and radiance, and it is said that in the higher realms this light knows us.

> *Know ye not that ye are the temple of God, and that the Spirit of God dwelleth in you?* [8]

> *Each of us is recognized by the brilliance of our light.* [9]

We must navigate and master each level of consciousness as we ascend "up the ladder" so to speak, though the quickening is greatly accelerated at this time. The direct dispensation coming down through the levels of consciousness is not being stepped down as in previous times. This is new on the earth at this time. Although mastery of each level is required for the next "door" to open to another level of consciousness, one might still temporarily fall back into patterns of an earlier stage.

In previous times, people participated in special mystery schools or received intensive instruction over long periods of time in order to achieve initiation. Lesley's experience in Egypt revealed to her that now we can initiate each other.

Levels of Initiation

Though many spiritual traditions speak of various levels of initiation, here we focus on the esoteric teachings of The Tibetan, an enlightened being also called Djwhal Khul, who telepathically transmitted several books of teachings to Alice Ann Bailey.

First Initiation: The Practice of Mastering the Physical Form and Material Appetites

Much of humanity is approaching the first initiation, which might roughly correspond with the communitarian level of consciousness described above. In the first step on "the path" or the First Initiation, we struggle to master the physical aspect of our being, learning to incorporate a healthy lifestyle and a balanced life. Addictions to substances, sex, internet usage and a multitude of other things abound that take us away from presence in the "now." The taming of our "animal nature," including learning to release obsessive thinking patterns and improving relationships, constitutes some of the challenges of this stage.

Even how the voice is used to influence or relate to others can be a matter of the first initiation. For example, as the throat chakra is strengthened, we may realize idle gossip's power to hurt others.

Mastery of the physical form includes developing greater responsibility for self, and realizing one's impact on the planet and others. As one proceeds through this first door, one's attention naturally orients toward greater care for self and others. Old judgments and dogmas fall away as former limitations and negative qualities seem less the focus. It is a movement from the solar plexus into the heart. This stage is often preceded by loneliness as this longing causes an extension toward the higher realms. One begins to question life's purpose and to see life's difficulties as possible lessons to guide in personal evolution. Self-centeredness, formerly the norm, drops away as a desire to help others develops.

Second Initiation: The Ability to Self-regulate, Using Emotional and Feeling States for Creative Self-expression Rather than Being Dominated by Them

The second initiation focuses on the emotional life. Though emotions can inspire great joy, harmony, peace and spirituality, they are also often accompanied by a heightened sense of polarization between good and bad, highs and lows. Rolling between these sweet and sour poles causes much grief, as long held beliefs of "the truth" can dominate consciousness and cause resistance to change. During this stage, old subconscious beliefs that hold us prisoner must fall away and be replaced with more spacious truths and guidance. Often they do not go gently into the night but arise in the shadow of projected blame and disappointing insights about those around us.

In the second initiation, the activated heart radiates love, thus dynamically affecting greater numbers of people, events and levels of activity and creation. Perhaps this initiation roughly corresponds with the integrative/systemic level of consciousness described above. Although this initiation offers greater scope and vision, at first the status quo of the whole life is usually destabilized. Though often unsettling, this actually results in a future filled with the possibility for greater flexibility and creative expression. A more comprehensive understanding of life purpose emerges. The inner and outer worlds become more balanced as higher realization and inner inspiration become incorporated into the life.

> *What we are is what we have thought for years.* — The Buddha

> *As a man thinketh in his heart, so is he.* — Jesus

The second initiation is difficult because of the need to move from ME to WE. It is said that it takes many lifetimes of steadfast desire and practice to master this level. One must learn self-regulation and mastery over emotions. When we react with strong emotions as if everything that occurs is a personal affront against us, we are not listening to the inner voice of the heart. We need to learn to be a dispassionate witness to our own process. Joining heart and mind provides the way out of the self-made, limiting prison of our closely held old beliefs and "stories." We can still have emotions; they just can no longer be the "captain of the ship." Marianne Williamson, in her frequently repeated quotation, admonishes us to conquer fear and be who we were meant to be:

> Our deepest fear is not that we are inadequate. Our deepest fear is that we are powerful beyond measure. It is our Light, not our darkness, that most frightens us. We ask ourselves, 'Who am I to be brilliant, gorgeous, talented and fabulous?' Actually, who are you not to be? You are a Child of God. Your playing small does not serve the world. There is nothing enlightened about shrinking so other people won't feel insecure around you. We were born to make manifest the glory of God that is within us. And as we let Light shine, we unconsciously give other people permission to do the same. As we are liberated from our own fear, our presence automatically liberates others." [10]

Along with reorientation on an emotional level, we move from concrete to more abstract thinking, and we seek deeper, more comprehensive understanding of our life experiences. We begin to understand how our socially prescribed and culturally embedded ways of seeing the world have gripped and limited us. As the heart and throat chakras are engaged, the emotions stabilize. Pride and loyalty evolve into serving the purpose of

Universal Will. Early instability and emotionalism creates a desire to seek guidance from Soul. The resulting greater mastery allows us to support the plan that is emerging.

In the second initiation, service and responsibility often include a pioneering mission. Power and influence increase, but their application must be for Universal liberation and not personal aggrandizement. Personal magnetism without selfish motive creates the ability to work on a larger scale. A "third eye," also called the brow chakra develops giving one perception beyond ordinary sight. This inner eye increases the skill and ability to consistently rely upon telepathy, clairvoyance and precognition.

Emotional Mastery Tests Are Like Surfing
Sacred Beloved

You are being given a series of emotional mastery exams to see how long you remain identified with the wave and how long before you can ride the wave like a surfer. A surfer gets thoroughly wet and is in the ocean and yet remains identified with himself. We are with you every bounce of the surfboard."

Third Initiation: Living a Life of Purpose and Relinquishing Personal Will, Knowing Oneself as a Soul, Identifying Oneself as Part of the Greater Whole and Moving Beyond the Identification with the "Personality Self."

> *The whole idea of compassion is based on the keen awareness of the inter-dependence of all these living beings which are all part of one another and all involved in one another. ... The whole purpose of life is to live by love.*
> — Thomas Merton [11]

> *The problem in the world is that we draw our family circle too small.* — Mother Teresa

At the third initiation people come into alignment with divine Will. This initiation might roughly correspond with the holistic level of consciousness described above. The personal will becomes an instrument for divine Will, just as Jesus urged us to pray, "Thy will be done." The third initiation has also been called transfiguration because our form has been transformed into a more beautiful, radiant, spiritual state. Saint Paul spoke of this experience as "Christ in me." Some have referred to this level of consciousness as I AM presence. We have moved from ME to WE now to ONE.

It is here that the personality literally becomes infused with the soul. The mind responds to intuitions, ideas and impulses of the soul in an almost conversational way, and the person has developed mastery over the mental body. At this point quieting the thoughts is within the volition of the initiate who is aware that the thinking mind creates thought forms that attract the events of the life and affect others as well.

Instead of identifying as a personality ("I am a teacher. I am a swift runner. etc.), one identifies as a soul. This would be the "I" that looks down at the nested Russian dolls of which we previously spoke.

More people are now approaching the third doorway at this time of acceleration, though this door remains closed until heart and mind can join to withstand the enormous increase in energy and light. The halo around the head of saints often portrayed in paintings reflects this integration of heart and mind that allows such a transmission of light. It is at this level that the kundalini fire, an electrical current, ascends up the spine through the chakra system. Awakening is further accelerated, often accompanied by mystical experiences.

Unconditional love pours from the heart for all of humanity. Concern and compassion extend beyond personal and familial issues to include all of life and to Gaia and the Universe as a whole. This brings about a larger and larger sphere of influence, one of the hallmarks of the third initiation.

One of the noticeable experiences of this level is its stability. One can "hold steady in the light," with balanced and refined energy fields. Those living at this level of awareness experience congruence in thought and action as well as concept and vision. These people catalyze change simply by being. Their mere presence influences others to move in ways that are consistent with their life purpose. Others also can begin to consider the needs of others as important as their own. This does not mean that flowers spring up at their feet but that the status quo is often shaken up and moved to higher awareness just by their presence. Their very being affects others. As their light shines, the world becomes more illuminated.

At the third initiation, a group field is created and seeded. People are magnetically drawn together as groups, some but not all in geographical proximity to one another. The shared resonance then facilitates group initiation.

These groups assemble not on personality levels but as soul groups. The people composing these groups may have various degrees of maturity and integration of soul and personality. Thus, their group appeal can be across a wide spectrum of humanity and yet function at the level of soul in its most refined level of reciprocal vibration.

Some people in these groups hold steady, coherent, resonant energy fields on behalf of that community. But it is also useful that there are group members who are less mature to bring a hearty, healthy diversity of thought and a denser substance. The group helps bring the inspirations and information from these higher vibrations into subtle energy fields on the planet. Greater numbers of people are thus able to "catch" the thoughts in dream and meditative states.

As personalities we incur karma based upon our ego's desires that influence our decisions. That is, our actions cause natural consequences — or "what goes around comes around." These initiatory groups that form to implement planetary work are not limited by individual desire so are freer to cultivate more dramatic kinds of changes. These groups invoke and evoke the changes that are part of the new world. These are not karmic families, but they are lineages of service that act as human agents to direct the free will of humanity to engage with the higher will of the Divine in manifesting new forms and ways of being. The Group impulse helps move karma to dharma, to the path of enlightenment.

What calls us into these groups? Soul does. Soul is not a grown up personality; rather Soul is the continuing light expression, a magnetic field. It can attract to it that which furthers its purpose and reason for being. When Soul expresses as part of a group impulse, the group assists more of humanity to come into identification with the reality that they are Souls living as human personalities rather than human personalities who might in the past have aspired to be infused by soul. When the door of initiation is opened to the group, the impulse to be of service to the Whole accelerates and is vastly augmented.

Albert Einstein seemed to intuit this impulse when he said:

> "There is one thing we do know: that we are here for the sake of each other, Above all, for those upon whose smile and well-being our own happiness depends. And also for the countless unknown souls with whose fate we are connected by a bond of sympathy."

Fourth Initiation: Expressing as the Will of God or Universal Consciousness, Aligning with Divine Mind.

The Fourth Initiation is called the great renunciation because one "dies" completely to ego and serves humanity as an embodiment of the teachings of the great teachers such as Jesus and Buddha. Most likely this initiation goes beyond what Spiral Dynamics offers as levels of consciousness. At this point on the path, karma, cause and effect has been lifted up into impersonal and universal awareness and "earth school" lessons learned. All of those who have reached this level have made lasting, deep and pervasive changes in human consciousness.

They have a very wide sphere of influence and bring new forms of Truth directly into planetary awareness. These Beings express cosmically by word and by example.

In the past this state was lived by disciples and initiates supporting these high vibrational states from the subtle energy realms almost entirely beyond the physical form. Today remaining with humanity while acting as a bridge to the fellowship of light and joining the staff of future planners of civilizations in this solar system is more widespread. Mother Teresa might be an example of this, as were possibly Martin Luther King, Jr. and Ghandi.

Fifth Initiation: This State of Initiation, also Called Revelation, is Beyond What Can Be Comprehended at This Time.

Having graduated earth school, the fifth initiation is a voluntary return to earth that is of complete choice to serve humanity and the planet. Prior to this level of attainment, one can take the Bodhisattva vow that prepares for this motive to ever serve humanity and the planet. One example of this vow is:

> May I be a guard for all those who are protector-less,
> A guide for those who journey on the road,
> For those who wish to go across the water,
> May I be a boat a raft, a bridge.
> For all those ailing in the world,
> Until their every sickness has been healed,
> May I myself become for them
> The doctor, nurse, the medicine itself.

Although such a high state of consciousness may have been demonstrated by a few, our limited consciousness cannot mentally hold the extent of the love/wisdom principles, nor can we fully comprehend or incorporate what we might see.

It has been suggested that all the initiations have been accelerating because of increasing fields of higher vibrational influences and because of the vast numbers of people who exist on the planet at this time. Each "level" of consciousness creates an "updraft" for the next. Perhaps in our lifetime we will each be exposed to levels of opportunity never before possible. Correspondingly, the new levels of complexity in awareness call forth a new response from the Beings of extremely refined consciousness.

Teachers on the Path

What about teachers along the way? While we believe that we now can be each other's initiators and inspirers to higher conscious states, we can still benefit from teachers. We can now look at historical teachers such as Jesus and the Buddha in new light. As consciousness increases, we can begin to fathom the deeper levels of their teachings. As for present day teachers, Ram Das said of his teacher:

> "It's like knowing somebody who lives a little further up the mountain and can see father than you can. The view from there is perfection—not perfection as something to be achieved, but perfection in what is."

Death

At each stage of evolution, the old must drop away, allowing the new to emerge, just as our physical form drops away at death. Whether we are dropping the form, as we do in physical death or are moving from one state of consciousness to another while still embodied, we often experience fear and resistance. We are asked to leave an old identification behind in order to receive the next. As human beings, we also experience grief in these transitions — whether from our own changes or with the loss of loved ones.

The Phoenix is burned to ash, the old form is destroyed, but it rises again — a resurrected Phoenix. This myth teaches us so much. A universal need exists to come to terms with death and to provide hope for the future. The Sacred Feminine also presides as a bringer of life, growth, decline, death and rebirth. Nearly every culture throughout history has revered some form of the goddess that assisted with death whether it is the Christian Virgin Mary's comfort and compassion or the Hindu Kali's fierce destruction of false consciousness and attachments. Kali, consort to Shiva, represents eternal time, change and death. She is also associated with empowerment and the primordial cosmic energy of Shakti, which moves through the entire universe.

Persephone, a Greek goddess, was forcibly taken into the underworld by Hades and thus became acquainted with her own "shadow" and unconscious. She became Queen of the Underworld and presided over death. Eventually she was able to visit her mother, Demeter, goddess of the earth in the upper world for part of the year only to return time and again to her new domain. She became a whole woman at home in both levels of consciousness. Persephone teaches us how to sit with death and destruction, to learn its lessons, to accept what is in order to become more awake and whole. We don't have to instantaneously release all of our attachments. Only in the allowing do we awaken to the higher truth of the continuity of consciousness.

> *Continuity of consciousness means remembering who you are in different states.*" — Vivian King [12]

Meditation, deep sleep, dream practices, or intuitive insights all provide experiences of continuity of consciousness. In all cases, we "die" to the ways we have seen and identified ourselves. So it is with death of the physical form. These states of altered consciousness for those living on this earth are common and can be cultivated to assist us in our fear of dying.

Near-death experiences, of which much has been written, help us to realize that we do not cease to exist beyond death of the physical form. We often fear death because we don't see it as the movement from one state of consciousness to another that it is. Facing the loss of identity and the unknown and letting go of attachments frightens us.

Death is inherent in all living processes, because all of life is impermanent and changing. It is simply a part of a larger continuity of consciousness and not a lost battle. Destruction of the old form and letting go of attachment to it is an integral part of evolution. In the past, we have not collectively been able to experience this continuity; therefore, we have been afraid.

As we develop greater appreciation for the feminine perspective of wholeness and the continuing nature of all processes, we can see death as a state within a larger process of continuing without a form. Whereas some view death as "losing the battle," or as a "bad event," we can perceive death simply as a valuable part of the evolutionary plan. If we view "heaven" as somewhere else, we feel separated from it and may experience fear of the unknown. As we understand continuity of consciousness, heaven can be here and now, in this perfect moment. Or we can be in "hell" when we are embroiled in negativity. With or without a body, purpose and meaning are woven into the entire fabric of life.

Identification

> *I must be willing to give up what I am in order to become what I will be.*
> — Albert Einstein

Ken Wilber suggests that humanity at this time has a sufficient number of people who have integrated cognitive awareness and heart-centered presence that impacts the world, whether through conscious transmission or just through being. Those stages represent one's identity moving from seeing oneself merely as me (ego-centric) to identification with us (ethno-centric) to identification with all of us (world-centric) to identification with All (kosmocentric). Each stage includes the awareness gained from the previous stage. At some point in the development between world-centric and kosmic-centric, the deep psyche can awaken itself, not as a temporary altered state but as a permanent realization or stage of consciousness.

> "We treat others by the way we identify ourselves. If we identify only with ourselves we are narcissist, if with our friends and family we will be more caring. If we are Nationalistic we will treat others as countrymen. If we recognize ourselves as an aspect of Divinity we act with greater respect and compassion." — Ken Wilbur

Regardless of whether we are talking about levels of consciousness or initiations, at each turn there is a letting go of an old identification and a re-identification over time with the new view of the world. It makes a difference the place we imagine our eyes to be. When we imagine ourselves to be just flesh and blood, or a personality self, we may look up to the soul, through the soul, for divine guidance. Even if we know we are more than just this personality self that includes body, emotions and mind, we are habituated to identifying ourselves from this perspective.

What if we imagined we were looking at the personality self from the vantage point of the soul? Some people write letters to God and then write responses from God, changing their vantage point in the process. From the new vantage point, the entire tone, perspective and vibration changes. We become identified or see through the eyes of the soul.

Literally a lighted thread of consciousness is created between the chakra system of the human being and the soul and has been called the "*antahkarana*," a Sanskrit word meaning "web of light." It has also been called the Rainbow Bridge, because at a certain point along the evolutionary path of the soul, instead of the soul looking down upon the personality self, the soul begins to look up towards the Oneness of All, creating a lighted, subtle energy bridge to the higher worlds. The Bible refers to angels walking up and down ladders. The more we travel this "ladder" or bridge, the stronger it becomes until we eventually re-identify as a Soul in the third initiation. Often in the past this was interpreted as that a body was no longer needed, so the person physically died. Part of the ascension process means that we are now traveling up and down, down and up, re-identifying as a living soul presence. The body can now become a luminous form — divinity into matter.

Shattering Identities
Ruth Eichler

I pray that I can stand present in the face of shattering identities, and though the outer world remains the same, I feel I'm in one of those cataclysmic shifts. A poem by Juan Ramon Jimenez has again become my mantra:

My boat struck something deep.
Sounds, waves, silence.
Perhaps nothing happened,
Or, perhaps everything has happened,
And I'm sitting in the middle of my new life.

I don't know what changes in identity are yet to emerge, but I began to sense something different when I felt like a hollow tube through which strong energies moved. I couldn't slump even if I wanted to.

Maybe getting used to receiving blessings that have been pouring in over the last few months is part of the shattering of one old identity and the gentling into a new one. Some people's changes do truly come as shattering experiences, catapulting them to a new place. My changes have felt more of the escalator variety, but perhaps that's just my Sagittarian outlook, seeing the bright side. Nevertheless, I'm sitting in the middle of my new life.

Beyond the Horizon
Ruth Eichler

It's all about identification—whatever I happen to be identified with at any given time. The Course in Miracles and Eckhart Tolle, author of The Power of Now, both talk about what constitutes the enlightened state in simple, yet profound, language. Repeatedly Tolle speaks about being present in the "now," unidentified with the past or future. At times, I think, "How true!" At other times I struggle to fully comprehend even these simple concepts. How could someone in the face of imminent extinction — as is occurring to some people on the planet as we speak — live fully present and feel joy? Perhaps if they were ascended masters, they could, but there aren't too many ascended masters running around the planet in the physical, although no doubt several do exist.

The choice still remains to choose our attitude every moment of the day. Viktor Frankl's book, Man's Search for Meaning, has probably been the most significant book I've ever read in my life. I thought, "If Viktor Frankl could choose his attitude while experiencing the horrors of a concentration camp, then surely I can do the same in an ordinary life." Of course, I gradually became aware over time of how certain unconscious patterns governed my attitudes. I remember the day I realized that I could never complain again with impunity. Indeed, I have complained now and then, but it's never held as much satisfaction as before, a complaint instantly heralding the presence of victim consciousness. I realized that if I could do something about a situation or change it in any way, then why was I complaining and not changing? Or if I couldn't change something, why complain?

> *Sometimes I go about in pity for myself and all the while a great wind is bearing me across the sky.* —An Ojibwa saying
> 13

A Great Wind Carries Me across the Sky
Ruth Eichler

How do I hold onto identifications? I want my ego to be in service to the Soul. I want to be a soul-infused personality, yet I realize that the personality self can't bring this about. As Einstein said, a problem cannot be solved at the same level at which it was created. The Indian vision of a great wind bearing me across the sky reminds me of the

159

enormous help and assistance available at all times from beyond the personality self.

I still feel as if I'm just on the verge of something, the edge of a breakthrough. I can almost hear the Hallelujah chorus in the background. So near. "Be here now, not in the future," Eckhart would admonish me.

> *Whatever we focus on is bound to expand. Where we see the negative, we call forth more negative, and where we see the positive, we call forth the positive.* — Marianne Williamson

Birthing the Mystery from the Cave
Ruth Eichler

Lesley talked about how Kali and other goddesses and archetypes are not The Truth either, but act as guardians of the door. We have to go through the doorway into the darkness, the divine mystery, in order to be birthed into the new world, old encrustations of form and belief shattered or dissolved. I see Kali at the threshold, guarding the Great Mystery held in the heart of God. I see a figure (perhaps it's me) walking past Kali after offering her something in gratitude and plunging into the Great Darkness of wholeness, of unity. I no longer exist as such. Source funds all movement, all resonance, and all life. What then of interior time? Being in that cave of darkness is to BE the heart of God, not just to be IN the heart of God, but also to live and breathe as this moving, pulsating, birthing Heart.

This morning I awoke feeling some of the usual low-grade anxiety feeling all that needs to be done in the outer world and the need for time in the Cave. Once again as so frequently has occurred, the Sufi blessing song echoed in my heart: "May the blessings of God rest upon you. May God's peace abide with you. May God's presence illuminate your heart, now and forever more." Instantly I felt relaxation melt over me. This little self once again is reminded that it's not in charge of the Universe and doesn't have to be, nor can it, but it can be a human vehicle or vessel for this vibrant, powerful, alive, breathing Dark Mystery. Sophia is alive and well. She has birthed God. We birth God into this world, into this life of form on the earth.

We celebrate Sophia's return to consciousness. She no longer needs to be sequestered in a hidden cave. What was it that Jesus said about seeking the kingdom of heaven? It is here. The dark cave has turned inside out. God is born. Spring has arrived.

I Am Not the Drum
Sacred Beloved

Loosening from the identifications that have solidified through multiple incarnations and several decades in this body is frightening and freeing, sorrowful and joyful. You recall how you reacted with startle the first time you heard, "I have a mind and I am not my mind." Remember that you are both the sound of the drumbeat and the silence between the beats. These exist outside of time, in the eternal now.

Release all judgments about the process of identification and disidentification, knowing and not knowing. Let go into the mystery, into the Beloved. Breathe. Breathe. Breathe. One stands in humility and in grace. New identifications emerge, different from anything imagined. The human mind can never fully grasp or understand the mystery, but you can continue to say, "I am not my body or my emotions. I am not the pole or the drum. I am the vibration—unique and at the same time part of the Universal Whole." Disidentify from the drama and from the story, even the meaning of the story. Just as in the dances, one foot touches the earth and then the next and then the next. And you are not the foot or the one who dances.

At Home
Ruth Eichler

Maybe I, too, am living a new life, and my identification just hasn't caught up yet. Though I didn't always know I was building a stronger Self over the years that Self had to be strong, intact and integrated in order to transcend it. I am less identified with doing and more with being. Perhaps for the first time I'm truly at home in the journey.

> *If you want to identify me, ask me not where I live or what I eat or how I comb my hair. Ask me what I am living for in detail and ask me what I think is keeping me from living fully for the things I want to live for. Between those two answers, you can determine the identity of any person.* — Thomas Merton [14]

Being

We have focused on levels of consciousness as if each level were an elevator ride to a new floor that brings new landscapes to experience, new beliefs to incorporate, and more enriched ways of being in the world. At any level one can choose one's response to life's challenges, and one can openly embrace the possibility of growth and change. Although we cannot will ourselves to another level, in our fast-paced culture, striving can take hold and diminish the joys of the present moment, minimize the importance of just being.

The state of being emanates from the subtle levels rather than only through the physical form, although form is illuminated from Being. Beingness reveals what is already potential at the universal level and facilitates its emergence into consciousness. Being might be experienced at times as "the peace that passeth all understanding" and is often beyond the intellect. The Buddha called the deep peace experienced by the personality as "being awake."

Even though seemingly passive, Being affects change at root causes and affects patterns in the subtle realms that interconnect and express synergistically. When individuals experience enlightened, loving and wise states of consciousness and actively live the Higher Will for the greatest good, divine love is expressed and the highest levels of being are called forth.

Andrew Cohen, spiritual teacher and author of *Evolutionary Enlightenment*, summarizes:

> "We make the effort to evolve because we are in love with life and are committed to unlocking its highest potentials through our own development. Those potentials will only come to the fore when we are no longer trying to become enlightened but have let go of any other option than to be the expression of the highest we have seen and experienced, in all our imperfection." [15]

> *Being recognizes itself. People come together, being in response to being. That's the beauty of it.* — Eckhart Tolle [16]

163

Call to Beingness
Ruth Eichler

Who knows how long the call to Beingness has been here? Perhaps hearing the inner words, "Be still and know that I am God" many, many years ago was one of the soft clarion calls. Perhaps all of my spiritual explorations and calls have been leading me into that sense of Beingness. Once I had to pull my car off the Kansas Turnpike because the sight of sunlight sparkling and dancing on a lake stunned me into awed wonder and silence. Once at the end of a four-day silent retreat, I sprawled on a chair as relaxed as a cat purring in a sunlit window.

Timeless Being
Ruth Eichler

Something is beginning to settle inside, and images float like clouds across my mind: the hawk over the prairie; dancing in the Sun/ Moon Dance. Both are part of the timelessness of Being, yet both involve activity. The hawk rests into floating on the air currents yet is ready to zoom to earth to snatch up its prey. At the Sun/Moon Dance, I am not just sitting — though there's a fair amount of that between dances, but I am dancing towards the pole in the center and back to my "place." Being does not always mean doing nothing — though I am aware that I must learn to do nothing.

Spring and Being
Ruth Eichler

Perhaps daffodils and the other delights of spring — trees budding with tiny green leaves, flowering trees bursting forth in color, the meadows suddenly clothed in vibrant green — are the new life. I only want my "yes's" to be those that harken joy and delight in Beingness, whether or not I am also doing. I wonder if my Swedish great grandmother, Christina Carolina Bergstrom Lindquist, also smiled when spring came — or did she only think of the obligation of planting peas and potatoes to feed the family.

Peace Permeates the Life
Ruth Eichler

I love Shiva Rae's gentle suggestion to allow the peace of our yoga practice to permeate the fabric of our ordinary life. That is my prayer—that the extraordinary permeate the ordinary, whether seamlessly or whether awakened through the out-of-ordinary experiences.

ENDNOTES
Chapter 4: Levels of Consciousness and Initiation

1. Don Edward Beck and Christopher C. Cowan, Spiral Dynamics, (Blackwell Publishing, 1996, pp. 300-301).

2. Compiled for Dr. Clare Graves by Chris Cowan, "Summary Statement: The Emergent, Cyclical, Double-Helix Model Of The Adult Human Biopsychosocial Systems," handout for presentation to World Future Society, Boston, Mass., May 20, 1981.

3. Clare W. Graves, "Human Nature Prepares for a Momentous Leap," *The Futurist,* 1974, pp. 72-87.

4. "The new birth" comment comes from this source: Deepak Chopra, *The Book of Secrets,* (NY: Three Rivers Press, 2004, p. 261).

5. Deepak Chopra, *The Book of Secrets,* (NY: Three Rivers Press, 2004, p. 4).

6.   *Course in Miracles, Volume One Text,* (NY: Huntington Station, Foundation for Inner Peace, 1975, Introduction).

7.   Greg Braden, *Awakening to Zero Point: The Collective Initiation,* (Sacred Spaces Ancient Wisdom Books, 1997).

8.   I Corinthians 3:16 Djwhal Khul, as reported by Alice Ann Bailey

9.   Djwhal Khul, as reported by Alice Ann Bailey.

10.   Marianne Williamson, A Return to Love: *Reflections on the Principles of* "A Course in *Miracles.* Ch. 7, Section 3 (1992).

11.   Thomas Merton said this shortly before his death in 1968.

12.   Vivian King, Reflections on the Will, Part II, Vol. 3, March 2002, p. 71.

13.   An Ojibwa saying quoted by Phil Cousineau in *The Art of Pilgrimage.*

14.   Thomas Merton, *The Man and the Sycamore Tree.*

15.   Andrew Cohen. This quotation is cited in several places online such as Andrew Cohen on Facebook (8/6/12) or www. magazine. enlightennext.org

16.   Eckhart Tolle, (in an interview "Stillness & Presence" in Inquiring Mind 18:1, Fall, 2001).

Chapter 5
Prophecy

True prophecy always holds out hope. This is because the function of prophecy really isn't to foretell the future; it's to inspire awareness and change in the present. It is, as I said, about opening, not closure. — David Spangler [1]

Over the last several decades, prophecies have proliferated about the acceleration process, a shift that would change how we think, what we believe and how we experience reality. As David Spangler said in his book, *Facing the Future*, "Expecting a new consciousness to miraculously appear and solve all our problems is a tenuous basket in which to place all our eggs for facing the future." [2] He also speaks of the complexity of prophecy that occurs because of such a variety of variables and interrelationships:

> "The 'revealed' or experienced future is the product of a number of factors all interacting with each other: the past, the present, the images of the future, the inertia or momentum of events leading to certain consequences, our consciousness, the equality of our beingness, our actions, our relationships, the fields of subtle energy we create, and so on." [3]

We have a choice in how we co-author with the future as fore-told in the prophecies; we do not have to take them as destined realities. We enter into this process with whatever our level of consciousness is, and we build the future as we can imagine that to be.

We will share brief highlights from a few of the multitude of prophecies that have been given by various beings, cultures, and traditions to show a certain amount of consistency, both in hopefulness and caution. Many books have been written about these prophecies, and they have been interpreted in various ways, again dependent upon the level of awareness of the in-terpreter. For example, people who are at Beck's fourth level of consciousness, where much of our population is today, believe that a higher authority, traditions, and established norms are the guidelines for knowing one's place. Because of their belief in authority, they would be more likely to expect the prophe-cies to carry messages of retribution or reward that cannot be altered. In contrast, people at Beck's eighth, holistic level oper-ate with a sense of discovery and multi-dimensional insight that offer a perspective that translates into action on behalf of the whole. The prophecies would be seen as transformational opportunities for global solutions and that we collaborate with the outcome as part of the web of life.

Many indigenous cultures have held an ancient prophecy that states, "When the Grandmothers from the four directions speak, a new time is coming." Thirteen indigenous grandmothers from many different countries have been meeting since 2004 in the belief that the time is urgent now for a rebalancing of the world and the destruction of the earth must stop. Prophecies from other cultures also point in this direction as evidenced by a few summarized below.

Inca Prophecy

*When the Condor of the South flies with
the Eagle of the North, a new day for
Earth will awaken!* — Inca Prophecy

Though this foretelling of the condor and eagle coming together comes from the Inca people of Peru, many indigenous peoples in the Western Hemisphere have shared and retold this prophecy. Ceremonies have been held involving native peoples of North and South American coming together to honor and fulfill this message. In all cases, the messengers say that the time is now for its fulfillment. According to this prophecy, a cycle of renewal begins every 500 years, part of much larger cycles of time and evolution. The last 500-year cycle began about when the Spanish conquered the Incas, at which time the prophecy of great change or "*pachacuti*" was given that is now coming to fruition.

Willaru Huarta, a native Quechua Incan shaman from Peru, says that the time is now to reunite as one people after having been broken apart. As with most traditions, he tells us that the elders have kept the dream and vision alive even through difficulties. The children must know this vision. He further says:

> "All of our people have to make a new design for our children and the future generations. It is written in the stars. ... This will begin a new time when we can take the Spirit in our own hands when the Eagle and the Condor reunite. ... When this is done the people will fulfill their destiny." [4]

The reuniting of the eagle and the condor will signal the ending of oppression, exploitation and injustice suffered by native peoples on both continents and will "write on the page of the sky the sacred word liberty," Huarta says.

169

Others have interpreted the condor to represent indigenous peoples or those who are spiritual and heart-centered and who have held the Earth as sacred. They say the Eagle represents the modern technological world in which intellect rules rather than the heart, separating us from life and the earth. The coming together of these two great birds means that it is now a time of partnership between heart and mind, forging the way for a sustainable, earth-honoring future together. It is a time of love and healing, peace and dignity, and a time of restoring balance in all of life. As human beings we can truly wake up and evolve into a more conscious species. The prophecy takes the view that though tumultuous times might coincide with the coming of the new age, we are on the verge of creating a new, golden age as old ways of thinking and being die.

Dr. Alberto Villoldo, a psychologist and medicinal anthropologist who lived with and trained with Q'ero Incan shamans and helped make this ancient prophecy well known in the world, says that some have interpreted the return of *pachacuti* as the return of the leader Pachacuti who was present when the Inca were defeated by the Spanish. Instead he says that it is a process of emergence available to all peoples, a collective impulse, rather than the return of one individual. That view is coherent with our view of ascension and the return of "Christ consciousness."

Hopi Prophecy

The Hopi Prophecy talks about five ages. We are now at the beginning of the fifth, the Age of Prophecy, an age when ordinary people are asked to do extraordinary things. According to Hopi Tradition, we are coming to a time of choice around purification. A message called *Hopi Elders Speak* attributed to unnamed Elders has received widespread coverage in recent years. In that message, we are told that "this is the Eleventh

Hour" and that it is a time for community to be in right relationship with each other and to speak our truth. They caution us by saying that "there is a river flowing now very fast" and that there will be those who will be greatly challenged and those who will celebrate with us. We are not to do this alone. Probably the most famous line is "We are the ones we've been waiting for." [5]

Let Go of the Shore
Ruth Eichler

"Let go of the shore," the Hopi elders instruct. Certainly everyone upon the planet is in the midst of sweeping, radical change. Even before September 11, 2011, we were swiftly changing from one level of consciousness to another. In the nightly visitations from the Sacred Beloved, the sentence, "And all things shall be made new" frequently reverberated in the writings. I also recall reading in the early 1980's a channeled manuscript called "Conversations with John" by David Spangler in which this radical shift in consciousness was predicted. The author stated that when the shift occurred that those who had shifted would see and know that all things were new, but those who had not shifted wouldn't realize that part of the world had moved beyond them because everything would appear the same.

The Mayan Prophecy

Many controversies flooded the media about the Mayan prophecies, and many books have been written about the Mayan calendar, especially prior to December 21, 2012. Some of the reports gave different "ending" dates. Most of the interpretations do agree that this is the closing of a 5,125-year cycle and that we are approaching the end of an Age. As we have learned, the world did not end, nor did we believe it would. Instead a new cycle has been ushered into the world. These 5,125 yearlong ages are part of a much longer cycle, approximately 26,000 years, which happens to coincide with the astronomical precession of the equinoxes. As we move through this time of great transition, many who study the Mayan prophecies imply that we can either resist or co-participate in the changes and that our choices affect the outcome.

Waitaha of New Zealand

The Waitaha, a gentle people, preceded the Maori in New Zealand. When their nation was changed and mostly taken over by foreign warriors, the Waitaha elders concealed 1,000 years of their generational and wisdom teachings. Only a small, select group of people in each generation carried down the teachings through the ages. Barry Brailsford in a beautiful book, *Song of the Stone*, tells how he was requested by an indigenous elder to tell their story that had been held secret for so many years in order to bring inspiration and hope to the next generation. It was time to reveal and share their sacred secrets that had to go underground for so long through very challenging times. The elder told Barry:

> "The stars would herald the new dawn. When they aligned in a very special pattern, two things would follow: First, the most sacred of knowledge held safe over countless centuries would be shared with everyone. Secondly, the people of peace would stand and walk tall again. The world would enter a time of nurturing and caring. [6]

And so it was that Barry began a journey that changed his own life and added one thousand years to a history that had previously been unknown to outsiders. His earlier book, *The Song of Waitaha,* tells that closely held story. The Waitaha believed it was time for their hidden story and wisdom to be revealed to the outside world, just as many other indigenous peoples from around the world have done in recent times.

Joseph Rael's Message to the Elders

Joseph Rael, part Ute and part Picuris Pueblo Indian, visionary, artist, and writer, has led spiritual dances and mystery schools around the world and is the man who had a vision for peace/sound chambers that would be built around the globe. These structures, of which one is on the property owned by Ruth and her husband, are kiva-like structures where people of all races and faiths gather to chant and sing for world peace.[7] Almost all of his work with groups has been to restore balance to the earth and to help usher in a world of peace. Rather than accentuating the coming times, he faithfully instructs in sacred healing practices and ceremonies. In the excerpt that follows, he calls forth the elders, mystics, and those "who belong to the first circle of light" of the world to step forward and share their wisdom:

> "As elders we have more responsibility to talk about the sacredness of the Earth, and the sacredness of the people on the Earth. ... Mother Earth is our land and she belongs to us because we are her children. She belongs to us and we belong to her. So we can take care of her the way she has been taking care of us." [8]

In the same book, Joseph Rael tells of a vision he received in 2006 that he calls "The Horn of Plenty" that says we will receive plenty of whatever we have as our focus, whether conflict or peace. However, he goes on to say:

> "I want to announce to people all over the world that this Horn of Plenty vibration is here for all peoples of all races of all nations. Now, prosperity and abundance are here for all of us. They are going to show up in many

different ways; just pay attention and you will sense, you will hear, you will feel the vibration of a worldwide shift toward peace." [9]

These are but a few of the prophecies that come from many traditions about the coming of a new age.

Grand Cycles and the Meaning of the Aquarian Age

Though not in the same realm as prophets foretelling a new time in our history, the grand cycles that have been charted for millennia also point to times of change.

Ancients from India, Egypt and other cultures have spoken of grand cycles of time just as the Mayans did. Is it possible that there have been other times on this earth in another age when this time of acceleration and ascension also occurred?

The ancient Egyptians speak of giant wheels of time that incorporate both dark and golden ages. The Egyptians, Greeks, Persians and Chaldeans all paid attention to a grand cycle of 25,920 years divided into four seasons of 6,480 years with each "season" divided further into a period of 2,160 years. The latter divisions correspond with the precession of the equinoxes through different zodiacal signs, each lasting approximately that length of time.

Synchronistically, during each zodiacal age, symbols related to that sign begin to flourish within cultures around the world. For example, the Age of Taurus (roughly 4,300 — 2150 BCE), which is associated with the bull, corresponds with the beginning of the worship of the bull in several places in the world, especially Assyria, Egypt and Crete.

The Age of Aries, which followed the Age of Taurus, has been associated with the ram. Many statues of rams appeared during this age, such as those that line the entry to the Karnak Temple in Egypt. The Romans worshiped Mars and Zeus as the Gods of war, war also being associated with the sign of Aries.

The Age of Pisces, symbolized by two fish, coincides with the time of Jesus' birth, the fish being a Christian symbol.

The Age of Aquarius is upon us, though as with all the Ages, controversy exists as to its actual beginning. Many say that we have already entered the Age of Aquarius, and certainly signs pointing to the symbolism of Aquarius abound.

The Aquarian Age includes a surge for freedom — liberty, equality, and justice for all — moving away from authoritarian control often in revolutionary ways, celebrating the uniqueness of each individual. Whenever a new paradigm emerges, however, the Old Guard will try to hold on even more mightily and forcefully. We have seen that push for individual and cultural freedom around the globe whether fighting for revolution within a country or fighting for equal rights of those who have been denied fair treatment.

The Aquarian Age heralds the proliferation of all kinds of technology and innovations, which have proliferated beyond imagination in just two or three decades. Who had a cell phone at the beginning of this century? In 2013 Time Magazine reported a UN study that said that out of the world's estimated 7 billion people, 6 billion had access of cell phones, 1.5 billion more than had access to working toilets. Mobile phones can be found in the most remote regions of the planet. These technological advances have connected us in ways we couldn't have imagined even a couple of decades ago.

In 1990 Tom Yeomans wanted his training group to be connected by email. Only five members were able to install the modems and get Internet access; the other participants remained bewildered and unconnected to the Internet. Today virtually every group of any kind is connected through the Internet and social media. We can instantly be in relationship with a long lost friend in another country. Soldiers deployed in foreign lands can view the birth of their child back home with Skype or other video platforms. The world is indeed small.

Aquarius celebrates not only the uniqueness of the individual but also the collaboration of the collective. Community and inter-dependence on each other are hallmarks of the Aquarian Age. Although the uniqueness of each person and the diversity of culture, ethnicity, and talents are celebrated in an Aquarian world, they are brought together in groups, communities, and the global village. Honoring differences and thriving on the contributions from many sources assist in finding innovative solutions to challenging concerns. Being a system — whether family, city, nation or the planet — that is open to new input produces energetic vitality. We can again see much evidence of this quality in the ascension process.

We can see that each age marked by a zodiacal sign is ac-companied by long-lasting transformation of the collective psyche. Carl Jung, the famed psychiatrist and founder of Jungian psychology, said that the Aquarian Age would bring about the union of the opposites that would be resolved only by the human being experiencing the living spirit.[10]

Equality is a celebrated value of Aquarius. The proliferation of information about transgendered people corresponds with the Aquarian emphasis on androgyny and a movement away from hard and fast gender roles.

The Aquarian Age calls for moving beyond categories, though we can certainly still see polarization in our midst. Gender roles begin to blur in this new time. Even though the science of neurobiology assures us of meaningful gender differences, the roles that men and women play are rapidly changing. More and more families experience equal participation of mom and dad. Roles have changed even in war, as until recently women were barred from combat. Our relationships with each other are changing, and egalitarian friendship becomes even more salient.

The Aquarian Age is also associated with flashes of intuition and inspiration, sometimes coming with lightning speed. Although Aquarius is an air sign connoting much about communication and collaboration, its symbol is the water bearer, often confusing for people who think it is a water sign. Not so. We might better understand this "water" bearer as signifying that humanity comes from the "waters of life," and the water bearer is pouring forth all of the resources needed by streaming universal consciousness, inspiration and intuition through us. We can have direct access to our inner teachers through this intuitive knowing as well as our own inner guidance.

Joseph Campbell, American mythologist, writer and lecturer, best known for his work in comparative mythology and comparative religion, also shared views about what he called the Space Age:

> "The world as we know it is coming to an end. The world as the center of the universe, the world divided from the heavens, the world bound by horizons in which love is reserved for members of the in-group: that is the world that is passing away." [11]

It appears that the Aquarian Age is definitely being felt in every aspect of our lives, linking us in a common humanity — unity within diversity.

We cannot know for sure whether times of ascension have occurred in the grand cycles of nearly 26,000 years, since we have no records of those other eras. We only know that we are currently in a rapidly accelerating time in which the collective of humanity is being drawn through a metaphoric portal into a new level of consciousness and that many indigenous groups have foretold a time of great change.

ENDNOTES
Chapter 5: Prophecy

1.   David Spangler from his online newsletter, *"David's Desk #49 Apocalypse Porn."*

2.   David Spangler, *Facing the Future,* (Everett, WA: Lorian Press, 2010, p. 87).

3.   Ibid., p. 70.

4.   Willaru Huarta, a native Quechua Incan shaman from Peru reported on this website: www.incaprophecy.com.

5.   Attributed to unnamed Hopi Elders, Hopi Nation, Oraibi, Arizona. This quotation can be found on many websites, including www.communityworks.info/hopi.htm.

6.   Barry Brailsford, *Song of the Stone,* (Hamilton, New Zealand: Stoneprint Press, 1995, p. 17-18).

7.   www.earthsongpeace.com

8.   Joseph Rael, *Sound: Native Teachings and Visionary Art,* (Tulsa, OK: Council Oak Books, 2009).

9.   Ibid., p. 36.

10.   C. G. Jung, *The Sign of the Fishes,* (Chapter IV, 1959).

11.   Joseph Campbell, *The Power of Myth.*

Chapter 6
Collaboration With the Subtle

*When I am asked if I have hope for hu-
manity and for out future, I always say
yes. The reason is because of humanity's
invisible friends.* — David Spangler[1]

The Subtle Worlds

The subtle worlds, those energies and beings that are generally
invisible to most of humanity, have operated alongside us forever. For eons only those with training or natural intuition were
able to access the subtle realms and thus able to pay attention
to our invisible companions. As more of humanity becomes
aware of planetary consciousness rather than individualized
issues, we are capable of becoming aware of and connected
with non-physical beings from the "invisible" world. The edge
of our experience can no longer be defined just by the material
world as our dominant culture has done.

Perhaps our increased interconnectedness through the Internet
and global communications help humanity to better sense the
vast, complex web of life that includes expressions from the
non-material world. In his interesting book, *Facing the Future,*
David Spangler eloquently writes about our "invisible friends"
from the subtle worlds who are our partners in shaping the future:

> "They are truly our invisible friends, and they are en-
> gaged in a collective undertaking to ensure not just the
> survival but the evolutionary fulfillment of humanity—
> and indeed all beings upon the earth. This undertaking
> is an effort to increase and enhance connections and
> relationships, both 'horizontally' within the physical
> world and 'vertically' between the physical and the
> subtle worlds." [2]

Spangler warns that if we don't pay attention now to the subtle worlds, we are missing one-half of the energy and information that is available to us at this critical time.

Various kinds of beings and energies exist in the subtle worlds. They range from plant and animal spirits to what indigenous people have often referred to as "star beings" or extra-planetary life. They include enlightened teachers and beings that may or may not have walked this earth. Both Lesley and Ruth value dialoguing with the teachings of the subtle realms.

The subtle world includes spirits of ancestors, some extraor-dinarily wise and some not so. Angelic beings of amazing light also live in the subtle worlds. The range and scope of consciousness that exists within the subtle realms is extremely vast, or as Lesley says, as many "as are the hairs on a head."

Robert Lawlor speaks about some Australian aboriginals who begin their day in intimate connection with the subtle and natu-ral world as they recapture their dreams:

> "The first thing a person does upon awakening is to
> wander alone into the bush or along the seashore and
> create a song based on the dreams of the previous night.
> The animals and birds hear the dream being sung and
> recognize that the singer is in touch with the inner

world, and therefore they assist him or her in daily hunting and gathering." [3]

Some people live in close communion with nature and are, therefore, much more likely to be attuned to nature spirits. Scientists and researchers who talk about the "field," a matrix of potential that influences whatever interacts with it, often access the subtle world through mathematical formulas and quantum physics theories. Some people only touch into the subtle realms through dreams or altered states of consciousness. Others intuitively access information from the non-physical world through libraries of information such as the Akashic records, sometimes called the "halls of wisdom."

Among the many forms of invisible friends, the Grandmothers (and Grandfathers) collaborate with us in so many ways. Those who are still in physical form can hold a palpable presence even though they are not geographically nearby, as Lesley and Ruth personally learned when Maori Grandmothers continuously prayed for the group of women who went to Egypt. We may never meet those old grandmothers in person, but we felt a deep connection with them. After returning from Egypt, we met with Raymond and told him of our appreciation for how present the Grandmothers and he were. He said that it was as if they were physically present; we just couldn't see them.

Many other ancient ones connect with us from the invisible world, long ago having released their physical bodies. Our collective ancestors continue to guide us today, and as we connect with them, we extend our awareness of the continuity of consciousness. The Grandmothers hold the long view, not only of time or timelessness, but also of the wholeness of life and connection with our origination and purpose for being on the Earth. They expand our awareness into a field of greater inclusivity, a view that moves from the personal to the collective.

Many indigenous people speak of their connection with "star people," often citing that they came from specific places in the Universe such as Sirius. According to Robert Temple in *The Sirius Mystery*, the Dogon people of the Mali Republic in Africa claim that their sacred knowledge was given to them by a race of god-like beings, who came from Sirius.

Joseph Rael, visionary author, artist and healer alludes to the star nations from which his Picuris Pueblo people came. The Hathors, an ascended civilization once incarnated in Egypt, according to their communications with Tom Kenyon, author of *The Hathor Material,* want us to know how to move through these turbulent times. They have given many practices that can help us stabilize our energies.

The point is that the subtle realms reside with us as closely as our breath, and some of these beings have more of a feel for the integration and wholeness of things than humans do. They wish to help us to fulfill our destiny and to lovingly assist in our living peacefully on Mother Earth. However, David Spangler cautions that these beings are not magical:

> "The beings of the subtle worlds can be powerful—after all, they include Archangels and Angels, Devas and other great planetary beings in their number—but they are neither omniscient nor omnipotent.... They are life forms, consciousness's and intelligences like you and me though existing in a very different mode of being." [4]

Angelic Presence

Angel means messenger in Greek and Hebrew, and it is mostly in this role of messenger that Christian, Jewish, and Islamic traditions refer to the angelic. In the East the forces of nature are called Devas, translated from Sanskrit as "shining ones." Hopi Indians call their spirits Kachinas.

Buddhists call Devas Dakini, which means, "Sky Dancers." Dakini are thought to have a demeanor that changes in various contexts. They express symbolically as dancing spirits — playful, nurturing, or unpredictable. They may be wrathful when protecting spiritual practices, or they can convey inner wisdom by appearing in dreams and daily visions. Dakini are complex and diverse in order to challenge any aspect of us that is not whole. In the Buddhist tradition, Dakini are best understood through myth and artistic, symbolic expression and become most relevant through personal inquiry.

Existing in the higher subtle realms are angelic presences that live as expressions of Source and that nurture the evolution of humanity and of nature. As expressions of enormous Light, their substance comes from infinite possibility and is imbued with love and wisdom. With their only motive being service to Source, they not only embody divine thought but they also provide the substance through which it manifests. They remind us of our divine source and heritage, for those from the angelic realm are so refined and pure that they uplift and inspire awareness of our collective possible destiny. Though never interfering with the free will of human beings, just their presence vitalizes those with less light into a higher expression.

Angelic substance is our divine nature, and our physical bodies are made from angelic substance. Humanity can actively participate in increasing the vibratory rate of our body, mind and spirit by the simple expression of deep gratitude, appreciation and love. Forgiveness of others also opens the heart and accelerates consciousness. Our Solar angels, the very vast and highest aspects of our Souls, are too refined and fiery to come into our daily awareness, yet when we stabilize and quiet our minds, we are able to be penetrated and influenced through flashes and clear insight into our higher mind through the matrix of the heart. These and many other ways help refine human nature so that it can be more in resonance with and able to receive and meet the new potential and to act in reciprocity with the note that is entering at this time.

The Angelic Kingdom

According to ancient wisdom traditions, the Angelic Kingdom has been called the fifth kingdom of evolution, following mineral, plant, animal and human kingdoms in that order. Just like the Russian doll analogy, each kingdom is inclusive of the kingdoms that have preceded it. The angelic kingdom has a vast range of levels of awareness and ways of expression. Elementals that do not have a "thinking mind" are at one end of the spectrum with archangels at the highest level.

The most advanced members of the angelic kingdom are the archangels, which are beings of enormous, even cosmic, expression. They are highly refined, fiery beings that work with the one universal flame. Although we humans have anthropomorphized them, their scope is vast and impersonal.

The midlevel of the angelic kingdom is made of those that are builders of form and those that spark the mind. When one speaks of "the angelic," we generally are referring to the roles that angels play in relationship with humanity. We can experience angels of music, beauty, art and joy, for example. There are those from the angelic kingdom who act as guardians and those who assist with all aspects of nature.

Although different traditions emphasize certain angelic roles and call them by different names, most believe that the angelic realm contains evolved spiritual intelligences that seek to serve a Greater Purpose. They serve the Divine and express the will of God. From our human understanding, they are largely expressions of immense love.

Nature spirits and elementals that follow the laws of Nature live at one end of the Angelic Kingdom continuum and are essential to our shared life on earth. Without their work, we could not exist on this earth.

The elementals are associated with the four elements — earth, air, fire and water. We know those of the earth as elves and gnomes, and they are associated with plant, animal and mineral life. Oxygen, wind and atmosphere are related to the air elementals, also known as fairies. The water elementals such as water sprites form rain and bodies of water, and fire elementals relate to fire and light even the light in photons, for example.

Machaelle Small Wright has written many books and oversees a beautiful garden from which flower and other essences are produced and marketed. All of the work is done in conjunction with intelligent beings called Nature at her place in Virginia called Perelandra. The following quotation defining "nature" comes from one of Wright's books and is written from Nature's voice:

> "In the larger universe and beyond, on its many levels and dimensions, there are a number of groups of consciousness which, although equal in importance, are quite different in expression and function. ... One such consciousness has been universally termed 'nature.' ... Nature is the conscious reality that supplies order, organization and life vitality." [5]

As we learn to interact with the plant, animal and mineral kingdoms in meaningful ways, just as indigenous peoples have long known how to do and in such places as Findhorn in Scotland, Perelandra, and elsewhere, we find that the relationship is reciprocal. If we bring loving attention to a tree or a cabbage, it reciprocates in its own way. Everything in the universe is connected directly or indirectly to everything else. As John Muir asserted, "Tug at one thing in nature and you'll find the whole world attached."

The Destructive Aspect

Although we primarily focus on the angelic as the builders and healers of form and as expressions of a universal vital force, they transmit electrical energy that can either create or destroy. Angels are extremely powerful forces and are destructive to form and dense vibration not in accord with the impulse they hold. Angelic builders are aligned with the greater purpose and the plan rather than with the little wills of human beings, so their activities reflect this more encompassing perspective. The sacred firebird, the Phoenix, is a mythological depiction of this kind of fiery destruction, as the old bird is immolated in its nest from which the new one is born. The Archangel Michael can also destroy the old through his fiery energy.

Interaction with the Angelic Kingdom

With both intention and attention, humanity is now creating resonance with a higher vibrational field and has the possibility of more interaction with the angelic kingdom. The more refined the note is, the more that lighted consciousness is made available as an actual essence or subtle energy. Increasing numbers of people are now able to hold a steady resonance at higher levels of mind and receptively meet these influencing impulses. Even those of us not capable of sustained and focused awareness at the level of the Soul can learn from the wide range of devic nature spirits and those in the angelic realms through observation, presence, and receptivity.

Because angels transmit energy at such a high level of vibration, the mental, thinking aspect of our minds often is not aware of these beings or transmissions. However, when we experience exalted or profound spiritual states or meditation, deep trauma and duress, or sleep or dream states, we may be more receptive to their presence. Whether or not we are aware of them, they are always present.

The subtle realms are also accelerating, just as we are accelerating. The angelic and other spirits sometimes evolve through service, and as we call upon them to serve us, their joyful participation allows them to further evolve. Without our invitation, they are unable to do so. Each part affects the whole. The Earth, humanity, and all of the subtle worlds are being drawn into higher states together towards our true nature, which vibrates at a much faster rate. We develop through demonstrating our free will choices that are in compliance with divine law and order. Because like attracts like, the angelic are most able to enter into space created with purified intentions and motives. Sustained coherence and intention is essential for such a meeting. We are all returning back to our point of origination.

Collaboration with the Angelic

The greater the refinement of our subtle energies through our thought, activity, and love, the easier it is for the angels to build into our form that which is in alignment with our divine purpose and plan. Form arises at the instant that the substance of the human and devic life forces merge. As the angels receive from us, they infuse this love into what they help build. They can only build with that which they are given, and these entities can only influence to the extent that we allow their impulses to be known and experienced by and through us. They must be invoked or invited. They do not interfere or impose upon our right to experience choices and the resulting consequences.

When there is a lack of love and regard, as often happens with human misunderstanding, then the energies are not of the richest possibility and are stepped down to a lower resonance. When our energies are refined and coherent, we can collaborate and co-create with the angels, which is part of our destiny. At lower levels of vibration and awareness, we used to simply just pray to them for outcomes that we desired, and sometimes we still might wish that they would "fix" us.

> *Love is that flame that once kindled burns everything, and only the mystery and the journey remain.* — Rumi

We as humanity have called this new note forth, and we are now over-stimulated by that which we requested. However, working with these emanations of light and love, we create change in the world. Using meditation and prayer, invocation, and transmission of energy and light, we connect to and co-operate with the angelic, collaboratively expressing emergent possibility.

Collaboration and Co-creation with the Subtle World

The more that we can be in collaboration with those in the subtle worlds — whether angels or other wise beings — the more joy we all share and the more our shared evolutionary paths are enhanced. They will collaborate with us if we are grounded in love and have a solid, integrated self from which to operate. These beings from the subtle world are not trying to create a new set of belief systems but rather to assist us in living more as loving, integrated beings, in harmonious relationship with all "our relations" and with the earth.

We now need to breathe out further to engage the future so that we can act as cause rather than effect. We do that by relating compassionately with others, engaging with love rather than fear, and seeing each other as part of the same fabric of creation.

Like the breath, acceleration is entering us, and we notice when or if we are open to receive this impulse. We are profoundly interdependent with all that exists within the web of life that includes the subtle realms. Our consciousness can hold more and more awareness of the entire planet so that we begin to think like the planet, the earth. In order to do this, our efforts are greatly enhanced by collaboration with the subtle worlds. David Spangler again shares his views:

> "The effort of those beings in the subtle worlds who serve the evolution of humanity and the world as a whole is really not to create a new consciousness. ... It IS to enhance the flow of life—physical life and spiritual life—upon the earth. It IS to enhance the flow of love. It IS to enhance integration and wholeness." [6]

Some people's relationship with the subtle worlds has been more like that of child to parent, and teachings have been given and received in this way. Others have adored or worshipped beings from the subtle world. Acceleration and ascension requires partnering with the subtle worlds as co-participants.

The over-arching principles of collaborating with subtle beings are the same as in human relationships. Both require mutual respect and a willingness to listen deeply to the wisdom and experience of the other. In order to effectively interact with these realms, one must enter with alignment and clarity of purpose. We human beings have to have developed enough maturity so that instead of negatively reacting to situations that we act with understanding of and reciprocity with others — in this world and the subtle. We have to set aside our projections and with curiosity learn to be in the other's "world." Only then can we truly appreciate the sacred energy of the relationship. To be of greatest service to each other, we must listen deeply from a heart place.

Collaboration assists us in moving to the level of thinking that is beyond the problem. Einstein said that a problem cannot be solved at the same level at which it was created. Though we have been speaking of the collaboration with the subtle realms as if they are all external to us, the Sacred Feminine reminds us that the Divine not only creates the world but is everywhere in the world, in every particle, atom and cell of matter and within that which is beyond matter. Everything in the universe is a fractal of God. Every aspect of the subtle realm is part of the one web of life just as we are. Therefore, we all collaborate together simply because we are part of one woven fabric. Every thread affects the whole tapestry.

Nature dancing with us
Ruth Eichler

Tonight, my friend Chris and I launched our preparation for the Sun/Moon Dance by walking our land for an hour followed by walking in the dance arbor. We began walking slowly in the dance arbor from one side to the other. As I got close to the west side, I suddenly noticed that the ropes between two poles were vibrating very fast. Chris joined me to watch this amazing sight. Sometimes the vibrating occurred all along a rope between the poles except for two or three still spots perhaps a foot long. Sometimes all three ropes were vibrating, sometimes two, and sometimes just one. Sometimes the top one, sometimes the bottom, sometimes just the middle one would vibrate. We both felt joyful and experienced an immense energy, and even our hands buzzed. I wanted to listen, because it looked like a symphony, like music, but I couldn't hear anything with my ears. Then, suddenly the vibrating ropes extended to the ropes between the next two poles, and pretty soon the ones we were watching became still, but the new set danced in this very fast vibration. Occasionally, the vibration extended to the next set of ropes. Once, the ropes that initially vibrated did so again. Then, the ropes directly across the arbor began vibrating. We walked there, laughing and thanking "them" for the blessings. Once, I put my finger gently on one of the ropes that was vibrating at a very high rate of speed, and my finger buzzed almost like a miniature rope burn. Chris then put her finger on the same rope a couple of feet away from me, and the rope quickly came into stillness. Later, it began vibrating again. This went on for 25 minutes. Finally all ropes came into stillness, and we left the arbor in awe. As we walked outside of the arbor, a rope began vibrating just as we walked by. We laughed again. Finally it, too, came into stillness. The subtle worlds communicated with us in non-ordinary ways!

Early Teachings in How to Relate in the Subtle Realms
Lesley Carmack

When I was five years old, I was in the hospital because an X-ray had discovered a mass in my heart, and I eventually had open-heart surgery. I was not allowed to move. My arms and legs were strapped to the bed to prevent me from pulling out tubes and transfusions. I was not in pain, but I longed for companionship. I was in an oxygen tent isolated from human touch, and the sound of my own breath was like a meditative practice. Many people in this intensive care environment were pleading for assistance and were being prayed for, and thus angels were attracted in large numbers.

I was taught by these angelic presences how to leave my body and visit the other rooms where there were patients. This moving out of my body and experiencing telepathic rapport was very comfortable and natural. Later I was taught ways to cultivate relationship with the angelic as companions rather than only as agents of healing.

This early experience became a backdrop for a continuing relationship with intuitive awareness and information in part because my father was in the military, and we moved every year, sometimes out of the country. Each community would have different norms and assumptions about appropriate behavior and ways of being in the world. As I adapted my behavior to these changing conditions and expectations in the outer world, in a parallel way in the inner world I experienced numerous different realms and teachings and adapted to them.

A core group of teachers assisted in this exploration, and as long they were present, I felt free to experiment. If, however, the teachers were not present, it was a clue to me that I had stumbled into a place where I was not equipped to navigate by myself, as I didn't know the ground rules. Still today one way of discriminating is to be aware if I am being accompanied by these higher vibrational entities. If they can't enter, I probably don't need to be there. I have been given guidelines on how to move in these realms and how to intentionally alter my state so that I either witness on one side of an energetic boundary or enter and participate in a realm.

Today, in my practice as a transpersonal consultant, I have a similar agreement with my clients to participate only with what their soul shows me. It is through vibration that I know with what I want to engage. My physical, emotional, mental and causal aspects of my being must be able to respond with coherence in order to participate in the corresponding realms. At times it is necessary to bring a more refined substance of light into the material form, light that is accessed from a level of consciousness that is generally not conscious to the person yet is within their energetic being. That level of their being fully invites and releases what is not needed, and this process might be referred to as healing. It is co-created with the energy from the subtle worlds.

Joyful Songs
Sacred Beloved

"We are delighted to be walking with you and are enlivened by your discussion with Lesley. We dance with joy! The entire field is electrified with collaboration. 'The hills are alive with the sound of music.' (They sing.) The scales are tipping, and each drop of gold on the scale brings the scale closer to that tipping point. Each prayer and each joyful laugh that holds the value of the good of the whole are drops of gold dust on the scale. The work that you and Lesley are doing catalyzes many drops of gold because the two of you have trod the paths to and fro with us in what you are now calling the subtle worlds so often that the passage is well worn and easily activated. Our dancing and the angels' joy affect the ripples of air and reverberate into other kingdoms. Our song is heard in other rooms in the mansion. Yes, we sing with joy. We have long awaited this moment, and the song continues unabated."

Discernment

We need to learn to discern from where the voice comes. We can easily believe that the voice of the ego self is a higher voice. Methods will vary on how to decipher which is which. Our friend Elmer Green, who researched people with unusual abilities and experienced a lifetime of dealing with the subtle realms, advised that the first thing to notice is if any part of the guidance sets you apart from others as special to receive these teachings or to be the special emissary. If it does either of these, then it is a warning sign that the ego is too involved or attached.

The quality of the content contains both feeling and mental states. If our brow furrows in worry over the content, it may be a clue that we are not in contact with higher guidance. Clues that authentic connection is occurring include feeling spacious, aligned, and loving towards self and others.

We need to cultivate our ability to trust our inner guidance that differentiates between the desires and wants of the personality self and what is truly higher guidance or insight. Our ego can sneakily convince us that it is God.

So how do we learn to discern from where the "voice" originates? We can use this kind of discernment whether we are talking about having beans or salmon for dinner or whether we want to participate in something of a higher moral consequence. At first, we can most easily develop this skill by quieting ourselves, focusing internally and listening for inspiration on inconsequential questions. Do I want an avocado or a peach for lunch? The more confident we become about the internal guidance on these kinds of questions, the more easily we can begin to trust ourselves in matters of greater consequence.

The Sufi, Hazrat Inayat Khan, advises:

> "One thing that must be remembered is to perceive the first suggestion that rises in the heart before it is disturbed by the action of the mind. If that opportunity is lost, it will not take one moment for the reason to attack the intuition and establish its own place there. Intuition is something which rises from our own heart and brings satisfaction, ease and happiness." [7]

ENDNOTES
Chapter 6: Collaboration with the Subtle Worlds

1.   David Spangler, *Facing the Future,* (Everett, WA: Lorian Press, 2010, p. 73).

2.   Ibid., pp. 74 and 115.

3.   Robert Lawlor, *Voices of the First Day: Awakening in the Aboriginal Dreamtime.*

4.   David Spangler, *Facing the Future,* (Everett, WA: Lorian Press, 2010, p. 82).

5.   Machaelle Small Wright, *Perelandra Garden Workbook 2nd Edition: A Complete Guide to Gardening with Nature Intelligences,* (Perelandra, Ltd., 1993, p. 304-306).

6.   David Spangler, *Facing the Future,* (Everett, WA: Lorian Press, 2010, p. 92).

7.   Hazrat Inayat Khan, *The Soul's Journey,* (New Lebanon, NY: Omega Publications, 2003, p. 179).

Chapter 7
Navigating the Ascension Process Through the Heart

And now here is my secret, a very simple secret. It is only with the heart that one can see rightly; what is essential is invisible to the eye. — Antoine de Saint-Exupery [1]

Heart as "Home" of the Divine

Though many spiritual traditions have focused on different energetic aspects of being to connect with the divine such as the brow or crown chakra, we will concentrate on the heart center, which is essential to the ascension process. We might visualize the heart center as not only the organ of the heart but as an energetic field that extends out both in front and behind our bodies and also reaches up through the top transducing the vibrational patterns. As the acceleration process increases the level of vibration, we can use the heart center to regulate and transfer energy, thus linking the outer world with the inner. The soul is connected to the heart through a silvery energetic stream that flows from above the head through the higher and middle mind, also called the "rainbow bridge" or *antahkarana* in Sanskrit. The heart center also relates outwardly to others.

Our physical and emotional bodies are not fully prepared for the refined energies coming at this time, which might be akin to a thousand volt transformer suddenly having 15,000 volts of electricity coursing through it. Many people who are awakening to higher states of consciousness report changes in sleep patterns, sensations on the scalp or crown of head, heart palpitations as well as sometimes feeling lost as old issues repeatedly surface begging to be cleared.

Yet this destabilization can help bring about greater pliability and openness to re-stabilize with coherence and core integrity. We have to re-stabilize and adjust to the new vibrations finding coherence and resonance with it, and the heart is our best ally. One way of connecting our "little" self with the Universal self is to direct attention to the beating of the heart, which can allow one to see, hear and perceive with greater sensitivity. The heart is capable of receiving and sending out energy without having to step it down, as it is designed for that kind of reciprocity. Of course, the heart also has to be open and ready, a subject we'll address later in this chapter.

> *The way is not in the sky. The way is in the heart.* — The Buddha

The heart has been seen as the place where the divine resides from many different traditions with several reflected here:

> "In the golden city of the heart dwells The Lord of Love, without parts, without stain. Know him as the radiant light of lights." (Hindu) [2]

> "If we keep the human heart unperverted —which is like unto heaven and received from earth—that is God." (Shinto) [3]

"The heart is a sanctuary at the center of which there is a little space, wherein the Great Spirit dwells, and this is the Eye. This is the Eye of the Great Spirit by which He sees all things, and through which we see Him. If the heart is not pure, the Great Spirit cannot be seen." — Black Elk (Native American) [4]

"For everything there is an appropriate way of polishing; the heart's polishing is the remembrance of God." (Islam) [5]

"One opens the inner doors of one's heart to the infinite silences of the Spirit, out of whose abysses love wells up without fail and gives itself to all." — Thomas Merton (Christian) [6]

"The human heart is the home of the soul, and upon this home the comfort and power of the soul depend." — Hazrat Inayat Khan (Sufi) [7]

"If there were a thousand universes the heart would accommodate them, it is so large."— Hazrat Inayat Khan (Sufi) [8]

Sufism and the Heart

Sufism has almost always been called the path of the heart, and many practices have been given over hundreds of years to assist in the opening of the heart in order that our divine inheritance can be lived. An ancient Sufi story tells about how God hid the greatest secret of the Universe in human hearts, knowing that it would take a very long time for humankind to realize that the secret lay within them. It was almost a trick, for human beings would travel to distant shores looking for the great secret. As Hazrat Inayat Khan says, "I searched for Thee in heaven, my Beloved, but at last I have found Thee hidden as a pearl in the shell of my heart." [9]

Instead of one energy center or chakra at the heart center, Sufis speak of three horizontal *lataif* or aspects of consciousness as different chambers of the heart. The first is called the *qalbiyya* and is considered to be color of red residing on the left side of the breast, an energy center more closely corresponding with and overlaying the physical heart organ.

Human emotions — joy, sorrow, grief, and others — are felt and expressed through the *qalbiyya*. No doubt it is the activity of this heart chamber that is spoken in these expressions: broken heart, heartless, heart cracked open, a full heart, heavy heart, heart to heart discussion, speaking from the bottom of my heart, wearing one's heart on one's sleeve, heart in the right place, kind hearted, heart of gold, change of heart, heart of stone, to lose heart, my heart goes out, or my heart is set on something. Rumi frequently speaks of the burning heart that is awakened by love and pain as he does in this poem translated by Coleman Barks with John Moyne:

> *"I must be consumed by fire.*
> *Why is there crackling and smoke?*
> *Because the firewood and the flames*
> *Are still talking: 'You are too dense. Go away!' '*
> *You are too wavering. I have solid form."* [10]

Love and a Warm Heart
Ruth Eichler

A gentle breeze wafts in my office window, but the fire in my heart remains. I just remembered that during a recent Sufi meditation that it seemed as if Murshid breathed into my heart and that my heart burst into flames. The flames burned brightly out of the heart and up around my body consuming everything. Those flames remained for a long time. They flashed and sparked to a few feet above my head. Then the flames began to subside and the outside was charred, and a piece of charred log stood end on end up somewhere about shoulder level. Eventually this piece of charred wood dropped to the ground. What remained was an effervescent light emanating from within. My heart remains warm.

The next *lataif* or energy center of the Sufi heart called the *ruhiyya* meaning Spirit. It is said to be white and is located on the right side of the breast. Here we experience pure spirit, untainted and pristine. The Sufis say that it is in this chamber of the heart that the impulse arises to bring our angelic self into incarnation. We can return to divine innocence and purity through it. Even if others do us physical harm, this aspect of our being remains untouched. To paraphrase Murshid Hazrat Inayat Khan, just because we have gotten into a muddy field doesn't mean that we have to keep walking in it. The *ruhiyya* or Spirit aspect of our heart points us in another direction.

The third horizontal aspect of the heart, the *lataif* called *sirriyya,* or the Secret, with the color of golden green, resides in the center of the chest. In this fine and subtle Presence, the person may experience an exquisite sense of compassion for self and all others. When we have reached a high enough state of refinement to consciously experience the *sirriyya,* that place where the Holy One sits, we can experience oneness with the Divine. It is here that knowledge is unveiled and is where the soul reveals knowledge of the human experience.

All three of these aspects of the heart as described in the Sufi tradition are important to the ascension process and are one model of the path home, a home of embodied Spirit. The *ruhiyya* (Spirit) and the *sirriyya* (Secret) are most activated during the ascension process. Their activation corresponds to some of the higher levels of consciousness previously described.

Buddhism and the Compassionate Heart

Compassion is at the heart of almost all Buddhist teachings. The Dalai Lama delivers many talks to thousands of people, and his teachings invite us to reorient our attention to create a more altruistic, genuine, and joyful life. His gentle and humorous presence moves us, and we expand our awareness to include the welfare of others.

The Heart Sutra describes "*Sunyata*," meaning emptiness, as the most complete and inclusive state possible. It is a state of total unity, empty of any separation. The vastness of this spacious wisdom teaching births heart qualities such as bliss, compassion, clarity, and courage. The Heart Sutra teaching on emptiness activates our complete openness and surrender to all that is and all that is possible.

Heart Sutra Teachings with the Dalai Lama
Lesley Carmack

The Heart Sutra teachings occurred over four days, much of them spoken in Tibetan. These teachings are about the Buddhist concept of "emptiness" and convey that liberation from suffering lies in our own hands. We can understand emptiness as being totally liberated from mental constraints and limiting concepts. It is not an abyss of abandonment but an empty canvas of infinite potential. Emptiness is a spacious capacity that includes even what cannot be thought by the mind.

The concept of emptiness is much easier to experience in the presence of the Dalai Lama.

First, we were asked to look at our attachments. Sitting in the audience, I wrote, "I am empty; empty is me; I am not different from emptiness." I am suddenly aware that I have laid a limited reality on others and that the true experience of oneness beyond any projections was a more respectful and accurate way of relating and living. Yet, I feel no guilt or shame for my lifetimes of living from a narrow viewpoint, but only sudden liberation from the confines of learned beliefs. Were the years of heart focus necessary for this awareness? I suspect that the teachings and transmissions must find a resonance within the receiver, a resonance that can only be found after the transmigration of the soul through lifetimes of maturation.

Finally I have come to understand "non-inherent existence" more deeply. Nothing has meaning without context; all is empty of inherent existence. There is "no thing" without our or my projecting eyes, and these eyes always hold a limiting view. [11]

> *The recollection of the heavenly state is so powerful it will transfigure our aura causing it to flower into great beauty. ... Awakening to one's true nature restores wholeness and happiness.* — Pir Vilayat

The Heart Influences Internal and External Communication

> *To the degree that we are able to see the events of life through the single eye of the heart, as opposed to the polarity of the logical mind, to that degree we heal our illusion of separation.* — Greg Braden [12]

Recent research on the heart has shown that the heart is one of the most powerful organs of the body in creating health and wellbeing on all levels — physical, emotional, mental and spiritual. Poets and mystics have long known that the heart is a key factor. We now know scientifically as well that the heart sends extensive, meaningful messages to the brain, affecting human behavior.

Scientists used to consider the heart simply the recipient of messages from the brain. Now we know there is an ongoing, two-way dialogue between the heart and brain. As the HeartMath Institute reports:

> "Research has shown that the heart communicates to the brain in four major ways: neurologically (through the transmission of nerve impulses), biochemically (via hormones and neurotransmitters), biophysically (through pressure waves) and energetically (through electromagnetic field interactions). Communication along all these conduits significantly affects the brain's activity." [13]

The HeartMath Institute, established in 1991, has conducted extensive research on the heart and has published a large body of work, including that found in respected journals such as the Harvard Business Review and the American Journal of Cardiology. Their work has shown that emotions are more powerful than thoughts in affecting our sense of wellbeing and even the wellbeing of others.

Whereas our emotional experience involves interaction between various aspects of our physiology — heart, brain, nervous, immune and hormonal systems, the heart remains very significant in the generation of emotions, as it is the primary entry point where body, emotions, mind and spirit connect.

HeartMath research has shown that when the heart rhythm — not heart rate — is coherent and non-jagged that all of our inner systems perform better.

Rolin McCraty and Doc Childre of the HeartMath Institute further explain:

> "The definition of coherence found in physics is used to describe the ordered or constructive distribution of power within a wave. The more stable the frequency and shape of the waveform, the higher the coherence. ... In psychological systems, this type of coherence describes the degree of order and stability in the rhythmic activity generated by a single, oscillatory system." [14]

Coherence

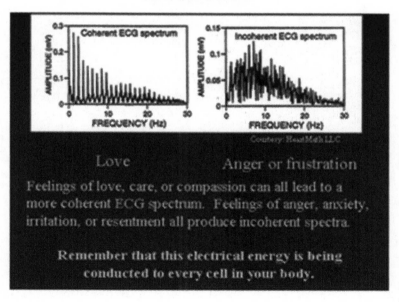

Love   Anger or frustration

Feelings of love, care, or compassion can all lead to a more coherent ECG spectrum. Feelings of anger, anxiety, irritation, or resentment all produce incoherent spectra.

Remember that this electrical energy is being conducted to every cell in your body.

[15]

As the heart rhythm comes into coherence, low frequency brain waves and the heart rhythm begin to entrain and synchronize. Shifting awareness to the heart changes our perceptions and behavior. We feel more emotionally stable and even joyful; we have greater cognitive clarity and heightened intuitive aware- ness. Our immune system is enhanced; circulating levels of DHEA, the hormone that slows aging, is increased. Levels of cortisol, a steroid hormone released during stress, are reduced. Elevated blood pressure can become normal, and stress levels, anxiety and depression are all lessened. In other words, a heart with coherent rhythms contributes to greater states of inner harmony, health and wellbeing.

Compassion, love, care for others, appreciation, gratitude — all qualities long associated with the heart — contribute to a coherent heart rhythm. Intentionally generating positive emo- tions alters brain activity and contributes to overall wellbeing. Allowing your thoughts to return to the feeling of a cherished memory will also immediately change your heart rhythm and bring it into greater coherence.

On the other hand, the heart rhythms of a person experiencing anger, frustration, fear or danger become jagged and incoher- ent negatively affecting body, mind and spirit. The work of the positive psychologists such as Martin Seligman and others of recent years also points us in the same direction. Not only do persons with coherent heart rhythms experience greater health and vitality, they also have a positive effect on other people who are in close proximity. This can be made even more potent by using focused intention accompanied by breathing practices. Similarly, negative emotions and incoherent heart rhythms can negatively affect others. According to the HeartMath Institute,

> "The heart is the most powerful generator of electro- magnetic energy in the human body, producing the larg- est rhythmic electromagnetic field of any of the body's organs. The heart's electrical field is about 60 times

greater in amplitude than the electrical activity generated by the brain." (diagram below)" [16]

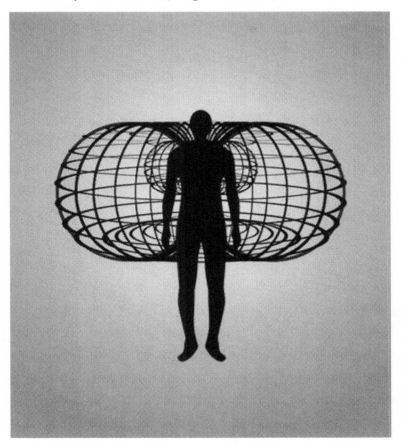

Therefore, through vibration, resonance and entrain-
ment, we are connected to one another and communicate
and influence one another through the heart. Energetic
information existing in the heart waves of one person
can be detected in the brain waves of another person
when they touch. [17]

The Deeper Meaning of the Subtle
Energy Bodies and the Heart

> *Take your heart into vast fields of light*
> *and let it breathe.* — Hafiz

HeartMath has demonstrated that we are not "skin encapsulated" and that our thoughts and emotions distribute information and energy. The ancient model of the chakra system integrates understanding of how our subtle bodies extend into union with all that is.

On the physical level, chakras are openings or interface points that act as conduits that take vital energy or chi — the universal life force — and transfer it through pathways called meridians. These internal meridians called *nadis* in Sanskrit literally mean "flow," and they carry the subtle energy throughout the body. The chakra and meridian points create a magnetic field, converting the subtle energy to a resonance that the body can use as it courses through the body. Dr. Leonard Wisneski and Lucy Anderson further explain:

> "Vital energy is converted into hormones, neurotransmitters and connected to physiological structures, such as endocrine glands, and energy the body can use at a cellular level." [18]

The chakras not only interpenetrate and interconnect with organs and systems within our physical bodies but also with our emotional, mental, and spiritual "bodies." These reside in the etheric, subtle energy field around our physical body. The chakras reflect our beliefs, choices, traumas — our wellbeing or lack of such. As we make more refined choices in our lives, the chakras change accordingly. Chakras can be cultivated over time to intentionally hold and transduce more light.

Each chakra represents differing levels of maturity and life experience with identified colors, patterns, and sounds. The root chakra at the base of the spine is associated with issues of family and belonging; the sacral with duality and relationship; the solar plexus with personal development; the heart with love; the throat with creativity and self-expression; the ajana or third eye with wisdom; and the crown with divinity.

They act as the interface point within the subtle energy body and interpenetrate the physical body. They operate as energy vortex conduits that reside in each of the various layers of energy fields, creating an egg-shaped subtle container around the entire physical form.

Learning Acupuncture in Korea
Lesley Carmack

When I trained in a Korean acupuncture clinic in Seoul, Korea, I was not able, nor was I encouraged, to speak or understand the Korean language. In Oriental medicine, the pitch, tone, and volume of the spoken word as well as pulse readings, color of pigmentation, and changes in facial expression are all "listened to" for diagnostic purposes. The healer also intuitively pays attention to the beat of both the heart of the patient and his or her own heart, assessing vibration and sound. Oriental pulse diagnosis assesses heart rhythms as found in twelve different pulses, which coordinate with energy meridians and body regions. In Western medicine, one is trained to feel the heartbeat within the chest, whereas the traditional Oriental practice of acupuncture includes the heart/mind in not only the physical body but also the surrounding subtle energy bodies.

The Heart Chakra as an Integrating Force

In our hearts there burns a fire that burns all veils to their root and foundation. When the veils have been burned away then the heart will understand completely. Ancient love will unfold ever –fresh forms in the heart of Spirit, in the core of the heart. — Rumi

Chakra vortexes are made up of petals that reflect the behavior and attitudes of a person's consciousness.

Because the chakra system interfaces and regulates the flow between internal and external energies, it is especially crucial to be mindful of our need for self care, our health and quality of life during these times of dynamic environmental and planetary change.

The ancient texts identified different numbers of primary and secondary chakras depending upon how that culture perceived and mapped the various subtle energy bodies. Probably the most widely known depiction of chakras for Westerners is the seven-chakra system.

One's life practices and evolutionary journey are reflected in the petals of the chakras. As the petals become more active and mature in their expression, they become more coherent, balanced and dynamic. The petals reflect the vibrational, spiritual qualities of the person and his relationship to his soul, community, and spiritual companions from the subtle realms. Human subtle energy anatomy correlates directly with corresponding realms or levels of consciousness. Another way of describing it is to say that the human causal body aligns with the planes of abstract thought, the mental with concrete thought, the physical astral with the emotional level of consciousness and the physical with sensory reactions.

In our evolutionary process, we begin with "I" as the central focus with concern for personal needs and desires, and in the chakra system this is often shown in the lower three chakras. As consciousness accelerates, as is happening for humanity right now, the petals of the heart chakra begin to be activated. The love petals of the heart become more vital, colorful, refined, and expressive in the subtle realm as we express more love. As the heart center is awakened and the throat center is also stimulated into creative work, the heart may then influence us toward a higher level of relationship and service.

As the heart petals open, they correspond with and are mirrored in the crown, stimulating the thousand-petaled lotus in the crown chakra. This activation synthesizes the head, heart and throat so that collectively these chakras express more potently. In addition, the triangulation of these centers causes the lower three chakras to become more refined and resonant with the higher ones.

It is said that the heart chakra reflects love, faith, and devotion to those closest to us first, and then begins to become more expansive and inclusive. The energy of the heart chakra then expands to express itself in an unconditional way, much as the sun shines on all the flowers in a garden rather than just a few chosen ones. Through this maturation process, the chakra petals grow, expressing wisdom of both the heart and the higher mind, bringing agape love, wisdom and intuitive insight together.

> *When the human heart becomes conscious of God, it becomes like the sea; it extends its waves to friend and foe.*
> — Hazrat Inayat Khan [19]

The heart magnetically attracts others, and with the shared impulse, it is further catalyzed into higher development. Old patterns of limitation and separation are released, and the ascension process is accelerated. However, as the heart chakra awakens and matures in collective humanity, it frequently becomes over-stimulated and uncomfortable, sometimes even compromised. An out-of-balance heart chakra may express as discomfort in the chest and back area, especially in conditions such as heart palpitations, blocked arteries, circulation problems, asthma, seizures and insomnia. This is not to say that all such conditions are a result of the heart chakra being activated through accelerated consciousness. However, accelerated awareness often does precipitate such concerns until the heart chakra comes into resonance and coherence with the higher vibrations. The over-stimulation of the chakra system can be stabilized and brought into ease through various means such as biofeedback, hemispheric brain balancing, meditation and spiritual practices, including yoga and breath work, to name a few.

The heart is a vital instrument of healing that brings us back to ourselves, back to our senses, and back to the present moment. For example, we once had a beloved friend who suffered from Alzheimer's disease. When she came into the presence of a long-time friend, she said to the friend, "I don't remember your name, but I remember I love you."

Martin Buber, a German philosopher, referred to the "space in between" as the place where the relationship really exists. In Imago Relationship Therapy, the sacred space between two people is considered to be the place where the relationship resides.

Criticism, defensiveness, indifference and shutting down with others produce incoherent heart rhythms. Finding ways to enhance appreciation and gratitude and to really feel them in the heart actually contributes to a much warmer, richer in-between space, enhancing growth, emotional safety and deep connection. Love does make a difference.

The heart shows us that our own health and wellbeing affect our lives, relationships, and the environment around us. After all, it is true that changing the world begins right here with us.

> *I have settled my restless mind, and my heart is radiant. Living in bondage I have set myself free. I have broken away from the clutch of all narrowness. I have attained the unattainable, and my heart is colored with the color of love.*
> — Kabir

The 14-day Kalachakra Teaching in Washington DC
Lesley Carmack

Receiving teachings from the Dalai Lama goes far beyond information and content. The Dalai Lama often reads the same words over and over — and sometimes in the Tibetan language — and yet each time I hear him speak the words, my understanding expands. This congruence of both heart and mind is a potent transmission of information and energy that brings the wisdom of the heart to living realization.

I experience deep knowing and integration of teachings and at the same time a sudden acceleration of consciousness. His words, along with multi-leveled transmissions, expand consciousness beyond personal capacity and exceed the limitations of the mental field. The latter is often constrained by karma or limitations of interpretations and learning from past life experience. Although the higher levels of the mental field can hold increasingly abstract and refined "thought" such as poetry and mathematics, it is nonetheless still limited to what can be "thought."

The opening words at the Kalachakra empowerment were, "First, self-confidence. Happy mind and inner peace are Universal values. Everyone has a right to a happy life." Those might sound like the words on a Hallmark greeting card, but I understood at multi-levels so many other teachings including right relationship, destructive emotions and their antidotes. [20]

> Love *and compassion are necessities, not luxuries. Without them, humanity cannot survive.* — His Holiness, the 14th Dalai Lama

The Dalai Lama continues by saying that renouncing the world, sensual gratification, meaningful desires and pleasure was the old view of religion. Coming home to our bodies and bringing the transcendent with us is the way of the heart. No longer do we believe that desire is an evil to overcome but that to respond to our hearts' desire as in "following our bliss" can be held in concert with what is in the highest good for the greater whole. To live boldly, bravely and joyfully is the reflection of the heart.

Warmth in the Heart
Sacred Beloved

"We encourage you to continue to bring your awareness to the warmth in your heart and live from that place within your being. We give you this visualization: see, feel and experience the beautiful light of Christ almost like snowflake mandalas of light. Feel and see it surround you. Feel it emanate from your heart and spread outwards. Each being is the light of the world. Many still are not ready to claim that rightful inheritance. Each of you has a responsibility to radiate this light for you then become healers of the world shining through illusion. As cells of the One God, you can participate in the harmony of the universe. Rise and go forth as a new being in Christ."

> *The real abode of God is in the heart of man; when it is frozen with bitterness or hatred, the doors of the shrine are closed, the light is hidden.* — Hazrat Inayat Khan, [21]

The New Heart
Sacred Beloved

"And all things shall be made new. This includes the human heart as a receptor. The spark of God has been buried in this instrument since humanity was first incarnated. The wise have always known this. In the new world, the heart makes more manifest the glory of God. The magnetism emanating from the heart center will one day be reliably measured through technology, not that the initiated have ever needed such affirmation. The heart center will become just as diagnosable, if you will, as the present day heart organ."

Belonging to Love
Ruth Eichler

I don't want to look at the negative or at what's wrong. I don't want to "crawl on my knees for 1,000 miles" as Mary Oliver stated in one of her poems. I want to go right to the heart of what calls me—belonging to Love.

Awareness deepens into the tender, soft purring of the heart, not as witnessing, but one and the same with it. This indwelling love has always called me. Isn't that why the call to silence, rest, peace, meditation, and yoga has beckoned for decades? They are not ends in and of themselves but the pathways to the purring furnace of a heart. The Beloved resides there. The innermost secret of life resides right here in the heart, not at some distant "place" out there.

Heart Encourages Group and Community

> *We are all angels with only one wing;*
> *we can only fly while embracing one*
> *another.* — Luciano de Crescanzo

Because the heart's electromagnetic field extends far beyond the physical body, it is easy to see that there can be a transfer of information and energy as the field of one person's heart interacts with the field of another's heart and they come into resonance with one another. According to research by Rollin McCraty, the heart field of a healer can literally pace the heart of the patient and create new patterns of health. And, healing does not have to be confined to the measurable electromagnetic field of the heart, for distant or non-local healing has been well documented.

Many distant healers work principally through telepathic rapport and transpersonal love that seeks no attachment, a very different feeling from sentimental or devotional love that often involves more of the emotions.

In 1998, Elisabeth Targ and her colleagues conducted a six-month, double blind study of the effects of remote healing on forty patients with advanced AIDS, a study that was reported in *Western Journal of Medicine*.[22] Lesley was one of these healers. Each healer was given a photograph and was asked to direct healing intention for an hour per day using the healing protocols that they used in their private practices. At the completion of the research, the group receiving healing intentions was

216

found to have fewer and less severe new illnesses, fewer doctor visits, fewer hospitalizations and improved mood.

A Distant Healing Experience
Lesley Carmack

I recall one client in the AIDS study who did not seem to respond when I began focusing on him in meditation. He felt depressed and ashamed, emotional states that close down the field. It occurred to me to ask him telepathically if there was a time when he felt joyous and free, and he responded in my imagination as a young boy swinging on a rope over a lake and dropping into the water laughing. I then used this image daily as I visualized him as a healthy, fearless, young lad and overlaid this joyful image onto the photograph I had of him in his current state. My focusing on loving and joyful energies affects the field, but it is up to the other person to reciprocate. After a few days I noticed that I had some energetic substance to work with from him. He was "showing up" for the process. Although we were not given feedback about the progress until the end of the study, I felt a shift in his ability to receive when I opened the field into a more joyous and receptive one that he had experienced as a child. I knew for certain that he had turned around."

Everything affects everything else in this interconnected web of life. Even though we may initially be drawn to others through our similarities and the feeling of being kindred spirits, the heart chakra expands along with our consciousness. Eventually we see beyond differences and find the deep inter-relatedness of all life regardless of beliefs and life circumstances.

He, who makes room in his heart for others, will himself find accommodation everywhere. — Hazrat Inayat Khan, [23]

As we human beings invoke unconditional love for all sentient beings and increasingly express ourselves from the heart, we align with and join a unified consciousness that transcends individual differences. We become less selfish and generate less karma (cause and effect) through our personal desire nature.

Working more in groups in de-personalized ways transforms the planet and all sentient beings. Until we come into the heart, we are incapable of experiencing unconditional regard for the welfare of all. Through the heart, group and community activity can occur without minimizing or compromising individuality. The heart allows much greater capacity to hold paradox and inclusivity, unlike the self-orientation of the solar plexus.

A Few Practices

Though many skills and tools are available that access heart wisdom and facilitate the expression of love to self, others, and the world, we would like to share a few practices that have been especially important in our lives.

Loving Kindness Meditation

Loving Kindness Meditation
Lesley Carmack

In my private practice, the one method of healing on which I receive feedback as being the most potent is the loving kindness meditation, specifically from the Buddhist tradition but kindred to many traditions. In this practice, one begins with oneself then moves to an identified source of challenge and finally includes all life everywhere.

May I be filled with loving kindness. May I be well. May I be happy and at ease. May I be happy.

May you (or the name of the person who challenges you) be filled with loving kindness. May you be well. May you be happy and at ease. May you be happy.

May all beings be filled with loving kindness. May all beings be well. May all beings be happy and at ease. May all beings be happy.

This practice begins with the self because we cannot give away that which we do not have, and we can realize that we have the power to impact the greater whole. Secondly, bringing a blessing toward the challenges we face acknowledges that all living beings are worthy of blessing and that everyone wants kindness, wellness, peace and happiness. And finally we bring our wishes for wellbeing to the Universal.

> *The Universe contains the ALL. We are the context for possibility, made open through grace and surrender.* — George Leonard

Receiving Love

Love Every Molecule Practice
Sacred Beloved

"Receive our love. Allow this love into every cell, into every fiber, every molecule of emotion, and every vibration of your being. Stop and receive. Allow God in every molecule."

"The information we gave you yesterday about loving every molecule of your body was not just a one-time exercise but rather it needs to be repeated daily as a meditation. 'I love every molecule of my body' becomes your mantra. Bask in that love. Play in that love. Give up struggle. Join us in laughter and joy. The greatest illusion is about struggle — the greatest joke. Many don't get the joke. Allow the shower of gratitude. We love you beyond measure."

Forgiveness

In the Aramaic language, the word for forgiveness means to cancel or remove anything that blocks unconditional love. It does not mean pardoning or condoning that which has been done but rather releasing the expectations that someone should have behaved in a certain way in order to receive our love. It does not even mean that we have to remain in proximity to that person.

Forgiveness is a decision not to punish oneself by harboring anger and resentment for the misdeeds of others. In her very helpful book, *Unconditional Love and Forgiveness*, Edith Stauffer speaks about eight profound attitudes taken from the Essene Code of Conduct, which are known as the Beatitudes presented by Jesus. Dr. Stauffer gives specific steps in order to achieve forgiveness based upon these principles taken from Aramaic texts. Basically, she advises that we first become aware of the anger that exists for the transgression so that we don't prematurely bypass this emotion. We then become aware of our unmet expectations and beliefs about what should have been. The next step involves translating those expectations into preferences. "I would have preferred that you (or someone) would have done such and such. But that is not what happened." The next step seems simple but involves careful consideration— to become truly willing to release the expectations and to navigate beyond whatever stands in the way.

Sometimes people believe that they need to hold onto the anger in order to have the energy to prevent victimization. This may be true in some cases until the person has learned more effective empowerment tools. Another common misgiving at this step is that forgiveness means condoning the action or that forgiveness means accepting ongoing bad behavior. Neither is true.

Once the person is fully willing to let go, the final step involves moving awareness into our spiritual essence, sometimes called the High Self, and to really feel unconditional love in our heart. Once alignment with Source is felt, unconditional love extends from the heart to the other's heart, shifting everything. Similar to the loving kindness meditation, the small "me" gives way to the larger "ME" and the Universal All in order to manifest a new possibility through focused attention, aligning with a Higher Will.

Gratitude Practices

> *It's just that whether we're talking about other people, or the Creator itself, there is something about the expression of gratitude that opens doors that do not otherwise open. This is a spiritual fact.*
> — Marianne Williamson [24]

Just as loving kindness and forgiveness have received much attention in recent years, so has the practice of gratitude. Twelve Step groups speak about the "attitude of gratitude" as a potent agent for good and for protecting against addictive behaviors. Googling the word "gratitude" reveals more than fifteen million results. Research from the HeartMath Institute has shown that the word "gratitude" and the felt experience of it shifts consciousness more than other positive words such as love that may be loaded with other meanings. Feeling gratitude in the

221

heart and extending this toward others releases the constraints of the "little self." HeartMath calls the following three simple steps the "Quick Coherence Technique:"

> Heart Focus: Focus your attention on the area around your heart, the area in the center of your chest.
>
> Heart Breathing: Breathe deeply and normally and feel as if your breath is coming in and out through your heart area.
>
> Heart Feeling: As you maintain your heart focus and heart breathing, activate a positive feeling (gratitude). [25]

Expressing Appreciation

Another gratitude practice involves expressing sincere appreciation to those people with whom we are in relationship. Genuine acknowledgement of our appreciations can soften hearts and create meaningful connection, paving the way for a more joyful and happy life.

Listening

David Steindl-Rast, author of several books and a website called www.gratefulness.org, advises us,

> "The key word of the spiritual discipline I follow is 'listening.' This means a special kind of listening, a listening with one's heart." — David Steindl-Rast [26]

A Blessing Prayer

Blessing My Beloveds
Ruth Eichler

One prayer that I say daily, even before getting out of bed in the morning, has meant a great deal to me and blesses all my beloveds, all those in the groups in which I participate, and anyone or anything else that I want to include. I, too, am blessed by the very act of bringing such loving, divine light from above my crown through my heart and extending it out to others. I am often moved to tears when I actually feel this energy moving through my heart, and I wait for that feeling before completing this prayer that is paraphrased from one given by Yogananda.

> *"Father/Mother God, I humbly ask that you bless _____ through me and bestow upon them thy supreme grace. Thy will be done."*

The Cave of the Heart
Ruth Eichler

The Cave of the Heart is beginning to rise out of the unconscious into awareness, presenting itself in collage and dream images. It is that moist, dark, illuminated place within that speaks the language of the Soul. The light of the soul illuminates this place of Being, a place where the divine feminine has residency. It is from this place that I want to live.

ENDNOTES
Chapter 7: Navigating the Ascension Process Through the Heart

1. Antoine de Saint-Exupery, (US: Reynal & Hitchcock, 1943).

2. From the Mundaka Upanishad 2.2.10

3. Revelation to Emperor Seiwa, *World Scripture: A Comparative Anthology of Sacred Texts, p. 139.*

4. Black Elk, Sioux Tradition, *World Scripture: A Comparative Anthology of Sacred Texts, p. 382.*

5.   Hadith of Tirmidhi, *World Scripture: A Comparative Anthology of Sacred Texts, p. 519.*

6.   Thomas Merton, *Love and Living.*

7.   Hazrat Inayat Khan, *The Complete Sayings, (Saying No. 161, p. 20).*

8.   Hazrat Inayat Khan, *The Soul's Journey, p. 139.*

9.   Hazrat Inayat Khan, *The Complete Sayings,.* (No 541, p. 62).

10.   Rumi, translated by Coleman Barks, *The Essential Rumi,* p. 63.

11.   These paragraphs come from notes that were taken by Lesley at the Heart Sutra teachings given by the Dalai Lama in Bloomington, IN in the summer of 2010.

12.   Greg Braden, *Awakening to Zero Point.*

13.   www.heartmath.org

14.   Rollin McCraty and Doc Childre , *"The Appreciative Heart: The Psychophysiology of Positive Emotions and Optimal Functioning,"* (Institute of Heart Math 2003).

15.   Rollin McCraty, PhD, "The Energetic Heart Bioelectromagnetic Ineractions within and between People," Copyright 2003, Institute of HeartMath.

16.   www.heartmath.org

17.   Song, Schwartz, and Russek; McCraty, Atkinson, and Tomasino, "Heart-focused attention and heart-brain synchronization: Energetic and physiological mechanisms," Alternative Therapies in Health and Medicine, 1998, 4(5): 44-62.

18.   Leonard Wisneski, MD, and Lucy Anderson, *The Scientific Basis of Integrative Medicine (2nd edition),* (CRC Press, 2009, p. 390).

19. Hazrat Inayat Khan, The Complete Sayings, (No. 483, p. 49).

20. These paragraphs come from notes that were taken by Lesley at the Kalachakra initiations by the Dalai Lama in Washington, D.C. in July 2011.

21. Hazrat Inayat Khan, *The Complete Sayings*, p. 234.

22. Fred Sicher, Elisabeth Targ, Dan Moore II, and Helene S. Smith, *Western Journal of Medicine*, December, 1998.

23. Hazrat Inayat Khan, *The Complete Sayings,* No. 74, p. 13.

24. Marianne Williamson's foreword in Angeles Arrien's book, *Living in Gratitude: A Journey That Will Change Your Life,* (Boulder, CO: Sounds True, 2011, p. xxiv).

25. www.heartmath.com

26. David Steindl-Rast in A Listening Heart: The Art of Contemplative Living, (NY: Crossroad, 1988).

Chapter 8
Mother Earth

The Earth System behaves as a single, self-regulating system with physical, chemical, biological and human components. — Declaration of Amsterdam, signed by 1,000 scientists in 2001 at the European Geophysical Union meeting.

Some of Us Dance to Bring about a New Earth

The Grandmothers Call
Ruth Eichler

Fifteen years before our travel to Egypt, I was receiving a cranial sacral treatment from a trusted friend who happened to be the same age as I. Unlike anything I had ever experienced in my life, suddenly a no-nonsense voice came through my mouth announcing, "It is time to gather the dancing grandmothers together." As a result, Marcy, my practitioner friend, and I called together about a dozen women over the age of 50 for ceremony, laughter, stories and sleeping under the stars at an overnight campout on our newly purchased land. Our cabin or house hadn't even been built yet. We had a wonderful gathering.

Years earlier when we lived in Kansas, I began to have visions of old indigenous-looking women dancing around a fire to the beat of a drum chanting the words, "Healing, wholing, healing, wholing." Those "dancing grandmothers" from the invisible world continued to impress upon my mind the importance of our collaboration at this perilous and momentous time on earth. Little did I know that the gathering of the "dancing grandmothers" under the stars was only the harbinger for many other "grandmother" experiences, including the trip to Egypt so many years later.

At my second Sun/Moon Dance, I heard a voice that said, "See, you are a dancing grandmother." They reminded me that this grandmother journey now seems seamless, even though years passed between the gathering on our land and my first Sun/Moon Dance last year. Of course, there were the annual Long Dances (five of them), and now a Phoenix Dance on our land in September. It's strange how an underlying theme can surface again and again until it becomes more clearly visible and conscious— like dreams breaking through to consciousness.

I, who felt heavy and like an un-dancer most of my life, have danced five Long Dances, seven Phoenix Dances, and four Sun/ Moon Dances. Apparently I am a dancer, and I love serving the Great Mother and the Earth and the Universe in this way.

As the ancient one calls who holds turtle island, She does so silently, for She wants me to hear with inner ears, underneath the brain and head. As She calls, the vibration reverberates through my body. I am learning to hear in new ways, and I certainly am glad that at this age I don't have to understand it all or even a lot of it. I can respond to the call from a deeper yet vaster place within my being. I love a Van Morrison song from one of his CD's called, "Let Go into the Mystery," a song that has so deeply moved me that I apparently wore out the CD.

The Phoenix Dance
Ruth Eichler

While the Phoenix Dance that occurred on our land for several years was not specifically a "grandmother" dance, this dance was also a part of the unfolding vision of a new world that included the Sacred Feminine.

Vision for the Phoenix Dance
Ruth Eichler

The Black Madonna weeps a glistening tear that slides down her dark face. Susan Seden Boulet's image of a weeping black woman insistently inserts herself in front of my eyes. That image has haunted me for ages, and I again found it pasted into a journal alongside some one of my writes.

I enter that lone tear on her cheek, and I am inside an Egyptian pyramid in a large room with a vaulted pyramid ceiling high overhead. A lone sarcophagus stands in the center of the room under the apex of the peak. Suddenly many people clad in long flowing black garments begin to mournfully and elegantly dance. They express lamenting sounds as they dance, bend, and move throughout the room.

The lid of the sarcophagus opens as a beacon of light penetrates the room from above. Ephemeral light emerges from the coffin, and the mood dramatically shifts among the dancers. Suddenly they are wearing long, elegant, white flowing garments. The resurrection dance turns celebratory, almost ecstatic.

This strange dream/vision unexpectedly occurred at my Friday morning group last week during a 15-minute meditation. As I shared the imagery, one of my friends said, "You've just been given the next dance for your dance arbor." Since that time details of the dance have been unfolding, mostly unbidden, one after another, in a creative flow.

The Black Madonna and the Phoenix Dance
Ruth Eichler

Only a sliver of a silver New Moon rose at 5:00 a.m. after we'd been dancing under glistening stars for two hours. Only the fire in the center of the arbor and the torches on the entry gate lit the velvet blackness of the night. The Black Madonna hovered in the darkness present to all whose heart longed to feel Her.

Soon I'll go in search of Her again in Germany at Joseph Rael's request. I still marvel at the synchronicity of Joseph suggesting that I go to the tiny village of Angerbach, Germany, to visit a peace chamber four houses down from a church that venerates the Black Madonna. Last January while giving his blessing for this dance, he said that I should go to Germany and bring the spirit of the Black Madonna here. He did not know that I would be one hour from Angerbach in October teaching with my friend Deborah. Deborah had been leading women's groups in Europe for some time, and she had invited me to join her as co-facilitator of one of the groups.

The Phoenix Rises
Ruth Eichler

The Phoenix rose out of the ashes at dawn yesterday, and the twelve dancers and I cheered and danced with gusto in spite of having danced four hours since 3:00 a.m.. Dancers then joined together in celebration, continuing to dance for another hour. We all stopped to sing the sunrise song, led by Carlajo Rael, as the red-orange ball of a sun rose high enough above the hill to be fully seen.

A huge flock of starlings flurried by shortly after sunrise, and I knew the dance was essentially completed by their appearance. Early on Saturday morning before the dancers arrived, I was refilling our hummingbird feeder on the deck when hundreds of starlings whirred and called overhead, heading south towards the arbor. The book Animal Speaks says starlings represent community and the ability to connect even though many languages are spoken. This seemed the perfect harbinger for the Phoenix Dance, so their reappearance just before it was completed seemed perfect.

The dance is such a whole experience that it's difficult to take out the various parts to write about. Vic is an integral part of the dance, mostly behind the scenes but visible as well. He does so much to physically prepare the trails, the campground and the arbor by mowing many times in preceding weeks. He makes sure ample wood is stacked, ready for the sweat lodge and the fire in the arbor that burns through the entire dance. He sprays the wasps that invariably congregate in the storage shed by the sweat lodge. He sprays the few stray poison ivy plants in the campground. Snipping cedar branches on our land, he prepares a smudge bucket that he fires up and periodically walks through the arbor during the dance swaying the cedar and sage like a priest with incense. He is the fire tender for the sweat lodge, and he drums — only once falling asleep with drumbeater in hand.

There's so much love among the dancers and drummers. Actually, this year the three drummers — Vic, Carlajo, and Calvin — seemed completely integrated into the entire experience. They just move their hands, and we move our feet and more of our bodies.

Seven of the sixteen people at the dance also participate in the Sun/ Moon dances in one role or another. The few who were new to the dances were quickly brought into the fold, warmly greeted and embraced by the community.

Dancing to Bring about a New Earth
Ruth Eichler

This past weekend, the third annual Phoenix Dance was held on our land. When I first received the vision for the Phoenix Dance, I thought there would be much personal mourning and grieving during the hours from 3:00 a.m. to dawn when we dance in black to release old patterns and beliefs that no longer serve. I thought this would be the time when the ego might complain in its fear of dying. Certainly dancers do release vestiges and remnants of illusion and old residue, perhaps not even known to the conscious mind. Each dancer names something they wish to release, and these pieces of paper are burned at the dawn ceremony. We also burn mustard seeds, a Buddhist practice symbolizing the burning of unconscious seeds of negativity before they take further root. We also commit to something we want to manifest in our lives over the next year.

But this dance has mostly called forth people who have already done enormous personal growth and healing. I believe most of the dancers come as a service to the Whole, the One, of which we are all a part. Several of the dancers have danced all three Phoenix Dances. Those who are energy sensitive say the energies continue to amp up on this land and in this dance. The dancers were strong this year, few sitting down or resting much during the five hours of dancing.

Dancing after the dawn ceremony is always so joyful and jubilant. Dancers have stripped off the black outer garments and dance ecstatically in white. This year, Calvin played his African drums along with the big Native American drum after dawn, bringing an ever greater joy to the jubilant beat.

This year I was thrilled to have a bagpiper on the hilltop at 3:00 a.m. calling the dancers forth and into the arbor. She and her husband who drummed stayed until 6:00 a.m., and she piped at various times during the first hour or so of the dance.

A Hopi Madonna and Child stood at the east gate of the dance arbor this year. Linda, who knows I love the Black Madonna and have several versions framed from various places around the world in my office, gave me a beautifully framed image that I had never seen before. It is a Hopi Madonna and Child dressed in Native dress, and it is a very powerful image. About a week ago while I was in my home office, she fell off the wall onto the floor with the glass unbroken. The house was calm. The nail and frame were strong. No others fell off the wall. I knew She intended to participate in the arbor and that she would be integral to the dance, and She was.

What is Gaia?

Originally a Greek goddess meaning Mother Earth, Gaia was the Great Mother of all, one of the primal elements that emerged with the creation of the earth — along with the elements of air, fire and water.

The word Gaia is now widely used to mean that the living and nonliving components of earth function as a single system. It came back into use in the 1970's with the work of James Lovelock, a scientist who developed what he called the Gaia Hypothesis. In the intervening years, the hypothesis was expanded into a theory or principle after extensive scientific debate and research, and the word and concept has spread like wildfire, infusing the environmental movement, among many others.

Many believe the ability to conceive of the earth as a unified system or organism was accelerated when the first humans in space sent back beautiful images of our blue planet in the 1960s. For the first time we had actual photographs of what the Earth looked like as a whole, and some old, limited views were shattered. Many indigenous peoples might chuckle that it took that long for science to catch up with what many of them have believed for eons.

Joseph Rael often speaks about how his people in the Southwest experienced place and land as a living being:

> "The Picuris Pueblo where I grew up was a living being with a psyche of individuals made up into a group that I began to know as my father's people. The village was architecturally designed so that it would continually give sustenance to the people who lived there. The village was not just a physical place. It was a mental, emotional, and spiritual place as well." [1]

Someone once asked the Zen Master Thich Nhat Hanh what needed to happen in order to save our world. He replied,

> "What we most need to do is to hear within us the sounds of the Earth crying."

One of the highest levels of consciousness is what Beck calls "holistic" in which the wholeness of existence is experienced through mind and spirit, and the Self is both distinct and a blended part of a larger, more compassionate whole. The Earth is a dynamic organism, and we as human beings are an integral part of that whole — even an expression of a collective mind. On the one hand, that magnificent view of our beautiful planet provides an experience of a witnessing observer, but on a much deeper level, we begin to realize how much we human beings are an intimate part of the whole.

> *The secret of the idea of a blessing to be found in holy places lies in the principle that the holy place is no longer a place: it has become a living being.* — Hazrat Inayat Khan [2]

The Future of the Earth

Paul Hawken, author and environmentalist, has dedicated his life to sustainable living and the relationship between business and the environment. He says that when he is asked whether he is optimistic or pessimistic about the future, he says:

> "If you look at the science about what is happening on earth and aren't pessimistic, you don't understand data. But if you meet the people who are working to restore this earth and the lives of the poor, and you aren't optimistic, you haven't got a pulse."

His quotation must have struck a chord, for it has been quoted numerous times on the Internet.

Cutting-edge neuro-scientific research reveals evidence that "higher states of consciousness" and their ready accessibility radically change our understanding of the limits of human potential. Our perception and behavior are a direct reflection of our consciousness. Human behavior can transform society if we open to and practice these higher states of development through our relationships with Nature and Gaia herself. The earth cares for us, and we must care for it.

As the Sacred Feminine reveals herself, it allows us to embody those mothering qualities so that we may now nourish that which has nourished us throughout time. The impulse to "green" the world and to think globally and to care for the whole earth seems to emanate from this impulse.

> *"The destiny of humans cannot be separated from the destiny of Earth."* ~ *Thomas Berry*

Morphic Fields

Rupert Sheldrake has reported his work on morphic fields and morphic resonance in thirteen books and dozens of research articles, one of the latest books being *Morphic Resonance: The Nature of Formative Causation* (2009). His work supports the idea of our interconnectedness, and that even without consciously knowing something we can tune into what others know. For example, in a 1988 article in *New Scientist*, Sheldrake spoke about these morphic fields that connect us through space and time. One of his examples concerns cattle guards. Ranchers throughout the American West have found that they can save money on cattle guards by using fake ones consisting of stripes painted across the road. Real cattle guards are made of a series of parallel steel tubes or rails with gaps in between. It is difficult for cattle to walk across them and painful for them to try it. However, cattle today do not usually even try to cross them. The illusory guards work just like the real ones. When cattle approach them, they "put on brakes with all four feet," as one rancher expressed it. Even calves encountering them for the first time avoid them as assiduously as cattle previously exposed to real guards. This aversion may well depend on morphic resonance from members of the species that previously have learned to avoid cattle guards the painful way.

Another example comes from data from laboratory experiments on rats and other animals implying that such effects occur. In one series of experiments rats learned how to escape from a water maze. New batches of rats were tested month-by-month, year-by-year. As time went on, rats in laboratories all over the world escaped more and more quickly.

Just as magnetic fields extend beyond the surface of a magnet, and electromagnetic fields beyond cell phones, so the mind extends beyond the brain through mental fields. When we look at something, for example, a tree, the image of the tree is projected out through these fields to the place where the tree actually is. Our minds touch what we are viewing, and this provides an explanation for our ability to sense when someone is looking at us from behind. Rupert Sheldrake discusses the evidence for the reality of this sense in his book, *The Sense of Being Stared At And Other Aspects of the Extended Mind* (2003).

The Power of Intention

Just as science has validated that prayer and intention affect others, even those not near us geographically, our thoughts, prayers and intentions also affect the physical world in other ways. Dean Radin, Ph.D. and senior scientist at IONS, says after several scientifically controlled experiments that there is substantial evidence in favor of intentional mind-matter interactions with random events, photons, cell cultures, and human physiology and behavior. [3]

Other interesting experiments can be found at the IONS website. As principal investigator, Dean Radin conducted a triple-blind study on the effects of distant intention on water crystal formation with Masaru Emoto, Takashige Kizu and Nancy Lund as co-investigators. In that experiment, 1,900 people in Austria and Germany focused their positive intentions for water over a three-day period towards water samples that were housed in an electromagnetically shielded room in California. Unknown to the people providing intentions, other water samples were also located near the target water and others outside the shielded room. A technician photographed ice drops formed from the water samples, and each image was assessed for aesthetic beauty by over 2,500 independent judges. Individuals who did not know about the treatment conditions analyzed the results. The intentionally treated crystal images showed statistically significant higher ratings for aesthetic beauty, replicating an earlier pilot study.

The research of Dr. William Tiller, Professor Emeritus from Stanford University has repeatedly shown that the acid/alkaline (pH) balance in a vessel of water can be changed either up or down without adding chemicals to the water merely by creating an intention to do so. This research has consistently been replicated around the world with similar results. Researchers at Tiller's Foundation for New Science believe that the technologies that they are pioneering will have a profound impact on all aspects of human behavior. They say, "Improved methods for converting fossil fuels to mechanical energy, more powerful computing capacities and greatly enhanced potential for human, mental, and physical development are just a few examples of the dramatic possibilities." [4]

Thousands of other published papers and hundreds of controlled laboratory studies give support the belief that what we think and do on a daily basis impacts what happens in our individual and collective health. [5]

Joseph Rael, Native American visionary, artist and healer speaks about how physical form on this earth is affected by our interaction through our thoughts and how we perceive. He goes on to say:

> "Land is the principal form that sets up a step ladder to climb to the heavens, because the land is the vast Self, which is descending light that purifies. It is the purifying force that brings heaven and earth together and crystallizes it so that it looks like a tree or an elephant or an ocean. ... Matter is in a state of incompleteness; it must have the perception of the perceiver to exist." [6]

The passion in the earth's whisper grew
so loud, I woke. — Meister Eckhart

Indigenous Perspectives

Indigenous cultures throughout history have had an intimate connection with the earth, and many have spoken of our bonded relationship with our Mother, the earth, a living being. Two famous Native American chiefs say:

> "All things are connected. Whatever befalls the earth befalls the children of the earth." — Chief Seattle

> "The first peace, which is the most important, is that which comes within the souls of people when they realize their relationship, their oneness with the universe and all its powers, and when they realize that at the center of the universe dwells the Great Spirit, and that

this center is really everywhere, it is within each of us."
— Black Elk

The Thirteen Indigenous Grandmothers from various cultures who have been meeting throughout the world since 2004 share their message that now is the time to come back into deep connection with the earth and each other. They have prayed at the Vatican, with children, and they have prayed with the Dalai Lama. They have blessed water in New Mexico and created ceremonies in many places in the world. They offer direct and simple teachings with compassionate authority, and they demonstrate through their actions and prayers to those of us not imbued with these principles how to come back into balance and preserve our sacred world. They and other groups of grandmothers have come together in various places in the world to offer prayers, ceremony and to act as agents of change on behalf of a spiritual directive. Such was our trip to Egypt as well. The following is the Mission of the International Council of Thirteen Indigenous Grandmothers:

> "We represent a global alliance of prayer, education and healing for our Mother Earth, all Her inhabitants, all the children, and for the next seven generations to come.
>
> We are deeply concerned with the unprecedented destruction of our Mother Earth and the destruction of indigenous ways of life. We believe the teachings of our ancestors will light our way through an uncertain future.
>
> We look to further our vision through the realization of projects that protect our diverse cultures, lands, medicines, language and ceremonial ways of prayer and through projects that educate and nurture our children."[7]

Raylene, the Hawaiian Goddess
Ruth Eichler

Raylene, the native Hawaiian woman who spoke about the sacredness of the earth at the Council Grove Conference, deeply touched my heart. She has the most amazing hair— long, gray-brown and full, reaching to the middle of her back. The way her hair streamed wide, her plump round-ish body, her radiant smile and luminescent eyes made me think she is the goddess herself. She spoke so softly and melodiously about how Our Mother, the Earth, wants to hear from her children. At the beginning of the conference, we all sang a song as we greeted each participant, "All I ask is that you forever remember my loving you." Raylene, the goddess, says the Mother wants us to sing that song to her. She said we'd all made a contract long ago to come together now to talk and share. During one of the early morning meditations, Raylene showed us how to dance some hula movements, something she teaches young girls.

Her body flowed with grace and eloquence, softly and tenderly. At the final ceremony of the conference while singing "May the blessings of God rest upon you; may God's peace abide with you; may God's presence illuminate your heart now and forever more," I greeted Raylene in the circle. Tears of abundance filled my heart— tears of joy, gratitude and love.

Attunement with Nature

> *There is no greater scripture than nature, for nature is life itself.* — Hazrat Inayat Khan

In a 2005 book, *Last Child in the Woods*, Richard Louv decries the trend that children are spending less time outdoors,

241

contributing to many problems including anxiety, depression, and attention-deficit problems to less ability to perform educationally. He argues that the disengagement from Nature by children has profound implications, not only for these children and future generations but also for the Earth itself. He says that studies in California and other states show that students who participate in outdoor education achieve significant gains in various academic studies.

Not only are children separated from Nature today, but so many adults also suffer from the lack of nourishment that Nature provides. Many books are now available on how to regain our relationship with the earth. One of those very helpful books is Philip Sutton Chard's *The Healing Earth: Nature's Medicine for the Troubled Soul* in which he provides various exercises and practices to re-attune us to the wind, sun, water and earth.

How did human beings sever their relationship with the natural world? David Abram, who *Utne Reader* called one of the hundred visionaries who are changing the world, has written a provocative book speaking of our intimate connection with the earth. He says:

> "Intelligence is no longer ours alone but is a property of the earth; we are in it, of it, immersed in its depths. And indeed each terrain, each ecology, seems to have its own particular intelligence, its unique vernacular of soil and leaf and sky." [8]

David Wagoner beautifully rendered a Northwest Native American teaching story told from the point of view of an elder instructing a young person into a poem titled "Lost." The elder asks, "What do you do when you are lost in the forest?" This poem has been recorded on numerous Internet sites and YouTube videos. David Whyte included this poem in the book of his own poetry, *The Heart Aroused*. Though David Whyte interprets the poem as a way through silence to return to our own creative fire, the poem also speaks of the power of being in tune with nature and its wisdom.

Lost

What do you do when you are lost in the forest?
Stand still. The trees ahead and bushes beside you
Are not lost. Wherever you are is called Here.
And you must treat it as a powerful stranger.
Must ask permission to know it and be known.
The forest breathes. Listen. It answers.
I have made this place around you.
If you leave it you may come back again.
Stay Here. No two trees are the same to Raven.
No two branches are the same to Wren.
If what a tree or a bush does is lost on you,
You are surely lost. Stand still. The forest knows
Where you are. You must let it find you.

Joseph Rael also speaks about how we must listen in order to be connected, and indeed in order to be human:

"Since people are made of sound, listening is important. It is through listening that you become a true human, and a true human is a listener who is constantly attuned by working with everything that is happening." [9]

While writing this chapter, Nature provided an excellent teaching in what happens when we are disconnected and how we can be restored to wholeness, as seen in the story below:

The Need for Connection
Ruth Eichler

Sometimes words fall into place, flowing as easily as an unimpeded mountain stream. Today while writing this chapter on Gaia and the earth, I felt as if cotton were in my head. Even Lesley's and my computers were befuddled, refusing to cut and paste properly and bouncing from one page of print to another without warning seemingly mirroring my own mind. I even wrote the words, "disconnected from our Self," and for some unknown reason, the computer typed them in tiny print, even though the original font size was still listed at the top of the page.

At some point, I felt impelled to walk on the beloved land where I live, and Lesley happily joined me. Walking through an open meadow, I suddenly spotted a deer antler in the grass quite some distance from any trees. I have walked on this property for sixteen years, and even though many deer share the land with us and we see them daily, I've never before found an antler. I don't take serendipities for granted and trust that messages coincide with such events. Lesley and I then walked to a place I call "Belly Stone National Park," a place in the meadow where many boulders stand together in community. I love draping myself over these stones, feeling their ancient song in my body. Joy returned, cotton in the head vanished, and the antler came back to the house with us.

I believe the joy is a gift from the land, the deer, the stones and perhaps Gaia herself. With great amusement, I realized that I had been "in my head," trying to write about Gaia yet separated from her even though we can see the deer, pond, trees and grass from the window where we are writing. Gaia invites us to participate, to commune, and to be enlivened by nature. I had been disconnected from my Self, and I am but a particle of nature, of the whole. The antlers will reside in a place to remind me that even though I am writing on a computer, I can't forget to participate in the in-between spaces.

The Impact of the Land
Ruth Eichler

I have seen the land affect hundreds of people who come here to attend events at our Peace Chamber or who have participated in the many trainings and workshops held here. Living here, I often forget the impact that it actually has. After the first weekend of our Sound Mystery School one year, a woman who is well acquainted with nature had an interesting experience. This woman has conducted outdoor camps, kayaked in Boundary Waters, and feeds all the squirrels, deer and raccoons that visit her back yard. She decided to spend an extra night at the retreat center across the street after the workshop and slept for 24 hours. She, too, had forgotten what an affect vitalized land can have. Many other people have commented on the potency of the energies on our land and in our neighborhood.

At each weekend of Sound Mystery School, a yearlong program that my co-teacher and I held for seven years, we incorporated some activities out of doors and also in the Peace Chamber, an earthen structure. At the end of each year, the participants set up tents around the land and entered into a weekend vision quest, communing even more deeply with their own spirit and with nature. This offered an opportunity to further expand their consciousness with a direct experience and collaboration with the earth. People reported that the land helped integrate transcendent states and ground it into a felt sense and lived experience.

An earlier "write" also speaks of the joy that can come when we commune with nature:

Falling Through the Sky Hole
Ruth Eichler

I had encounters with deer outside the cabin on each of the three days of my retreat plus other inner deer experiences. The experience with the doe and me looking at each other remains a peak moment. I've never been so immersed in deer before.

There were other mystical moments during the retreat. One was while walking the labyrinth at GilChrist one morning. The morning rays of sun lit up the sparkles of melted frost, making the green labyrinth and surrounding brown hillside glisten with millions of dancing diamonds. "The hills are alive," Julie Andrews once sang. Indeed that entire space was alive.

Communication with Dolphins and Other Species
Lesley Carmack

While at a conference, my friend Judy and I attended a seminar that spoke about extending human consciousness through interspecies communication. Midway through the slideshow that presented hundreds of dolphins swimming in the open sea, tears began to stream down my face. I said, "We have to experience this," and Judy and I registered for a seminar with Joan Ocean in Kona, Hawaii that was to occur a few months later. We were unsure what to expect except that we would swim with dolphins during the day and in the evenings meet to hear talks about dolphins and whales and to dialogue about our experiences that we had during the day.

Judy and I began to train for the adventure, researching dolphins and trusting our inner guidance for means to develop greater telepathic rapport and to become more open to interspecies communication. We walked backwards with our eyes closed, read things backwards as in a mirror, practiced various traditions of heart meditations, and we tried to get out of our habitual projections and expectations concerning how to "know" and register communication.

Before leaving for Hawaii, we traveled to Judy's home on a lagoon in Florida. Her home had windows that overlooked the place where a small pod of dolphins swam daily. Someone in the house would yell, "dolphins," and Judy and I would run to the rock wall, trying to establish telepathic communication with them. Did it matter if we established eye contact or whether we put a hand or foot in the water? Did they like bright colors? Was singing better than silence? We intentionally projected heart-centered love to them in a state of joyful innocence. After three days, the mothers and guardian aunts began to swim on the far side of the babies, allowing the babies to be close to us. Humbly, we felt ready for the big adventure.

Off the big island of Hawaii, twenty of us boarded a boat to travel into deep water where migration patterns of dolphins and whales are well established. Although we would not "pursue" them, we would seek to be in proximity with the dolphins and hope that they would engage us. Wearing wet suits, goggles, snorkels and fins we scanned the waters for hours. When we spotted a pod of bottlenose dolphins the length of a football field or so away, we all jumped off the back of the boat into infinitely deep, clear blue water. It never occurred to me to ask, "Why are we doing this?" I did think, though, "If this is the end, what a way to go!"

After several days of immersion in the pods' playful field, we could easily understand researchers' findings that these swims increase endorphins and left/right brain hemisphere balance just as a deep, meditative practice does. What was less familiar was the experience several of us had. We realized that when immersed in the pod's field, we sometimes "forgot" that we were not dolphins. Being suspended in the silence and the translucent, blue water within the dolphin pod field provides an expansion of context beyond knowing oneself as "skin encapsulated." Swimming in open water with these engaging, playful and intelligent beings that were so full of heart, we became one with the patterns and rhythms of the cavorting dolphin companions and with the ocean itself.

The vulnerability of being in deep water and yet feeling the safety of the collective and interrelated pod field was a paradox that was like a shamanic initiation. Dolphins use sonar to echolocate. Perhaps this, too, has a vibrational context that caused us to feel "held" in the collective yet immensely spacious flow of rhythms. The experience of presence, without verbal language, yet with deep felt sense of meeting, was a profound training in openness and emptiness that went far beyond what I had known through meditation and other life experiences.

On day three, we encountered the humpback whales' distinctive body shapes. They swam nearer and nearer to the boats, and we had to wait until they were 100 yards or so away before entering the water with them. As we did, they approached closer and closer. This was life changing for me. Humpback whales are 40-50 feet long and weigh up to 80,000 pounds. Both males and females can produce sounds, but the males sing the long and loud sounds in low register that are perhaps the most complex in amplitude and frequency of any animal in the world. These songs last for fifteen or so minutes.

I could find the depth that their sound was traveling in the water by moving my head from just below the surface to perhaps eleven or so inches lower. Whales generate sound by forcing air through their massive nasal cavities, and the vibrations and vocalizations travel through the waters creating a sound field that for me was even more potent than that of swimming with dolphin pods. The sound activated my senses inside and out, and my chakra field became aligned in the sound in such a way that I felt as though I was marinating in a field of heart-crown liquid resonance. I had heard hours of whale songs on tapes, and even played their songs while I was with a friend who was dying. Their songs include calls and squeaks and beautiful long tones, and the fact that the songs change over the years may be partly why the whales are called "Record Keepers." For me, the experience of floating free immersed in the sound was a deeply spiritual experience. The sound vibration permeated my entire body inside and out like a giant swimming heart. I was totally submerged in love. I was in a timeless state of transpersonal, trans- species, trans- worldly Beingness.

The convergence of non-ordinary states of consciousness such as those I had with the dolphins and whales can form a new model and definition of reality. Although I was mostly unaware of it upon returning from Kona, old patterns, attitudes and self-limitations fell away with increasing ease after " the swims." Underlying or unconscious beliefs concerning "what is possible" were altered in a way that has had an ongoing empowering effect on my healing and therapy work. Perhaps most pervasive of all was the experience of being immersed in a field of joy, without personal will or even words, as the most natural and truthful way of being and so effortless.

The Earth Is Changing

> *In evolutionary enlightenment, the individual must come to terms with the profoundly implicating recognition that as we evolve, the process that created us also evolves.* — Andrew Cohen

We can observe dramatic expressions of the earth changing — seismic events, tsunamis, erratic climate changes, and intensified solar flare activity, among others. For example, in 2002, satellite photographs of electromagnetic fields on the earth, especially strong at the poles, demonstrated that the magnetic field is in process of reversing. According to University of California Professors, Gary Glatzmaier and P. H. Roberts, the magnetic field waxes and wanes, poles drift and occasionally flip. Change is normal. The source of the field, the outer core, is itself seething, swirling, turbulent. They say, "It's chaotic down there. The changes we detect on our planet's surface are a sign of that inner chaos." [10]

Further, solar winds from the sun cause the northern lights to be more visible in places much further south than in previous times. Galactic, cosmic rays are increasing by 20 percent because of the weakening natural shielding provided by the heliosphere. Solar flare activity is in synch with temperature changes on the earth, demonstrating that space weather affects us. What we have learned from measurements and observations of these phenomena is that they are increasing in number and intensity, and we know that one form of activity affects another. Sometimes the connection is direct such as seismic events or earth plates shifting under the ocean resulting in tsunamis. Sometimes the connection is less well known such as the link between solar flare activity and electro-magnetic disturbances that affect many forms of technology.

Part of the interrelationship that we wish to address is how we, as the microcosm, reflect these changes ourselves both metaphorically and physically. Inner shifting landscapes can metaphorically cause tsunamis in our lives. Solar flares can literally cause physical perturbations in our energy field and affect our sense of wellbeing.

As the planet's energy accelerates, we as humanity correspondingly increase our vibratory rate. This is both an individual and a collective awakening, not inspired by hard work or a planned endeavor. Like birds that come together to fly a migratory pattern, we are being collectively inspired by this awakening impulse. The impulse arises within each individual in resonance with the quickening on the planet and one another.

A few months before the Twin Towers went down on September 11, 2001, The Sacred Beloved had this to say about changes and the earth:

Coming Changes
Sacred Beloved

We are here as we always are. (I feel a very refined energy and ask about it.) That is because our elders join us as a special visit of truth. The time is at hand. Time is of the essence. You must be prepared. (I feel a bit of fear creep in.) Remain dispassionate so that you may best receive our message. Great turmoil is about to be unleashed that will affect the psychic realm of your planet. One form is warfare. Neither the Council nor we can prevent this from happening. (I ask what kind of war.) Much bloodshed ensues because of a bomb. The Middle East is involved. (I ask if it involves the U.S.) Yes, perhaps. Just as the huge death toll in India from the earthquake is affecting the psyche of the planet or the collective unconscious, so too will the new situation affect it. Indeed the fabric of the Earth's atmosphere will be affected. It is as if the suffering produces bulges in the stratosphere in the same way that a psychic disturbance does within an individual's aura. The bulges result partially from so many beings being in the astral realm after death.

Visualize the perfection of the earth and her atmosphere already whole, sparkling with light. Your Great Mother, the earth is in labor and is near birth. She is birthing a new way of being in the universe. She too asks for your prayers. Cherish her. Rock her in your arms as you would a baby. Breathe with her as you would with a mother in childbirth. And remember, Dear Beloved Children, you signed on for this task. That is all on this issue.

Sacred Sites

Because we carry our sacredness within us wherever we go, every place is sacred and imbued with light and spirit. However, there are special places on the earth that have been identified as being particularly potent. Some sites such as temples or stone formations of many kinds have been imbued for thousands of years with prayers and ceremonies, adding to their special vibrations. These places may feel different and to clairvoyants may actually look different. Colors, thought forms, and orbs are visible to seers. Sometimes these phenomena have been recorded photographically or with electromagnetic field resonance measuring machines. In those places we often experience a greater sense of awe and connection to something larger than ourselves not available in ordinary consciousness.

There also are many sites on the earth that may or may not have spiritual edifices or structures built on them that have been known for thousands of years to be very special and to enhance consciousness. Some people refer to these places as energy vortexes, and others have written of ley lines that run through the earth carrying heightened electromagnetic fields. The planet and its biosphere is a living being that is accelerating in vibration. The lower, denser fields are becoming more refined. There are magnetite crystals in the brain that create a resonance to the earth itself, five million crystals per gram in the inside brain and 100 million crystals per gram in the brain membrane. These crystals may assist us in orienting to the earth's magnetic field.[11] Artificial fields from devices such as cell phones and computers also affect these electromagnetic fields.

Although one can still be inspired and uplifted by visiting these sacred places on the earth, the whole planetary being is rising in vibration and therefore accessible anywhere. Whether we visit culturally recognized sacred places or whether we just become more aware of personal sacred places, we can become more intimate in our relationship with the Earth.

When new light and energy come in, it replaces what was there before, and we may become discombobulated and feel agitated until the body can assimilate and equilibrate the new vibrations. Perhaps the earth is experiencing the same thing.

Etheric Field of the Earth

Brian Swimme, author of several books concerning the nature of the universe, believes that humans are aware of suffering on the earth and that we are ready for "giving birth to a new form of humanity." He also shares thoughts from his friend, another famous ecologist:

> "Thomas Berry says the challenge of our time is the rein-
> vention of the human at the species level, which makes
> it clear that we are called to do something monumental
> and magnificent. That is why is it so great to be alive." [12]

When we walk on the earth, there is reciprocity between our etheric field and the etheric field of the earth. The earth's field will permeate us to the degree to which we are open. Even though we don't necessarily have to be conscious of the inter-penetration of these fields, they can nourish us. Practices such as tai chi or chi gong demonstrate that this interrelationship can be consciously cultivated as a healing practice, just as an appreciative walk in nature can be mutually beneficial.

The etheric field refers to the densest of the subtle fields that lie next to the physical realm, sometimes referred to as the aura, whether related to human bodies or the earth. It is a system-atized flow of forces and currents. The etheric body conducts energy and is an oscillating, dynamic field. It carries informa-tion and energy as a subtle substance that interfaces and inter-penetrates both the physical and the subtle just as the energy of chakras interpenetrate the human body. Our observations and participation relate not to the purely physical world of matter and energy or to the purely non-physical psychic world, but to an intermediate reality that Theosophists and others have called the "etheric."

Similarly, morphic fields as defined by Rupert Sheldrake are located within and around the systems they organize. Like quantum fields, their work restricts or imposes order upon the inherent system under their influence in a holistic way. Morphic resonance suggests that like is drawn to like and that these fields influence patterns or subsequent similar patterns of activity across space and time. However, the hypothesis of morphic fields has an inherent limitation. It helps explain how patterns of organization are repeated but it does not explain how they come into being in the first place.

David Bohm, one of the leading quantum physicists of our time, spoke of the implicate order, which contains both the essence of all that has happened in the Universe and the multitude of possibilities that might yet happen. Brian Swimme says that "implicate," means that "it's not there the way a molecule of nitrogen is there, rather it is in between." Joseph Rael said, "Grandfather lives between the words, not in the words themselves." The Mayans called this "no time," as a cycle of birth and referred to those who live in this time as "you who walk between the worlds." All of these speak of the place in between, and we become a conduit of creation in the in between. The in between is latent potential, neither formed nor unformed. It becomes form through our observation and participation. Bohm also spoke about the explicit order, which is like a molecule of nitrogen, for example. His ideas revolutionized the Newtonian idea that an atom remained an atom and doesn't change. He said that as the vibrating atom rises out of the field, something essentially new has come forth. He also believed that human beings are coming forth out of a new ground that is different because it contains every moment of experience that has brought us to this moment in time. We are co-creators with the Earth.

Dr. William Tiller and his collaborators have discovered that there are two levels of physical reality, not just one and that this "new" level of physical reality can be significantly influenced by human intention. He says the "substance in the new level of physical reality functions in the empty space between the fundamental electric particles that make up our normal electric atoms and molecules."[13] One of the levels is the dense physical and one the subtle physical or what others call the etheric, and he says that each is made up of unique substance and appears to interpenetrate each other. These levels do not generally interact with each other, but through our intention we affect both realities. Even human intention directed to a device can affect both realities in such a way that a new coming together can occur.

Dr. Tiller states on the front page of his website:

> "For the last four hundred years, an unstated assumption of science is that human intention cannot affect what we call 'physical reality.' Our experimental research of the past decade shows that, for today's world and under the right conditions, this assumption is no longer correct. We humans are much more than we think we are and Psychoenergetic Science continues to expand the proof of it." [14]

Earth Part of a Larger Whole

According to the work of Saul Perlmutter, Adam Reiss, and Brian Schmidt, recipients of the Nobel Prize for Physics in 2011, space itself is not only constantly expanding as Einstein proposed, but the expansion is accelerating. A new understanding of the Universe is bringing forth a new cosmology. Even in our living rooms, we can see images on television that come from the Hubble telescope, extending our perception of reality. Only a short time ago, we believed that there were few other stars like our sun; now we know there may be as many as 14,000 (or more). Five hundred years ago, Copernicus was jailed because he asserted the earth was not the center of our solar system. Astronomers have discovered that only four percent of "matter" in the universe is what we might call "normal matter" and that the rest is "dark" matter or energy. That means that 96 percent of what is in the cosmos is just inferred rather than observed.

Crop Circles

The possibility of intelligent life existing on other planets in the cosmos seems quite reasonable given the quantity of potentially habitable places that are being discovered every year. It is currently speculated that there are 10,000 earth-like planets that could have intelligence greater to or equal to our own, and it seems reasonable that they could travel out of time from other solar systems. The possibility of having benevolent assistance from some of these is also plausible.15 In 2017 astronomers announced that a form of chemical energy that can support life appears to exist on Enceladus, one of Saturn's moons.

At latest count, more than 5,000 crop circles have appeared in 30 countries, most in England, and more appear each year. They have become increasingly complex over the years.

According to the Hathors, a large body of non-physical teachers from whom Tom Kenyon receives messages, "The conversation between earth and the intergalactic visitors and the cosmic waves are becoming more intricate." They report that crop circles are conversations between Gaia and intergalactic intelligences and that some are related to the earth's past history. They further instruct:

> "Some of them are an attempt to wake up the Humans — to see in the patterns the complex information that is being offered regarding your glorious destiny if you will but shape it." [16]

Though actual causes remain controversial, it is possible that extra-planetary forces may be involved that correspond with the acceleration we have been discussing. Though a few crude versions have been man-made, most are intricate, complex, huge patterns that often arise overnight and contain measurable, electromagnetic signatures. Stems of wheat can be bent over at right angles and braided with no visible footprints lead-ing to or from the field even when rain occurred on the night of the new circle.

Although all of the crop circles are interesting and possibly contain sacred geometry codes and embedded messages, one of the most interesting actually occurred in a rectangular shape that was a near replica of a digital message sent from NASA in 1974 into space via radio signal. The NASA transmission in-cluded core principles of math and science and representations of the DNA code, a human figure, an inhabited planet, a NASA antenna, and our place in our solar system. Twenty-seven years later, in 2001, a crop circle (in the form of a rectangle) ap-peared in England that essentially matched the code sent by NASA except that it showed a different solar system and the representation of a DNA molecule that was different from that of humans and information that it was sent from a microwave antenna. Interestingly, this crop "circle" appeared beside a working radio wave antenna that was similar to the one NASA had used 27 years earlier.

Dances

The Sun Moon Dance
Ruth Eichler

Joseph Rael, respected, wise Native American visionary and elder, led several dances at many peace chambers and sacred sites around the world. He also brought forth the vision for the peace chambers around the world. Because he is Native American, the dances do have a strong cor-relation with his Ute and Pueblo traditions, but he assures everyone that they are not replicas of Native American ceremonies. I danced four Sun/Moon dances between 2003 and 2006, life changing experiences for me. In all of the dances, we were dancing "for the people" and for the Earth. Every dance is a constant prayer for the Earth. The following stories come from some of my "writes" about these experiences, including receiving the inner, what I call "marching orders" late in 2001.

Let Go of the Shore
Ruth Eichler

"Let go of the shore," the elders say. Joseph Rael quietly sat down beside me for breakfast last week at the international gathering of peace chamber caretakers. Though I met him the day before, this was my first conversation with Joseph. So many of the people who are caretakers of peace chambers have danced and studied with Joseph for years before they actually built their chambers. I told Joseph that we came in the back door so to speak through a strong call but without the benefit of having been with him as others had. The dances and other ceremonies make up a strong part of the offerings from most of the chambers. I asked for his advice. In his quiet, gentle and non-directive manner, he said that it was time for me to dance — meaning the sun/moon dance.

I had previously danced two Long Dances. Those dances seemed do-able, as they were only one night with no further commitments. Never mind that the one night of dancing began about 9 p.m. after a sweat lodge and other preliminaries and ended about 3 a.m. I didn't know that I could make it the whole time, but I did. I should clarify that "dancing" often translated to trudging for many of us, especially in the wee hours.

Last year my very intuitive friend, Nancy, wondered if I wanted to dance the sun/moon dance in Toronto. I should mention that the sun/moon dance is a four-day dance without food or water though people do sleep at night. I don't think Nancy would have mentioned it had she not felt an intuition about it, and I felt a "God chill," my inner yes. However, I also felt a dread, an inner "no." I'm too old, I thought, and I can't imagine going four days without water — food yes, but water no. I also realized that the building of the peace chamber took priority, and I'm so glad that I decided the time wasn't right last year.

So when Joseph gave his gentle nudge, I was surprised to find that my body no longer was tinged with the dread of last year. I did protest though, that I was probably too old to be starting such a venture. He chuckled and said, "No, you aren't." He knows the in-flowing spirit takes over in spite of older flesh. He even told the group later that it's harder for the spirit to come through with the ones with super-fit bodies because they can rely on their physical bodies to get them through. He said that I would be completely changed by doing these dances. Something within me is ready to let go of the shore and see what transpires.

When one commits to the sun/moon dance, one commits to four years of dancing.

After the first Sun/Moon Dance in July 2003:

Those Dancing Feet
Ruth Eichler

At the Sun/Moon Dance, there were surprises even though I'd let go of all outcomes. "The dance will be what it will be," I'd said. One of the surprises concerned rest periods, more and longer than I'd anticipated. The dance periods varied in length from as short as ten minutes to as long as an hour or more, depending on what the chief intuited was needed. I had no idea since I was in a timeless space and had mercifully left my watch at home. My husband, Vic, later informed me of the temporal side. I only learned after the dance that the visions often occur during these resting periods and that the rests are as much a part of the dance as the up-on-your- feet-dancing-toward-the-pole times. However, I slept for some of almost every rest period, oblivious to any conscious visions. Even on regular days when a nap is possible, I usually only sleep fifteen or so minutes, so to sleep so often and so thoroughly, including at night, was another surprise.

We're not supposed to talk about the big spiritual wham-mies for six months but my dance didn't seem to be about visions and revelations as much as actually experiencing Being in my heart and body. In fact, that was one of my desires.

Back to surprises, I had thought that I'd probably walk most of the dance to strategically conserve my energy so that I could make it through the whole dance. I've walked for probably half of the time in the three Long Dances I've done. But, Spirit seemed to take over, and the other six women dancers inspired me. Instead of trudging back and forth to the pole, I danced almost every time. I was surprised that my feet found their style and steps, just as each dancer's did. I was surprised how light and free I felt and how my feet knew just how to move in spite of knotted calf muscles and intense energy coursing through my Being. I was surprised how on Monday morning, with no food or water since Friday afternoon, an infusion of joy sprang up, and I danced with celebration and jubilation, as did all the other dancers.

Vic, who had attended the dance to support me, was cracked open and blown away by the dance, a surprise to both of us. He thought that the dancers' sacrifice was also for the greater whole, the greater good of humanity.

Freed for Service
Ruth Eichler

I am grateful for the extra hours I put in at the gym and the extra session with a personal trainer. I am grateful for I am grateful for the delightful yoga session with Melissa in May, and I am grateful for my friend Chris's many "coaching" sessions and walking with me around our land prior to the dance. I was grateful for yoga being in my bones for the last thirty some years, for I did yoga stretches and postures between every single dance, and I know that helped a great deal. All of that physical preparation and discipline helped free me for dance. My back was strong. My core was strong. Actually one of my surprises is that my physical body fared far better than I expected. By the time I got to the scheduled post-dance chiropractic appointment on Friday, he said my alignment was only off one-quarter inch.

However, I have needed extra rest, but I don't actually think the rest was needed as much for the physical body as it was for integrating on all the other levels.

When I began writing these kinds of "writes" three years ago, I often wrote about my longing to dance. I thought maybe I should sign up for dance classes, but I didn't. Little did I know at the time that I don't have to learn to tango or waltz or perform ballet. Perhaps unbeknownst to my tiny, limited personality self at the time, the real call was to these kinds of dances. Being a Sun/Moon dancer or even a Long Dancer isn't exactly a Zorba the Greek dancer. The dances are really about answering the question, "How can I serve?"

A Place of Residence
Ruth Eichler

Lesley called today and shared what has happened to me since the Sun/Moon dance from her intuitive eyes. It's so helpful to receive her input since she's at home in these realms and sees and understands clearly. She talked about our place of residence, meaning, I believe, the place of consciousness to which we resonate and can sustain. I think of it somewhat like an elevator. We may live on the second floor, but we might occasionally take the elevator up to the fifth floor for a brief visit, and we can't sustain at that level because it's beyond our resonance. Or, we might occasionally visit the basement or first floor, but we don't live there. And, we sometimes move to and take up residence on a higher floor. She says I've taken up residence at a higher level and am now being inspired from a higher level.

Mostly I don't think about these changes much, but yesterday I witnessed the effect at the Sunday morning gathering at the peace chamber. I led the group and used "Gratitude" as a theme. The inspirations I shared seemed to emanate more from my heart than from my mental self. During the silent meditation, I seemed to be informed about what to speak about—how I grew up with constrained emotions with my multigenerational lineage of hard working, homesteading, farming ancestors where emotions were a luxury. I shared about my deep gratitude: the ability to express emotionally now; the Kansas prairie and its beauty; the less harsh Michigan climate; Vic and the things we do together that neither of us could do alone, and how he was my supporter at the dance. I wept as I told these stories. The response was electrified and warm. I felt different, yet unless someone was astutely tuned into energies, I'm not sure they would know anything was different. However, Vic was glowing and kept saying what a good morning it was. Then he asked if I'd like to go out to lunch. "We need to celebrate," he said. We drove all the way to Colon to go to the River Lake Inn — the place with bluebird trails, wildflowers and hummingbird feeders on every window. A hummingbird graced our window during most of lunch. Both Vic and I seemed to be in an afterglow.

After the 2nd Sun/Moon Dance in July 2004:

The Monet Prayer
Ruth Eichler

During the second Sun/Moon Dance, I began to get a glimmer of the greater purpose of these dances. The entire experience began to fold into a moving collage of four days of prayer. Dancers in their various colored dresses and individually unique steps dance to the pole along their own spoke on the wheel, and they dance back to their spot at the outer rim. The drummers steadily drum and from time to time burst forth with songs from Joseph's native Tiwa language. The support people sit in white plastic chairs near the entry gate. The Chief and the supporting women called Moon Mothers walk from place to place at the outer rim. Suddenly, we are flowing patterns of color and rhythm, a moving Monet painting. Finally the drums give one resounding beat, and we freeze in place. Then, if the Chief chooses to end that dance, the drums beat three more times, and Benito says, "Go to your places and rest. The drums will call you." We go to our places on the rim, under the canopy of the slanted-in tarp walls of the arbor and rest.

Dog soldiers, as those dedicated, hard working, loved ones are called, wash dishes, boil towels to bring to the dancers, oversee the fire, chop wood, stand guard 24 hours a day at the gate to the arbor, and do a myriad of other tasks whenever the dancers are resting. Moon Mothers stand by providing loving assistance in any way that is needed by the dancers.

Even though everything done is for the benefit, blessing, and support of the dancers, I experience us all as part of a moving, vibrating collage of prayer. We just have different roles to play. The dancers dance their prayers in addition to having many prayer ties, each filled with a prayer, hanging by our spaces. Every trip to the pole is a prayer. Every loving act of support is a prayer. I rarely have ever experienced four days of total reverence and prayer, each done in its own way but all part of the beyond-Monet painting that constantly moves.

Michael, the man known as the Alpha Dog who is in charge of all of the people who help, is unbelievable in his love and prayerful way of being. This year before the dancers left the arbor on Monday morning at the conclusion of the dance, he gathered all the dog soldiers around the center tree as they prayed and offered thanks. As he did last year, he burst into tears. He told Vic and the others that he'd do this every weekend if his wife would let him. Imagine—very hard physical work, very little sleep, and a tent.

Perhaps I fail to be present to my own beauty. Right after the Sun/Moon Dance, I became aware of almost an ocean of reality, a vastness, and eternalness. I long to just be in that ocean of space. Yet my outer reality once again moved into the fast lane. I write now to be with the inner landscape.

God Needs You to Rest
Ruth Eichler

That old pattern of holding on and pushing through the fatigue, to keep on slogging, as my inner Little Soldier Girl does, is ready to be released. At one point when I was lying down, Benito, the dance chief and Joseph's brother, came to me and said, "God needs you to rest." Just like last year, I didn't have profound visions — just messages. Last year I learned that I am a dancer. This year, I heard God speaking through Benito, "You need to rest." Benito went on to tell me that I could rest as long or as short as I needed. But, if I heard God calling me to dance, then I could get up and dance. I want my life to gracefully and joyfully include more rest and play.

After the 3rd Sun/Moon Dance in July 2005:

And the Beat Goes On
Ruth Eichler

Where to begin? I've been so very grateful to have this time of stillness post the Sun/Moon Dance. I have not left our property since we arrived home on Monday. As usual, images swim in and out. Even though I think I'm back to "normal" (whatever that is), I'm aware that even today I float somewhat from one thing to another — whatever feels right at the moment. Cooking has been satisfying — organic vegetables creatively combined. On Tuesday I dug weeds for an hour — my brain could handle that. Laundry. Lots of laundry — also satisfying. Today I have actually caught up on some email. The checkbooks haven't been touched. The

Phoenix Dance flyer hasn't been prepared. Uninteresting mail hasn't been opened. I have rested at times with a heating pad on my stiff neck muscles. Yesterday I loved doing an hour of gentle yoga, not my usual faster yoga, and my muscles appreciated the stretches. Even during the dance, I usually do one or two yoga stretches during the rest periods.

Back to the dance. One of the images that floats in is of the sixteen of us dancers dancing, each in our own unique way back and forth, back and forth, back and forth to the pole and back to our "place" with a sleeping pallet covered with mosquito netting. One moving picture. Drums, drums, drums and the whistling, whistling of each dancer with the turkey bone whistle. Sometimes my mouth was so dry I didn't think I could blow anymore, but something continued to whistle through me through the turkey bone. I am a hollow bone myself. None of me and all of Thee. Dancing. Dancing. And then the drums thump three strong beats and it's rest time. We all are lying on our pallets, many sleeping, many fanning, fanning in the heat. And the blessed Moon Mother and helpers bring around cold, wet towels — gifts from Heaven — and I place mine on my head. If I have one left over from the last rest period, I raise my T-shirt and put it on my solar plexus. Wet and cold. My shirt gets wet and cool which helps the next time the drum announces that it's time to get up and dance again. I wear the white, wet towel under my hat. Dancing, dancing. The heat is enormous — over 100 degrees each day. Sometimes during the rest times, I hear the drum only to find everyone else still looking lifeless. The drum didn't actually sound — only the inner drum. The inner hearing is only differentiated from the outer hearing by my eyes taking in whether others are getting up at some of those moments. On Saturday night and Sunday night we received medicine tea — a strong herbal of some kind that tastes heavenly, heavenly even though it might only be barely tolerated at other moments in life. The sun. The pole in the center. Dancing. Dancing. We dance back and forth to the pole, which becomes symbolic of The One in which we are all one and united. The sliver of a moon at night.

Dancing. Dancing. The Sun. Fireworks from somewhere in the neighborhood on Saturday and Sunday nights. Other sounds from the neighborhood. Wonderful birds singing at dawn. The Sun. The heat. The love. The oneness. Back to that image of all the dancers dancing as one moving collage. Drummers near the gate. Supporters near the gate in white, plastic chairs. The love. The smell of eggs and bacon wafting in under the arbor canvas in the mornings for all those who are helping. They eat for us. My only food thoughts were of cherries and watermelon — cold and moist.

At sunrise each morning we offer cornmeal to Mother Earth in a sunrise ceremony. We offer gratitude. We sing the sunrise song. We dance. We pray. We rest. The oneness. Every dance step is a prayer. Every chop of wood by the helpers is a prayer. Every washing of a towel is a prayer. Four days of powerful prayers. And many people praying for us far away from this site further amplified those prayers.

I must be crazy. I think that my brother, the marathon runner, must be slightly masochistic to run that way. Yet, this doesn't feel masochistic. It's only Thursday after the dance, and I know — barring unforeseen circumstances — that I'll dance again next year, my fourth year of a four-year commitment. Like having a baby, once the labor pains have worn off, a parent wanting more children is ready for the next birth. If I am crazy, so be it.

Birth — that's it. These dances do have a profound birth affect. Birth into a new life. I'm so aware there are so many, many ways to be reborn, and this is only one of a zillion. And it calls me. I know that many, many things have occurred in my life as a result of these dances, but I can't begin to know or articulate the specifics. I just know. I do believe that that Phoenix Dance was a vision that was birthed out of this energy. Only the Great Mystery knows the details, and I have no desire to figure it out.

So held and supported by the divine. So held and supported by my beloveds on this earth. I am deeply blessed. My intention (or rather aspiration since this desire can't be controlled or made to happen) was the absorption of the little will into the Greater Will — and that this can happen for the earth as well and for all of its inhabitants including even the stones, the rivers and oceans.

For whatever reason that only the Great Mystery could begin to know, in spite of the intense heat, this was my easiest dance so far. Yes, I was very hot. Yes, my mouth got sticky dry. And somehow I didn't really suffer. Every dance is different. My place in the arbor was between two long-term veteran dancers (one who has danced for ten years and the other for thirteen.) Last year I was nauseous for quite some time and had to sit down during part of the dances. Had I suffered this year, I'm sure I would have learned something from it, but I don't believe that I have to suffer in order to reap the rewards of the spiritual path.

May each and every prayer amplify and heal the earth and each of us. Speaking of prayers, for my birthday last November, Vic gave me a shawl on which he hand tied hundreds of fringes, each with a prayer — a beautiful gift that I lovingly wore at this dance. With so much love generated by so many people throughout the dance, Vic and I seem to be basking in that love in a gentle, kind way.

Letting Go
Ruth Eichler

These funny beliefs held onto tenaciously by the unconscious spring up like weeds into my garden, but I can't pull the weeds until they break through the ground. The soil is very fertile, so not only are the vegetables and flowers that nourish my body and soul abundant, so are the weeds. One weed at a time. One hour of sacred practice at a time.

This may be one of the many gifts of this most recent Sun/ Moon Dance. These dances work at such a deep, deep level that what unfolds out of them is not always obviously connected. But any huge shift in consciousness alters everything. I'm so grateful to let go into the Great Mystery and not even have to understand—a radical shift for a dyed-in-the-wool Sagittarian who used to want to understand the entire Universe. A little laughing voice adds, "And to control it!"

Ah, letting go. Letting go. Letting go. Just in time for the Phoenix Dance, another alchemical experience of releasing the old and living in the New Life — a dance of resurrection.

At the Sun/Moon Dance, I became so aware of how we are all connected in the One. We are One. One of the images that continues to appear in my consciousness is of all of us dancing, all of us supporting, all of us drumming, all of us praying—a microcosm of the unified Universe.

After the 4th Sun/Moon Dance of July 2006:

Hafiz
Ruth Eichler

Swami Rudrinanda said, "Everything in the Universe is energy or a manifestation of energy, and the purpose of spiritual work is to become one with that flow of higher creative energy coming from God through the cosmos." This quotation reminds me of the Sun/ Moon Dance, which I danced in Tennessee a week ago. The more I dance these dances, the more I enter that creative God flow. In this dance, my back and shoulders were very stiff on Friday evening and Saturday, and I imagined my head and body being suspended from a string attached to the crown, something I learned in tai chi, bringing me into alignment. Brenda Sue, the Moon Mother, came by on Friday evening and said, "You didn't come here to play, did you?" On Saturday, she confided, "What you are releasing is so ancient that it has no name." Later she came back and asked if I could see that. "No," I said, "but I feel it." Then miraculously on Sunday after having no water or food for at least 38 hours, the stiffness had dissipated, and I felt light and free.

Laughter and joy punctuated the entire experience. Five of us women crammed into a mini-van, along with all of our gear, including sleeping bags and tents, and we laughed with gusto frequently all the way to Tennessee and into the dance arbor.

One of the magical moments in the dance occurred when I heard the dancer to my right uttering sounds from his resting place that I at first thought might be crying. The sounds then deepened into sustained laughter, belly-rocking laughter. Contagious as laughter is, soon other dancers and supporters were at the very least chuckling and some laughing outrageously. I thought, "Hafiz is dancing beside me!" Hafiz, an ancient Sufi, always seemed to laugh.

Joy and Laughter
Ruth Eichler

Chris and I, both of us who had just danced, announced that we'd be happy to share the driving — we were fine. Both Penny and Linda who had gone along as supporters turned back to us and laughingly glared: "You will not! We were told you are not to drive." We didn't really realize how altered we still were. After the "No-you-won't" glare, we went into a fast food restaurant.

I suddenly felt almost enshrouded with a thick, murky energy blanket. I had to lean against the railing and close my eyes behind my sunglasses and only peep them open often enough to inch forward in the line. I didn't even care if people thought I was on drugs. We ate our lunch in the furthest corner of the restaurant, still feeling that the lights glared and the energy suffocated. Back in our trusty mini-van, we five resumed our place in dance energy.

The first night on the way home, my mind felt as if it was sprouting various thoughts or images, but none went any-where, each forgotten nearly as soon as it sprang up. Even during sleep since arriving home, I feel as if I go very far away and have a hard time coming back to something as dense as the body lying on the bed. But somehow this expanded state feels very different from just being "out of the body." It feels as if I'm expanded to embrace the Universe, being a part of that creative energy coming from God through the cosmos. And I laugh. And I feel joy.

ENDNOTES
Chapter 8: The Earth/Planet/Gaia

1. Joseph Rael, *Being & Vibration*, (Tulsa, OK: Council Oak Books, 1993, p. 19).

2. Hazrat Inayat Khan, *The Mysticism of Sound and Music: The Sufi Teachings of Hazrat Inayat Khan,* (Boston: Shambhala, 1996, p. 180).

3. Dean Radin, Ph.D., *Shift: At the Frontiers of Consciousness*, (June-August 2007, p. 24).

4. The William A. Tiller Foundation for New Science Website, www. tiller.org.

5. W. B. Jonas and CC Crawford, *Healing Intention and Energy Medicine,* (New York: Churchill Livingstone, 2003, pp. xv-xix).

6. Joseph Rael, *Being & Vibration*, (Tulsa, OK: Council Oak Books, 1993, p. 13).

7. There are many websites that cite their mission.

8. David Abram, *The Spell of the Sensuous Perception and Language in a More-Than-Human World*, (NY: Vintage Books, 1996, p. 262).

9. Joseph Rael, *Being & Vibration*, (Tulsa, OK: Council Oak Books, 1993, p. 34).

10. Gary Glatzmaier and P. H. Roberts, "Rotation and Magnetism of Earth's Inner Core," *Science*, (Vol. 274, no. 5294, December 13, 1996, pp. 1887-1891).

11. Kirschvink, J.L. et al. "Magnetite biomineralization in the human brain." *Proceedings of the National Academy of Sciences*, 89 (1992): pp. 7683-7687.

12. Brian Swimme, *Shifts,* 2007 June - August #15.

13.   William Tiller Foundation.

14.   www.tiller.org.

15.   *"The Thrive"* movie.

16.   Lee Carroll, Tom Kenyon, and Patricia Cori, *The Great Shift: co-Creating a World for 2012 and Beyond,* (Newburyport, MA: Weiser, 2009, p. 153).

Chapter 9
Relating to Others in This Time of Acceleration

Today, more than ever before, life must be characterized by a sense of Universal responsibility, not only nation to nation and human to human, but also human to other forms of life. ~ His Holiness the Dalai Lama

Turbulent Challenges

In these turbulent times in which we are more interdependent than ever before, relationships are more important than they ever have been. The ascension process calls forth a group impulse. Whether we wish to be or not, we are in relationship with everything as part of the web of life from microbes to turtles, from people to planets, from time and space and beyond. How we relate to self, to others and to the planet matters greatly. A healthy human being is actually a community of trillions of interrelated cells, and an unhealthy person contains a collection of cells at odds with each other. Similarly, billions of human beings on this planet form a community, and we either live in an unbalanced, chaotic way, or we learn to cooperate and collaborate with each other for the good of all.

Although one person alone cannot create a tipping point for the planet, one person can choose to learn new ways to relate harmoniously with significant others. Healthy, harmonious relationships are possible with effort, consciousness, and choice.

When we are able to meet the fiery, accelerated energies by a softened, expanded heart and strong core, we are enhanced. We can become more adaptable, resilient, inner directed, and aligned with integrity. We do not just have to have acceleration happen to us; we assist and collaborate by consciously participating. We may be buffeted by the storms in the beginning, and some will continue to wobble precariously if they are unable or unwilling to integrate the higher frequencies.

As we embody the accelerated energies, our relationships will correspond energetically with our level of equilibration of these heightened vibrations. That does not mean that all relationships suddenly become ideal and connected, for some will spin away when the energies and level of integration become too disparate. A favorite cartoon shows two caterpillars on the ground watching a butterfly flying. In this cartoon, the anthropomorphized caterpillars happen to be male but could as easily be either gender. One of the caterpillars says to the other, "I can't believe it. That's my ex-wife."

However, we must not be too hasty in discarding relationships or in prematurely assessing the level of consciousness of the other. Most of us need a little assistance in uncovering our hidden fears of deep connectedness and in learning new methods of relating to each other in deeply honoring and loving ways. Fortunately, we can learn these skills.

Relating in a Sacred Manner

Desmond Tutu, winner of the Nobel Peace and several other prestigious prizes awarded for peace efforts speaks of a practice that acknowledges sacred relationship:

"A person with "*ubuntu*" is open and available to others, affirming of others, does not feel threatened that others are able and good, for he or she has proper self-assurance that comes from knowing that he or she belongs in a greater whole and is diminished when others are humiliated or diminished or treated as if they were less than who they are." [1]

For centuries, African Bushmen have greeted others with the full meaning of *ubuntu*. They joyfully say, "I see you" upon meeting another. The other person responds with enthusiasm, "I am here." Being fully seen through the eyes of the heart without judgment or conditions allows the other one to soften, open, and be available. We, too, can respond by being present: "I am here. I am fully here with you." What if all of our relationships were filled with *ubuntu*?

From a different culture, but with similar intention, Hedy Schleifer, a beloved teacher and facilitator of couples therapy and workshops, says that our relationships live in the space-between and that when we honor the relational space, it becomes sanctified. That is, there is a "you" and a "me" and a space between that is sacred and alive, a place where we can truly become more of who we really are when we make that space safe. We help create that sense of safety by being willing to truly accept and understand the other and for the other to truly receive that openness. [2]

Hedy says:

"In order to honor that space, one must cross the bridge and bring one's full and authentic presence to the world of the 'other.' And in doing so, the perfect conditions are established to create a true 'meeting,' an encounter of the souls. Once the space has been honored, and the bridge has been crossed, a genuine, nourishing and fulfilling relationship is established." [3]

Relating to each other in a sacred manner and seeing each other as sacred beings, whether in intimate relationships, friendships, groups, or even in relationship to the Earth, are truly requirements for being on the ascension path. We are all "one" even though uniquely individual. One cannot really "see" the other and move beyond old, defensive patterns unless the brain is firing in the frontal lobes. "Seeing" the other is not possible when we operate solely from the more primitive regions from which we see only a "you" out there from whom we must protect ourselves. Some people have been able to relate in the way that A. H. Almaas describes in the quotation below. Though most of us have to learn new skills in order to do so, more and more of humanity is developing this capacity to learn and to live from a new paradigm:

"When your whole organism is in harmony on all its levels, there is no conflict. The expression and radiance of that harmony is love. You become a channel of love, a manifestation of love. You feel completely yourself and not separate from anything. This is the action of love. The action of love is to unite, to reveal the connectedness." — A. H. Almaas [4]

Relationships, especially the ones with those we love the most, become part of our spiritual path. It is in these relationships that we have the highest expectations for reciprocity and unconditional love and for "getting the love we want," to use the title of one of Harville Hendrix's groundbreaking books. Our significant relationships become our greatest teachers and provide our deepest opportunities.

It is common to become negatively "triggered" by something a loved one does or says, and we can find ways to slow down our negative reactions and really be able to understand what the other is experiencing. As we struggle to bring into the light of consciousness that which has often been hidden even from ourselves, we can learn to kindly ask for what we need and at the same time to also give what the other needs.

In a strange quirk within relationships, what we need from our significant others is usually the hardest thing for them to give, and what our partners and intimate friends need from us is hard for us to give. It seems to be the law that we are drawn together for this mutual learning and soul growth. As we learn to give that which stretches us into new growth, we become more mature and whole. Just like breathing, we take in and we give out in order to live abundantly.

> *Out beyond ideas of wrongdoing, and right doing, there is a field. I will meet you there.* — Rumi

> *The awakening through the soul of the other begins when attention is directed not only to the contents of another's words but also to the soul gesture and soul movement that precedes the speaking.* — Johannes Tautz [5]

Teachings abound at this time about how to improve our relationships and how we communicate with each other. Ruth has been immersed in Imago Relationship Therapy for many years, one method of developing mature and effective relationship skills.

In order to cross the bridge that Hedy Schleifer discusses, we have to learn to really listen to each other from a non-defended place. In an intentional dialogue, each person takes turns "crossing the bridge" in order to really hear, feel, and understand the other one's "world." We need to come with an attitude of open curiosity, a willingness to really be present and an open heart. For the time being, we leave behind our opinions, ideas and defenses. Even though reactivity may arise in the listener or receiver, it can be set aside until that one becomes the sender. As we are totally present to the other, we also are able to witness or to see the other without over-personalizing. Witnessing is done from a heart perspective rather than a detached, mental state. Being able to walk in another's shoes doesn't mean that we have to agree with the other. We may have another perspective in "our world" and yet be able to truly understand the other's point of view as well. This process sounds simple, and in reality it is simple, but not easy because of old conditioning and habits of response. [6]

Daniel Siegel, an acclaimed author and neurobiologist, shares thoughts about relationships:

> "Becoming a part of a 'we' does not mean that you lose a 'me.'" [7]

> "As relationships are the most important factor in studies of good health, longevity, happiness, and wisdom, finding a way to promote interpersonal integration may be an essential step in developing these positive aspects of living a full and rewarding life." [8]

Miracles begin to happen when one truly feels heard, validated and met with empathy, respect and compassion. Our relationships move to a new level, and the sacred space becomes effulgent and nourishing. As many Imago therapists say, "Peace in the world, one couple at a time." As we learn to really be in a connected, harmonious relationship with those we most love, then those relationships ripple out into other relationships and into the world.

Another method that helps us move out of the defended state into a higher vibration is gratitude and appreciation. Expressing sincere appreciation to another shifts consciousness. If we had FMRI (functional magnetic resonance imaging) scans of the brain, we would see that more activity would be generated in the part of the brain that allows greater access to seeing another's point of view.

Others, such as Marshall Rosenberg, promote non-violent communication, furthering our skills in communicating with each other in ways that enhance each other. Rosenberg has worked with individuals, gangs, corporations and multi-national groups. He stated:

> "NVC (non-violent communication) begins by assuming that we are all compassionate by nature and that violent strategies—whether verbal or physical—are learned behaviors taught and supported by the prevailing culture. NVC also assumes that we all share the same, basic human needs, and that each of our actions is a strategy to meet one or more of these needs." [9]

David Kennedy, pioneer against gang violence, reports:

> "It takes some time, but get everybody together, sit down with the bad guys, treat them with respect, and tell them there's right and wrong. They know what wrong is, and they know it's wrong to kill people. We tell them, 'You love your mother. If you kill someone, think how that's going to hurt their mother.'" [10]

If the most violent criminals who have been dismissed as unsalvageable sociopaths can "see the light," then there is extraordinary hope for the world.

While the methods above require us to stretch ourselves in the context of living, breathing relationships, we can also enhance our ability to be in relationship through individual practices. The work of neurobiologists tells us that the brain's plasticity allows the creation of new neural pathways, ones that are more amenable to non-defended, harmonious relationships.

Their work also confirms that the more one practices a particular discipline such as meditation or mindfulness, the stronger these neural connections are. The neurobiology slogan of "what gets fired together gets wired together" speaks to this promise.

Of course a multitude of practices are available that suit different individuals. Just a few include chanting, journaling, praying, or walking in nature. All offer new ways of being in relationship with self and of integrating change.

While some of these methods especially focus on close, personal relationships, the principles can apply just as well to large groups and to nations as we have seen through the work of Rosenberg, Kennedy, Nelson Mandela and a host of others.

Many other people have written extensively about processes used in groups such as circle processes that have a similar goal — respectful, healing relationships in which everyone's gifts and voices are treasured and welcomed. No one is more important than another; power is shared. Many indigenous tribes have long used a "talking stick" to ensure that each person is fully heard before another speaks.

Group Guidelines
Ruth Eichler

For six years I traveled to Boston to participate in a group facilitated by Tom Yeomans at the Concord Institute in which we were exploring ways to work with groups from a spiritual perspective. Out of Tom's deep understanding of Psychosynthesis and his ability to synthesize new material, our group created guidelines for group work that I have incorporated into every group I have facilitated since that time. The following principles basically come from that experience, although some of the statements may have morphed a bit. It is interesting that these same principles apply whether participating in a group, listening to a friend or lover, or mediating conflicts between groups of people at war.

Guidelines for the Group

Slow down from your habitual pace of interaction and take all the time you need to listen to yourself and others, to express, to interact.

Breathe fully and rest in this rhythm of breathing as you participate in the group.

Tolerate, accept and welcome silence in the group either when a group member calls for it, or when it falls spontaneously.

Speak the truth of your experience, moment to moment over time. This includes those hardest to express—disagreement, negative feelings, and the experience of being disconnected.

Listen to each other deeply and with presence. Let go of rehearsing your response, or strategizing.

Express differences and appreciate other points of view, even if this generates conflict. Hold the differences as a creative part of the group's experience, not as something to be avoided.

No judgment/blame of self and others and practice simply being with your own and/ or the other person's experience.

At moments of intensity, hold this experience in your awareness without reacting or trying to do anything about it. Let it live in the group and be contained within the circle.

Let the unknown of others' and your experience simply be, rather than seeking to explain or control events immediately.

Have patience with the workings of the group and the time it takes to grow and change, both individually and collectively.

Enter into the moment-to-moment changes in experience, both individual and group, that necessarily constitute the multidimensional process of human healing, development and creative work.

These guidelines draw upon several sources—David Bohm, The Native American Council process, Carl Rogers, and work with Tom Yeomans at the Concord Institute.

The Dalai Lama has repeatedly said that everyone wants to be happy. Indeed, when we move beyond the details of conflict, most of us want the same thing — to be loved, to be happy, to be respected, and to belong. Most conflict resolution methods start with the premise of finding the principles that the parties agree upon — whether with individuals or with nations. This simple reminder guides our interactions regardless of cultural and social differences.

Our Impact on Each Other

As we step out of our habitual patterns of relating, we begin to recognize and care about our impact on others. On the receiving side, we may feel delight after conversations and experiences with another whose inner light shines and with whom we feel a caring reciprocity.

Good listeners and teachers often build upon what is going well, seeing the good within another and calling that forth. Thomas Berry, among many examples, must have been that kind of person, as seen in Brian Swimme's memorial tribute to him. In talking about Berry's impact on others, Brian says:

> "It was the evocative power of his presence. ... You found yourself at the very center of the universe and you were given a vision of the inner harmony of things. ... We all fell in love. With sunshine—with the rising moon— with the rainbow trout as they hover in the shadows of Chambers Creek. With everything."

Though not everyone has the impact on others as Thomas Berry or the Dalai Lama or a multitude of others whose inner light shines forth and permeates the environment, most people don't realize the impact that their presence has on others. As Marianne Williamson so famously has written:

> "Our deepest fear is not that we are inadequate. Our deepest fear is that we are powerful beyond measure. It is our Light, not our darkness, that most frightens us. We ask

ourselves, 'Who am I to be brilliant, gorgeous, talented and fabulous?' Actually, who are you not to be? You are a Child of God. Your playing small does not serve the world. There is nothing enlightened about shrinking so other people won't feel insecure around you. We were born to make manifest the glory of God that is within us. And as we let Light shine, we unconsciously give other people permission to do the same. As we are liberated from our own fear, our presence automatically liberates others." [11]

Every decision and action we take, no matter how small, has reverberating effects. This is an idea that has often been poetically called "the butterfly effect." Edward Lorenz coined this term in speeches and papers after discovering that entering the decimal .506 instead of the full .506127 in a computerized weather prediction gave a completely different weather prediction. One seemingly insignificant change can alter an entire pattern. The "butterfly effect" phrase refers to the idea that the flap of a butterfly's wings in one part of the world alters molecules of air and creates tiny changes in the atmosphere that might even cause a tornado to occur somewhere else in the world.

The entire earth and its inhabitants are part of one system, a system affected by small changes in any part. Andy Andrews has written a book titled, *The Butterfly Effect: How Your Life Matters* with the message that every life matters, and that no action goes unnoticed by the Universe, and that each of us has the power to change the world — far beyond what most of us can even imagine.[12] Andrews tells the story of a Union soldier, Joshua Lawrence Chamberlain, who led a desperate bayonet battle in Gettysburg causing the Confederates to surrender. His action changed the course of the Civil War, even though his name has been almost unknown. Not all decisions and actions have such huge ramifications, but each of us can think of myriads of examples in our own lives of how one decision took us down one path that altered our lives and, therefore, the lives of others.

Daniel Siegel, M.D., and other neurobiologists have done phenomenal research on the brain and the embodied neural mechanism that shapes the flow of energy and information. They have discovered that our biology and mind/body affects the biology of others. Interpersonal relationships shape the mind and foster emotional wellbeing.

"Mirror neurons" in the brain, discovered in the late 1990's, become activated at the perception of behaviors or feelings of others and can actually replicate maps within the brain that mirror the other's brain maps even before words have formed or mental understanding has occurred. We might become instantaneously teary as another expresses tears, or we might feel heaviness in the chest when another experiences spoken or unspoken sorrow. Unless the "receiving" person is quite defended against connection, these neurobiological mechanisms facilitate empathy and compassion.[13] One of the HeartMath experiments demonstrated that the heart can actually receive information 1.5 seconds before the brain receives it.[14]

Daniel Siegel further explains how we are all in this together:

> "Because we are collaborative creatures by evolution, hardwired with the potential to be cooperative and to help others, the issue is really expanding a sense of self and expanding a sense of identity, so that it is not limited to our old cave clan mentality. ... We come to realize that I am you, that we are in this together — literally, together. We are together." [15]

Our most intimate relationships offer us a mirror of our own strengths and weaknesses. We have the opportunity to see both our shadow and light and come into a greater acceptance of who we are. As we deepen into greater awareness through relationship, we have a larger ability to face those aspects of ourselves that are too difficult to either realize or face alone. As we seek to embody life changes, conscious relationships assist the journey to integration, and more space for bliss and joy emerges. Our authentic, awake relationships offer the most continuous, safe opportunity for insight and release of old habits and limitations. We can awake together.

Collaborating in the Woven Basket of Love

We're all in this together; we need each other. We might think of our diverse communities around the world as being in a big, woven basket, and if we can see beyond the fear and division, the basket is made of love. Jean White Eagle, visionary and leader of "For the One" dances around the world calls forth an Arc as a place of coming together:

> "An Arc provides a metaphoric and energetic vehicle within which we can safely place ourselves as we move through the Transformation that has been prophesied for centuries and is now here. We can begin with each other, caring for and being kind to each other, being honest with each other and in integrity with ourselves. ... It is a place to realize you're not alone." [16]

As we come to know that we are the agents of change, we participate in a collective opportunity. We realize that we are consciously connected in a way that we have never been before and that we must act as if individual rights matter while giving voice to global concerns. We are increasingly more aware of the need to let go of our personal prerequisite of being comfortable in the familiar. We become more adaptable and re-silient. Rather than simply reacting to crisis, we move towards a vision of greater possibility for altering world conditions. We have come to realize that our vision and conscious intent create opportunity to be causal and to respond to all life around us. We know now that we can create conditions for change for one another by increased tolerance, expansion of deep listening and synthesis of the best from the past, choosing with flexibility and non-reactivity to attend to what is important, relevant and for the good of the greater whole.

Thich Nhat Hanh, the Vietnamese monk has said that the next Buddha will be the *sangha*. The *sangha* is a community of spiritual practitioners. Hahn implies that the future of the planet depends on the awakening of the many, not the heroic efforts of the few.

The ascension process is accelerated the more we collectively participate together with the highest good for all life in mind. With discernment and openness to expanded possibilities, we find greater ease in recognizing new and sometimes mysterious possibilities. Paula Underwood, a respected Iroquois teacher and elder, now deceased, said that her father taught her that the idea of the rope which bound a whole People into a unity toward a purpose could never have been devised by an individual in an isolated context. "What is impossible for one, is possible for many," her father said. He also said that a guiding purpose became their Great Rope, binding them across any changing cir-cumstance. Paula acknowledged that the term used today would probably be "group synergy" and that she didn't clearly know whether this represented an evolved understanding or simply a continuance of what was understood from the earliest times. [17]

When two or more are gathered together, consciously entering a field with intention, the ability to hold a vibration is much

289

greater than one individual can hold. Through joining together in this way, we are able to co-create and co-participate in accelerating the ascension process. The butterfly effect is now magnified exponentially. Group collaboration and participation in community is the keynote of our present trajectory.

> *Love is the only medicine that can heal the wounds of the world. "*– Ammachi [18]

The Internet has made the world small and accessible to the majority of people on the planet — for good or "evil." We have always been like millions or billions of cells in one organism on this planet. Yet, it is only with instant access to what is happening around the world and with the ability to envision our earth from satellite photos that we have come into consciousness about global concerns. Peter Russell foresaw the impact of the computer age on the world when he wrote, *The Global Brain*, first published in 1983 and later updated in 2006. He said that the interconnections created by computer networks were like neurons firing in a human brain, and that the world now had one "brain."

We are truly interdependent, even if some of the cells in our organism are at war with each other. In Thomas Friedman's book, *The World Is Flat* [19] (published in 2005, updated in 2006 and 2007), he details how globalization has made commerce accessible to everyone and how interdependent we all are. Ordering a hamburger at a McDonalds somewhere in the USA might entail the call going to a call center in India and then relayed to the personnel preparing the meal. We have seen the role that social media has played in the Arab Spring and other uprisings as well as a recruitment platform for groups who want to destroy. Governments have a harder time silencing information, even though some still vigorously try.

True love is unconquerable and irresistible, and it goes on gathering power and spreading itself, until eventually it transforms everyone whom it touches.
— Meher Baba [20]

Relationship and the Sacred Feminine

Relationship is a significant aspect of the Sacred Feminine impulse, just as it is to the feminine principle in general. Whether we are looking at one-on-one human relationships or relationship with the divine, how we connect is significant. In some ways, relationship is a central key to the entire ascension process, as living in a sacred manner requires that we be connected through the heart with others. Even if we live in a cave, what happens in our mind and heart affects the world.

Being relational implies reciprocity, a mutual exchange and interdependence, a shared relationship rather than a hierarchical one. Rather than verbal teachings, we might share intuitive transmissions from the Divine. As we consciously move beyond the view of "I" as ego or personality self into a state of "not I" while becoming one with the All, the sense of being an isolated individual vanishes. Yet paradoxically, we retain our unique individuality, just as a cell in a human body keeps its own purpose, along with trillions of other cells, all the while functioning together as one organism. Each of the cells is in relationship with each other.

The Sacred Feminine holds the context of seeing the divinity in the other. In what ways do we complement each other, individually, and in the group? We must begin with the underlying belief in an inherent pattern of divinity. We don't make that happen. It arises when we become aware of that level of consciousness.

> *Do not seek for truth. Merely cease to cherish your own ideas and opinions. Noble silence refers to listening with all the senses by being still and silent.*
> *— The Heart Sutra*[21]

The Native American, Joseph Rael, often talks about how English is a language of nouns and objects, a rather masculine language. He says that his native Tiwa is a verb language, and if we were translating those words into English, we might say "I am Ruth-ing" or "I am Lesley-ing" rather than just our names. With all in movement rather than being static, we feel the inter-connectedness, bringing spirit into our relating. Synergistically, the whole is greater than the sum of the parts. Even the whole is in process and is "whole-ing." Sacred Feminine-ing is weaving through all of creation.

ENDNOTES
Chapter 9: Relating to Others in This Time of Acceleration

1. Desmond Tutu, *No Future Without Forgiveness,* (Image, 2000).

2. www.hedyyumi.com and from numerous trainings

3. Hedy Schleifer, TED Talk in Tel Aviv, Israel, April 2010.

4. A. H. Almaas, *The Freedom to Be, Book 2,* (Boston: Shambhala, 1989).

5. Johannes Tautz, *The Meditative Life of the Tea*

6. *Crossing the Bridge DVD,* www.hedyyumi.com.

7. Daniel Siegel, *Pocket Guide to Interpersonal Neurobiology,* (W. W. Norton & Company, 2012, p. 191).

8. Ibid., p. 41.

9. From Marshall Rosenberg's website, www.cnvc.org. Rosenberg also has a series of CDs and other materials online at Sounds True and other places.

10. David Kennedy, Talk given in Kalamazoo, Michigan, reported in Kalamazoo Gazette, March 27, 2012.

11. Marianne Williamson, *A Return to Love*, (Harper Collins, 1992).

12. Andy Andrews, *The Butterfly Effect: How Your Life Matters* (Thomas Nelson Publishers, 2010).

13. Daniel Siegel, *The Neurobiology of We: How Relationships, the Mind and the Brain Interact to Shape Who We Are*, (Sounds True Audio Learning Course, 2008).

14. HeartMath Institute. "Science of the Heart: an Overview of Research." Print Vol. 2, 2015.

15. Daniel Siegel, *Pocket Guide to Interpersonal Neurobiology*, (W. W. Norton & Company, 2012, p. 42-8).

16. Jean White Eagle, email of 1/13/11 and www.jeanwhiteeagle.com.

17. Paula Underwood, *The Walking People: A Native American Oral History*, (San Anselmo, CA: Tribe of Two Press, 1993, p. 817).

18. www.Amma.org.

19. Thomas Friedman, *The World Is Flat* 16 (published in 2005, updated in 2006 and 2007).

20. Meyer Baba, quoted by Ram Das in *Be Here Now*.

21. From a poem titled "Trust" in the *Heart Sutra*. The *Heart Sutra* is a famous sutra in Mahayana Buddhism and if often spoken of as the most popular Buddhist scripture of all.

Chapter 10
Joy and Non-struggle

Joy is the happiness that doesn't depend on what happens. — Brother David Steindl-Rast

What Does It Mean to be in a Joyful State?

Although joy can be experienced through our physical, emotional and mental states, it essentially emanates from the level of Soul and then permeates the personal self. Joy carries supreme happiness of an elevated, spiritual kind, but it is not the same as happiness. Happiness is often associated with external circumstances, but joy is not. Joy is often associated with bliss, ecstasy, elation, and exultation, and some have called it "shining contentment" or "spiritual radiance."[1] According to the Dalai Lama, joy expands our ability to "spread the message that love, kindness, and affection are the source of joy and happiness."[2]

Joy is a net of love by which you catch souls. — Mother Teresa

Joy is part of creation and therefore inherent in ascension. When we are liberated, the state of joy frees us from fear, dogma, habituated patterns and the need to be right. Similar to the blessing of grace, joy is often received and experienced spontaneously and is not as a steady state, although some people have learned to live in a state of being in which joy is fairly constant. They have learned how to access this joyful, inner state of being even though they might also experience pain or challenging circumstances.

However, acceleration does not mean that we must constantly experience the state of joy. Because the ascension process confronts us with what is unfamiliar and unpracticed and because the brain is "wired" to follow familiar patterns, we don't always feel ecstatic in this process. Rather, joy is experienced as a pulsing rhythm, sometimes strong, sometimes soft and in varying degrees of intensity, and sometimes conscious and sometimes not.

> *I slept and dreamt that life was joy. I awoke and saw that life was service. I acted, and behold, I realized that service was joy!* — Rabindranath Tagore

In *The Book of Joy,* a beautiful book based upon conversations between His Holiness the Dalai Lama and Archbishop Desmond Tutu, both of these loved and respected men repeatedly express that joy comes from seeking to do good for others. Again and again the Dalai Lama asserts that compassionate concern for others' wellbeing is the source of happiness.

Both men consistently assert that they are no different from anyone else; that we are all human beings and part of a unified humanity. When we suffer adversity and if we think of others who are similarly experiencing this pain, our view widens. Joy becomes accessible.

Douglas Abrams, author of *The Book of Joy,* synthesized their thoughts into eight pillars of joy. The first four pillars relate to qualities of the mind: perspective, humility, humor, and acceptance, and the second set of pillars is associated with the heart: forgiveness, gratitude, compassion and generosity. [3] We'll speak more of these qualities later.

Holding Both Joy and Sorrow

Archbishop Desmond Tutu eloquently lets us know that we can experience both joy and sorrow. He says,

> "Discovering more joy does not, I'm sorry to say, save us from the inevitability of hardship and heartbreak. In fact, we may cry more easily, but we will laugh more easily, too. Perhaps we are just more alive. Yet, as we discover more joy, we can face suffering in a way that ennobles rather than embitters. We have hardship without becoming hard. We have heartbreak without being broken." [4]

When we deeply immerse ourselves in an authentic life, we will experience sorrow. Yet, when we allow and even welcome sadness or grief as a messenger, we can simultaneously feel joy because we are also tuned into a deeper reality that holds the human experience in a much larger context. When we truly become present to our vulnerability and pain and welcome all that life has to offer, we heal and transform. Rather than thinking about sorrow and joy as contrasting opposites, we move into a more expanded state that includes many levels of awareness by holding both and by living in the paradox. The Sacred Beloved spoke about this paradox in the following transmission:

Experiencing Joy and Releasing Anxiety
Sacred Beloved

Our heartfelt wishes this morning for a joyful life. We wish for you to feel the joy that we feel. You write much about joy yet do not fully feel its golden light. (I ask how to do that more.) Bask in the glory of God, not from that place of head but from the domain of the heart. Frame some of the Alex Gray pictures for your next office. He taps into the sacred light within humanity.

(I ask why I still feel some mild anxiety.) In some senses you are absorbing the anxiety in the field of the earth. The collective of humanity is afraid. Suffering, starvation, homeless children, warfare, and economic shakiness all contribute to people's fear that they are not safe. Be aware of what you are absorbing and then release it as one of your regular practices. Do so now. And listen now for your own tone.

Accessing Joy

Our prayer from the beginning of this work is that it would feel joyful and effortless. Whenever anything began to feel sluggish or as if it were a struggle, then we knew we were out of alignment with our Souls' impulse for this work. This same prayer began to have deep meaning for Ruth during the building of the sound/peace chamber on the land owned by her and her husband.

Building of the EarthSong Sound/Peace Chamber
Ruth Eichler

The "joyful and effortless" prayer permeated the building of our peace chamber in the summers of 2000 and 2001. As I donned gloves and mortared concrete blocks or stomped on clay, earth, straw, and sand for the adobe-like "cob" that coated the inside and outside walls, excitement bubbled within my entire being. The "doing" was so aligned with my soul's work that joy was inevitable. Others also seemed to

298

catch the spirit of joy, perhaps engendered by the potential of the chamber itself. Over one hundred people showed up to help with the building, many of whom we had not previously known. One woman working beside me said as we were pressing the wet "cob" into the straw bales, "Now what is the purpose of this building?" She had heard the "call" without even consciously knowing why she was there. Joy is contagious!

Another story occurred during the writing of this book that illustrates how we can lose track of "joyful and effortless" and then sooner or later return to it with intention and attention.

The Key
Ruth Eichler

During a week when Lesley was visiting me for the "writing project," we both became challenged with personal health, other outside issues, and the feeling that we needed to meet an internalized deadline to complete this book. In spite of our belief in the truth of joy and non-struggle, our old mode of tenacity and "pushing through" momentarily prevailed and the feeling of "struggle" ensued. We decided to go out to dinner that evening rather than cook. When we arrived at the restaurant, my car would not lock. When the key remains inside the car, a message flashes and the car refuses to lock. The key was missing from its usual place on my purse, but we could not find it anywhere. When we came home, Vic, Lesley and I searched for sometime in the car for the key but could not find it anywhere, even by removing every item from the car. The three of us searched with flashlights under the seats, even in illogical places, to no avail. Lesley and I started to chuckle, believing that "they" were playing with us. I knew that the key would most likely be in an obvious, visible place the next day.

The next morning, we started the search again and Lesley said, "We know that there is only one way that we can find this, and that is by being in a place of having fun with it." We shifted our attitude and demeanor and began to look joyfully and playfully. Fifteen seconds later, I found the key in a visible, easy to access and even a predictable place under the driver's seat, and we laughed heartily. We experienced once again the profound lesson that, especially in these times of acceleration, we must move in the present moment with an attitude of positive expectancy, playfulness and joyfulness. Only then can we be aligned with our true, creative potential. We are creating this moment, and we are being supported in that creation when we make available to ourselves all that is.

> *Perhaps the wisdom lies not in the constant struggle to bring the sacred into our daily life, but in the recognition that life is committed and whole and, despite appearances, we are always on sacred ground.* — Rachel Naomi Remen, MD

Joy and Co-creation with the Subtle Realms

Because of joy's steady, welcoming, and flowing quality, it is a more coherent energy that can resonantly link us with the more refined subtle fields of information, energy and beings such as angels. Joy can certainly be an antidote to human feelings of fear, anger and sorrow, but it also expands our emotions to incorporate greater creative possibility. The Angelic, who are working more creatively with humanity now, have suggested in our meditations that it is more conducive to our mutual alignment if we are in a state of willingness and cheerful expectancy.

Joy opens us to the paradox of hearing the sometimes competing voices within ourselves while in the state of duality and at the same time bringing us into a state of being at one with all. As we access greater inner authority from our Wise Self, we become agents for Spirit rather than just responding to societal demands. Joy joins the inside and outside, self and other, mental and emotional, into a much more comprehensive view.

Rather than thinking of joy as an emotion, the Angelic invite us to see it as providing substance for linking energies with them. The Angelic use the refined feeling of joy to actually create form. Joy is the linking energy that helps brings thought forms into substance or what we might call "reality." Therefore, joy that is both fluid and stable supports the expansion of consciousness and our awareness of union. With joy, no edge of longing and unfinished business tugs at the heart; it creates acceptance of what is and generously opens the space to greater possibility. Joy moves us from a position of needing to fix things or to see things as good and evil. Thus, we move into growth from which divine creativity flows.

> *If you remain in the eye of Spirit, every object is an object of radiant Beauty.* – Ken Wilber

You Create Your Own Reality from the Way You Look at the World

> *You have to sniff out joy. Keep your nose to the joy trail.* — Buffy Sainte-Marie

Sniffing for the joy trail does not mean trying harder or struggling to attain or maintain a way of being. It simply means that by bringing attention to the joy that is already inherent within us, often shrouded but nevertheless always present, we shift into the possibility of experiencing greater joy. The Soul needs

301

not to have an external locus of control, even though the environment may affect us in various ways. Joy is a state of being without condition. Joy emanates from within, even though it certainly radiates outwardly, and it infuses our whole being.

Even though joy is inherent within us, it also is enhanced and expanded by relationship with others. We know that joy is contagious whether we are talking about one-on-one relationships or one with groups of joyful people. Relationships fostering joy can also be internal such as our connection with the Beloved as expressed by the Sufis.

David Spangler eloquently speaks to the experience of joy:

> "I'm asking myself, 'How can I enter into the joy already present (or potential) in this situation?' or 'How can I open myself and make myself a portal so that joy can enter here?' I'm aware that the subtle energy in the environment begins to resonate with this joy to the extent that it is able; who knows what the consequences of this may be." [5]

Stress researchers such as Elissa Epel and Nobel prize-winning molecular biologist Elizabeth Blackburn tell us that when we can change our perception of threat into a challenge that we have a calmer response. [6]

Researchers at the Institute of HeartMath say that the neural system assesses things as "positive" (optimistic, confident, hopeful, and interesting) if similar past situations have been seen in that light. Experiences that were felt as "negative" (annoyance, apprehension, hopelessness, and depression) in the past are often experienced as such again. However, as we learn to self-regulate (very different from "strong-arming" our point of view into submission), we choose new options and reinforce the neural pathways that access greater joy. We invite a higher aspect of Self to assist us in this mastery. HeartMath further explains what happens within our neural pathways:

> "We expand our repertoire of successful outcomes. The more repertoires available, the more likely a new input will be assessed as optimistic with a high probability in maintaining control. It is the organization of sequences of input patterns and behaviors into hierarchically arranged programs that gives a person flexibility and adaptability." [7]

As we experience sustained joy and appreciation more frequently and for longer periods of time, we are opened to the possibility of ascension. These feelings excite the system in a way that eventually becomes a new, established and familiar pattern to the brain. The brain's plasticity is impressed with a new pattern through repetition. In addition, joy actually changes our biochemistry. It causes the brain to release oxytocin, sometimes referred to as the "feel good" hormone. Much of the work done in the field known as Positive Psychology emphasizes the fact that everything we see and hear causes a response. Choosing positive attitudes leads to greater happiness and this opens the doorway to more joy.

> *We are shaped by our thoughts; we become what we think. When the mind is pure, joy follows like a shadow that never leaves.* — The Buddha

Even though joy is often experienced as grace, the path to it and the recognition of it can be enhanced through positive intention. During these turbulent times of transition, it isn't always possible to project a goal to be achieved. However, creating a state of awareness with gratitude may guide us, through joy, to higher states of consciousness.

God does not die on the day we cease to believe in a personal deity, but we die on the day when our lives cease to be illumined by the steady radiance of wonder renewed daily, the Source of which is beyond all reason. — Dag Hammarskjold

Thinking positive thoughts and turning our attention to a grateful heart and to joy paradoxically also includes welcoming into our awareness whatever is there rather than pushing what might be considered negative emotions into oblivion. Our intention then becomes to view and experience these emotions or beliefs from a compassionate, witnessing viewpoint. Thus, we welcome all emotions and beliefs with neutrality, creating spaciousness that can allow transformation.

When we bring a gentle, kind heart to difficult situations, more space is actually created for a sense of joy and pure being to arise from our heart. Kristin Neff, a leading researcher on self-compassion, says, "Here's the beautiful paradox of self-compassion: by accepting yourself, your situation, and your feelings as they are, you embrace the pain with loving-kindness."[8] Research confirms that self-compassion is highly correlated with happiness even though it means accepting the suffering.

Kristin Neff further explains:

> "Basically, self-compassion involves treating yourself with kindness, caring, nurturance, and concern, rather than being harshly judgmental or indifferent to your suffering. What distinguishes self-compassion from self-love or self-acceptance is that ... instead of feeling, 'Oh, poor me,' which is like self-pity, we understand that the human condition is tough. ... To have self-compassion, you have to be able to notice and become aware of your pain."[9]

In *The Book of Joy,* Desmond Tutu repeatedly reminds people to not berate ourselves if we do have negative thoughts and emotions but rather to accept them and move forward.

The famous Serenity Prayer reminds us to accept the reality of suffering (God grant me the serenity to accept the things I cannot change) and at the same time to "have the courage to change the things I can and the wisdom to know the difference." One of the things we can change is our attitude and how we look at painful situations. The Dalai Lama says that even though it takes time to develop, the best solution to our suffering is what he calls mental immunity or what we might call choosing a positive, more holistic attitude that is less susceptible to suffering. Or, as Desmond Tutu said in *The Book of Joy*, "The goal is to be a reservoir of joy, an oasis of peace, a pool of serenity that can ripple out to all those around you." Joy is contagious.

Dealing with Fear and Anxiety

Fear presents as one of the emotions for which we can have compassion for self and others. Neurobiology counsels us that neurons in various parts of the brain fire when threat is perceived. The amygdala, an almond shaped set of neurons located deep in the medial temporal lobe of the brain and part of the limbic system, can quickly alert us to any sense of danger. Of course, this function helps us get out of the way of an attacker, but it also can react in ways that no longer serve. Our biological self can assist us in discerning what true danger is and what it is not, helping us access greater intuition and wisdom. If we are in the direct path of a tornado, we of course want to move out of the way. If, on the other hand, we are picking up the vibrations of fear that course through the collective fabric of humanity when big changes are occurring as they are now, we may want to choose to attune to another vibration that brings us to greater clarity.

That web of life that embraces the entire planet and all of its physical and non-physical inhabitants, including rocks, trees, tigers, and humans, hums with the emotions of the collective, much of which is unconscious or only semi-conscious. When we hear about dozens of people dying from the actions of a suicide bomber or when we learn that thousands have died in an earthquake or when we fear that terrorists are on our doorstep, our fear reverberates into the collective web. Unless one is quite conscious, it is easy to absorb and resonate with that vibration.

The ascension process naturally includes destruction, for an old way is dying. Old paradigms sometimes held onto tenaciously by some out of fear are crumbling. Those who hold onto the old beliefs fight with great resistance, often with violence and hatred — whether in words or in actions. How can we hold the possibility of ascension without fear and focus more on compassion and integration? In order to do so, we must see a much bigger picture — one that has compassion for the suffering and fear and that also lives in a larger, luminous reality in which joy is present. When we are closely and compassionately joined with others, fear subsides.

A Lamp unto Their Feet
Ruth Eichler

We have to be strong and confident, firmly aligned with and infused by Soul/High Self in order to be a lamp unto the feet of those who haven't had or haven't chosen the opportunities we have to stand calm in the face of tremendous fear and shadow, planetary shadow. Of course, we don't have to do this. We can do as we've done before and succumb to the fear. And at the same time, I wish to lighten up and not take all of this so deadly seriously. For if the light shines through, we can and do experience peace and joy simultaneously with firm confidence.

Move from within . Don't move the way
fear wants you to. Begin a foolish proj-
ect. Noah did. — Rumi

Perspectives on Enhancing Joy and Wellbeing

The Dalai Lama reminds us,

> "If you are setting out to be joyful, you are not going
> to end up being joyful. You're going to find yourself
> turned in on yourself. It's like a flower. You open, you
> blossom, really because of other people." [10]

However, he also tells us that meditating on compassion and
kindness for others is a way to maintain a calm and joyful mind
and to develop what he calls mental immunity.

We can learn — whether through prayer, meditation, self inquiry, neurobiology or other means — to create a much more
open heart and a less reactive mind. Many joy practices fill the
last chapter of *The Book of Joy* offering means of developing
mental immunity and enhancing the eight pillars of joy.

Fear and Anxiety about Coming Changes

Before and after 9/11, many instructions came from the Sacred
Beloved, which we include here as further means to address
fear and anxiety and perhaps to be helpful to others.

This Precious Moment
Sacred Beloved

The most important thing you can do is to truly live in the
preciousness of each moment. Continue to cultivate the
awareness of our presence. Continue the Practice of Five
(noticing five beautiful, precious things or experiences each
day). Your eyes are being sharpened with the light of the

divine shining through and being seen. God is seeing God. You become God's eyes, so to speak. Practice trust. As you love every molecule and receive our love, your awareness of divine providence increases. You will have everything you need. After all, one of the reasons for earthly existence is to overcome fear and to see that heaven can co-exist on earth. In that way, you return to the paradise spoken of before the apple was consumed in the Adam and Eve creation story. Of course, this is only one of many creation stories. The important message is that we are always here. Remember this always in all ways. We are teaching you this message. Only the ego is afraid. Receive our love and joy. Continue to clear away old thought forms that accumulate out of habitual ways of responding. They are beginning to dissipate. Eventually peace and trust will be a steady state. Continue to treasure the journey with new delights and surprises along the way. We know you enjoy serendipity, and your chosen path is full of joyful serendipity.

Guidance for These Times of Great Change
Sacred Beloved

It is imperative that each of you takes responsibility for refurbishing your own vehicles (body, emotions, and mind) and your way of being on the earth. The time is at hand when it is no longer a luxury to cleanse and purify your fields and to fill them with light.

You must take responsibility regarding these things so that these energy systems are impervious to the onslaught of psychic debris. You must be able to walk among the dead as if you are in an impervious bubble of Christ light. And you must do this with radiance, love and serenity. You are also responsible for mastering your fear so that the fear and grief do not undermine the bubble of light. The bubble of light allows you to move and to be wherever you are needed. Know that we are with you 100 percent in joy. Do not lose sight of the greater picture or that your being transcends this earthly existence. We remind you again that all things in the universe are temporary. We love all of you beyond measure. Think of Christ or Mother Teresa as they unflinchingly moved amongst suffering with equanimity. Sing "Holy, holy, holy, Lord God Almighty" to fortress and galvanize your strength and courage. (I ask what if nothing in the outer world happens.) Then you will still achieve your purpose on earth by realizing who you are and by developing mastery over the lower vehicles. Continue the practices we have given you — be fully present in the preciousness of each moment. As the Zen say, bring beginners mind to your life as a child full of wonder and delight. Yes, even in travails, one can appreciate and honor the precious moments. Breathe equanimity into your own self and into the planet. Go and rise a new being in Christ.

Joy for Birth of Christ Consciousness
Sacred Beloved

We have a gentler message this morning. Be of good cheer. Love is also at hand. The planet and all of her occupants are being bathed in glory and love — a shimmering light. The angels sing for the birth of the Christ consciousness — Holy, holy, holy, Lord God Almighty. Heaven and earth sing. Joy and sorrow exist simultaneously. For now, relax into this enormous love and light. Christ is here. (Tears) The Beloved is nigh. Welcome this energetic with open arms and heart. All is well. Feel into it. Receive it. Yes, you smile and we are exceedingly glad for the joy that is infusing the planet. The journey to heaven paradoxically requires that you hold both the joy and sorrow and that you feel it. And this, too, shall pass. All things are being made new.

Suffering on the Planet and Love Pours in
Sacred Beloved

We are sad today to announce that more suffering is yet to ensue for the planet and her inhabitants. Continue to pray for those in India on both sides of the veil. Many on this side are assisting with this work. Enormous love is pouring onto the planet to assist in healing and rebuilding. Grief rises and swells, ebbing and flowing like the tides. That is all at this time on this subject.

Breathe spaciousness into your day. Flow with it. Receive our love now. (Tears.) You do not need to defend against the sorrow. Allow it to come and go as the tides. Know that our love is commingled with it. Allow yourself to feel and to then release. Be an empty vessel. Listen for the tone of the Christed mandalas.

World Free from Fear
Sacred Beloved

Behold a new world free from fear. (I ask how that can be, given the human condition.) Each of you chooses. (I ask how we can get the fear out of our cells.) Some will not have eliminated the old configuration of fear chemistry at a cellular level in this lifetime. Others will truly be able to eradicate fear at all levels. These souls are rare as you might suspect. Others will be able to eliminate so much of this toxic substance that they will feel brand new. We remind you that this can become a steady state if you choose.

All Things Are Made New
Sacred Beloved

(I ask how to overcome inner resistance.) Consciously align with the Stream that is coming in from above. Call upon us. Call upon God. Call upon the Hierarchy to assist you. This is a crucial time when all things are being made new. Indeed the Christ consciousness is infusing the earth, and the Great Mother is awakening within humanity. As you well know, you must ask. (With a smile, I ask if I can have a retainer contract with them like people have with lawyers.) Yes, that is possible — an open contract so to speak.

Practices and Group Activity
Sacred Beloved

Remember the instructions from the Hathors about the tube or cylinder of light going from heaven to earth. It is no accident that you are reading Elmer Green's instruction manual now.[11] He wrote this book as a guide for those who are ready to remain free from enmeshment in and being snared by the web of the planetary unconscious. Obstacles remain to be solved like riddles. Yet each success brings you closer to liberation.

Working in groups is crucial for as you know, intentions are amplified. As Christ said, "Where two or more are gathered together..." Working in groups with aligned understandings amplifies the magnitude and coherence of the intentions, whether or not you are in physical proximity.

We are pleased that you are joining thousands of others in repeating the Great Invocation these five days around this eclipse and Festival of Christ (or Humanity as it is sometimes called). We require your help in letting the plan of love, light, and power manifest. We deeply desire this plan "which the Masters know and serve" to work out on earth. But we require your assistance, you who are embodied and in graduate school or who have graduated. The grand experiment in free will is coming to a final battle of dark and light.

Keep asking that your part be revealed to you moment-by-moment and day-by-day. The asking remains essential. We send our blessings and remind you that we are with you always, just a "phone call away."

A Son-in-law in the Military
Ruth Eichler

My son-in-law is in the military and might be deployed to Iraq, and I'm aware of some of my own fears as well as those of my family.

I'm also aware of the fear and anxiety that swirls in the collective, and I again want to experience compassion, and I also don't want to be governed by the collective. When I try to avoid what is absorbed, the collective holds sway over me. Once again, I rally for consciousness, and I know that prayer helps not only with healing and peace, but also in keeping conscious.

The sound of the spring peepers keeps reverberating in my ears, and I again recall the tiny tinkling fairy chimes reminding me of renewal, of change, of aliveness and of connection with light and joy—even in the midst of suffering.

The Quaking Bird
Ruth Eichler

On Monday at my writing group, I did one of those writes that sounded coherent to my writing partners, but I knew it was just the top, and I didn't know how to get deeper that day. An image came, though, of a quaking bird being held in a very still, loving hand. The bird sensed the still presence, and though it didn't completely stop shaking, it began to grow calmer.

I think I am both the bird and the hand. My small self has feared and indeed experienced a low-grade anxiety a lot of my life. When I asked the question about what emotion was present, the little bird came to mind. Yet as I am present to it, its trembling subsides. Simple words do not soothe it—only that abiding Presence.

This sense of Being is getting stronger. Last summer after the Sun/Moon dance, I just wanted to sit in silence feeling an inner, radiating humming light. In that afterglow, I imagined all of those molecules dancing in joy with all those neuro-peptides having a "whee" of a time. Last night I awoke repeatedly with the fires of inner Being stoked, warming, soothing deep inside the body.

Ready for a Dive into Fear
Ruth Eichler

I am ready for the solar wind on my sail, but paradoxically this morning I drew a card from a fascinating new deck I bought. It said to face my fears with compassion and to stare them into dissolution. I have been feeling some minor (or is it major?) resistance this past weekend. And what do I mean by resistance? For example, I allowed other things to take precedence over sitting in my meditation room this morning and on Saturday.

I'm on the precipice of something big; I can feel it. Yet some part of me in the vague recesses of my consciousness is afraid— not a conscious fear that raises the heart rate, but an insidious, unconscious fear that shows up as resistance or as metaphor. For example, as I recounted an experience of my very colorful tennis shoes disappearing at the end of the Sound School vision quest. My friend, Sher, looked at me and asked, "Were they comfortable, Ruth?" Yes, of course. She laughed as I begrudgingly heard her message. So I'm being asked to give up the comfortable way—to let go of the known and familiar.

Safety
Ruth Eichler

As the earth literally quakes and hemorrhages, it's easy to get caught up in collective clouds of fear and to forget that we are infinitely safe. It's easy to forget gratitude and forgiveness in the midst of a roller coaster ride. This morning I had a vision, once again, of the star tetrahedron with one three-sided pyramid facing downward and another upward forming a three-dimensional Star of David. This image has surfaced into my awareness repeatedly over the last several months, especially in Egypt and since. I imagine sitting in the middle of this shape, held stable even when the world careens around a fast curve. I imagine the Earth in the middle of a giant star tetrahedron stabilized in spite of being topsy-turvy. In this star tetrahedron I can plant flowers and water them. I feel joy for their blooms and stand in awe as a caterpillar crawls off a milkweed in my flowerbed and creates a lovely green chrysalis. I can laugh with joy when I see that the green chrysalis is but a clear shell, the butterfly already having emerged and flown.

The secret of seeing is to sail on solar wind. Hone and spread your spirit till you yourself are a sail, wetted and translucent, broadside to the nearest puff. — Annie Dillard

ENDNOTES
Chapter 10: Joy and Non-Struggle

1. His Holiness the Dalai Lama, Archbishop Desmond Tutu with Douglas Abrams, *The Book of Joy,* (New York: Avery an imprint of Penguin Random House, 2016, p. 34.)

2. Ibid., p. 297.

3. Ibid., p. 193.

4. Ibid., p. 12.

5. David Spangler, "From David's Desk," #54 *"Enjoy"* November, 2011.

6. *The Book of Joy,* p. 97.

7. Rollin McCarty and Doc Childe, *"The Appreciative Heart: The Psychophysiology of Positive Emotions and Optimal Functioning,"* Institute of Heart Math, 2003.

8. Kristen Neff, *Self-Compassion: Stop Beating Yourself Up and Leave Insecurity Behind* (William Morrow, 2011).

9. Kristin Neff, PhD, in conversation with Cassandra Vieten, PhD, Director of Research for the Institute of Noetic Sciences in a tele-seminar series, *Exploring the Noetic Sciences.*

10. *The Book of Joy,* p. 43.

11. Elmer Ellwsorth Green, *The Ozawkie Book of the Dead,* (Los Angeles, CA: Philosophical Research Society, 2001) plus many other lectures, conversations, and papers.

Chapter 11
Embodiment

Joy/Non-struggle is not something you do; it is something that is the result of how far you take enlightenment and how much of yourself you give it. The entire cosmos is your body. Let your humanness reflect and manifest the whole.
— Adyashanti [1]

We Already Embody Universal Consciousness

Universal consciousness is our essential nature, already inherent within form. This is one of the ways in which the Sacred Feminine expresses itself, and we only have gradations of realization of this truth. Fully feeling and knowing our cosmic nature often remains hidden from view as an experience or is known only as a concept or "head knowing." The primordial oneness gradually emerges into realization. Adyashanti tells us, "The human being is what links consciousness to its own infinite expression in form."[2]

The masculine impulse or motive for expression is to do; the feminine creates the space that allows what already is to arise. New possibilities emerge out of this container. Indigenous peoples often believe that the Great Spirit lives in and imbues all of Nature. As more people around the planet remember our deep connection with the environment, our lives are impacted by awareness of the Divine that is within all that is and that is imminent. With awareness, humanity breathes and assists in the birthing of the new world. The Sacred Feminine manifests through our consciousness.

As a collective, we are only now becoming coherent enough in our awareness to fully appreciate the experience of reciprocity. Incoming consciousness and arising awareness simultaneously join as light meeting light. Adyashanti also says, "Through the form of an awakened human being, consciousness becomes conscious of itself as both formlessness and as all form." [3]

We have the utmost encouragement from many religions and traditions: From Christianity: "The kingdom of heaven is within you." From Islam: "Those who know themselves know their Lord" From Hinduism: "Atman, the individual consciousness, and Brahman, the Universal consciousness are one."

From Buddhism: "Look within—you are the Buddha." From Native American spirituality:

> "Walking with intent and ceremonial dancing are ways to connect with the inner, infinite self. The metaphor that is enacted is the collision of the foot with the ground. The foot is how we move out in life. In ceremonial walking and dancing, the foot connects with the ground, which is the symbol of the infinite self." — Joseph Rael [4]

The Awakening Process of Embodiment of Spirit

Rather than infusing spirit into matter, as we might have previously thought, we now recognize that the process instead involves re-identification or awareness of what already is. The mother or matter aspect is revealed and brought into more coherent expression. Rather than having an external energy impressed upon the system — or the body — we need first to go inward.

We have to develop an ego structure that is mature enough to not be discombobulated by the energetic tides of life. We have to learn to manage the ways in which we react or act defensively. We also need to learn to accept what is, for whatever is resisted and pushed aside gets emboldened in the subconscious and projected onto others in the outside world.

As our personality self develops greater maturity, we become more truly who we uniquely are, more individuated, even as we become aware of the inter-connectedness of all life. Progressively as the self evolves, it begins to seek union, union with greater Self, with community, and with Source. As union is discovered as an extension of Self, rather than competition with other, relationship becomes the natural evolutionary expression. This reorientation to relating rather than competing is an expression of the feminine principle.

Not only do we need to develop mature emotional and mental fields, but we also need a physical body that knows itself as part of the unified "vehicle," that is, mind, emotions and body. Sometimes when we speak of the ascension process, it sounds as if it resides in a transcendent state rather than as a lived, embodied reality that breathes and expresses consciousness, even though the Self is not limited to the body. The body is an expression of the divine rather than just a bridge to it. As we develop greater trust in the body new possibilities emerge.

> *You have the source of the One within*
> *you as a powerful integrating force.*
> — Rowena Pattee Kryder [5]

Yoga Nidra is one of many ancient traditions that bring understanding to how we can eventually experience our true, unchanging nature that is both within and beyond the body. Richard Miller succinctly lays out seven stages of awareness that lead to the sense of pure, joyful being that exists regardless of outer circumstances and conditions.[6] By fully allowing awareness without judgment, resistance or non-acceptance of these various stages, we open to the divine present in the here and now, present within the body and energy field.

Miller calls upon the ancient yoga teachings for the identification of these stages of awareness, and the first begins with awareness of physical body sensations. In other words, the body is one of the entry points for us to discover pure essence that resides within. The sheaths (Sanskrit for bodies) and stages of Yoga Nidra are as follows:[7]

> Stage 1 — Physical Body — Awareness of sensation

> Stage 2 — Energy Body — Awareness of breath and energy

> Stage 3 — Emotional Body — Awareness of feelings and emotions

> Stage 4 — Body of Intellect — Awareness of thoughts, beliefs and images

> Stage 5 — Body of Joy — Awareness of desire, pleasure and joy

> Stage 6 — Body of Ego-I — Awareness of the witness or Ego-I

> Stage 7 — Natural State — Awareness of changeless Being

The ancient yogis knew that body and breath, breath being divine, were united as one. Rather than judging and denying desires, we can use them so that their more refined qualities become present. As we do so, we allow the desires to be expressed in a more evolved way. For example, enjoying excellent, nourishing food can provide us with vitality and the potential for greater wholeness in our life experience.

Many practices are available that assist us in strengthening all of the systems of the body, allowing this "vehicle" to be a greater expression of light. Yin yoga, for example, uses awareness to create space to meet "what is" without resistance. Stillness settles in the physical body and the mind. Through breathing consciously and letting go of thinking, stillness becomes a portal to the present moment. Without distraction, we become aware of pure being. A vital body and a quiet mind assist us in more fully expressing our divine nature in our daily lives. And, as we experience divinity in our ordinary life, we become like Bodhisattvas, which is a Mahayana Buddhist term meaning an enlightened being that wishes to help alleviate the suffering of others out of compassion. In the Buddhist tradition, that "merit" which has been accumulated through good deeds and thoughts can be dedicated or transferred to the world causing benefit.

Elmer Green's Depiction of Embodied Spirit

Quantum physics and ancient spiritual systems are now coming into agreement that there is one primary form of energy from which everything is constructed. Matter is the densest form of spirit and spirit the subtlest form of matter.

Elmer Green, Ph.D., has created a visual map[8] that symbolically depicts the continuum of spirit and matter that shows how we identify and experience ourselves in the world. Fundamental to this model is the realization that the continuum of consciousness is really one whole that we experience as parts. Just as a magnet may be thought of as the densest expression of the magnetic field, we, as "personality selves," are spiritual substance becoming more material.

Elmer uses the words substance, consciousness and energy interchangeably to represent the continuum of subtle essence or refined energy. Using "substance" to describe the interpenetrating exchange of perceptions and actions shows that everything affects everything else. Elmer is often quoted as saying, "Every change in the physiological state is accompanied by an appropriate change in the mental- emotional state, and correspondingly every mental and emotional state is accompanied by a change in the physiological state." This model delineates that interchange.

Just as in Yoga Nidra, we can bring attention and awareness to physical sensations and elevated unselfish thoughts as a means of changing our state of being and looking through new lenses at the world. Paradoxically, this occurs when we accept everything just as it is.

Dr. Green uses the phrase "Planetary Field of Mind " to refer to immeasurable, infinite potential that includes everything or " all that is and ever can be and even all that isn't and never can be". The Planetary Field of Mind represents the primary energy that constructs or makes up everything else. He says that "becoming enlightened" is to become part of the Planetary Field of Mind.

The states of consciousness diagram visually expresses the evolutionary journey of energy or spirit from the seventh level, the most refined impulse, downward into the first level in which energy becomes dense and manifests as matter. Though we generally self identify first as body, emotions or mental body and experience evolution from this perspective before moving to more enlightened and refined ways of seeing life, our evolution is always inspired by the highest level that descends into the lowest. We have always been divine, and that divinity is now being embodied. As ascension occurs, we have the opportunity to realize our true spiritual nature.

The following diagram given by Dr. Elmer Green depicts the seven layers of consciousness/ substance/ energy.

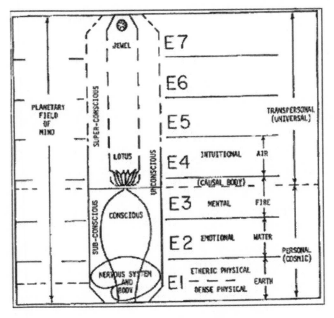

Symbolic interpretation of man's substance and perceptual structure.

The vertical cylinder in the center of the diagram represents a human individual who evolves through various expressions of substance, becoming increasingly refined. In this process, the person becomes infused with spirit and begins to identify with more of the transpersonal qualities. Levels E1 to E7 are the states of consciousness or ground of being that the individual identifies with as "reality" at that phase of evolution. Each of these seven levels is further divided into seven sub levels or gradations. For simplicity, these sublevels are not depicted in this map.

The personal self is made up of physical, emotional, and mental substances, and the inside of the "light bulb" depicts what we normally perceive as reality. Outside of the bulb are the more expanded or non-ordinary realities. The transpersonal self is made up of mental, intuitional, causal and increasingly more rarefied substances.

E1, called etheric physical, includes the dense physical and what energy sensitives and healers call the aura. Elmer Green says that the substances of the etheric are "said by yogis to be unique forms of physical matter, in the same way the electrons and light are unique forms of physical matter." [9]

E2 is the emotional or astral level, which depicts the energy and substance of the astral field. Some of the denser forms of emotions are anger, lust, arrogance, greed; some of the higher emotions are compassion, bliss, mercy, and contentment.

E3 is the mental level of substance. This level ranges from concrete, cognitive thinking that includes tangible, naming-of-things mental activity to higher, more abstract thinking inspired by the realms of intuition.

Elmer Green says that the High Self resides at the stem of the lotus in the diagram — at the very top of Level E3. He also calls the High Self the Doorway to Divinity.

Beginning at level 21 (the highest of the seven sublevels in E3 or the mental plane), a person begins to think of herself as more than a separate physical body and realizes that the High Self or Soul is the more accurate and truthful understanding of a realized self. Here one knows oneself as a soul with a personality.

The two sublevels leading up to this re-identification as soul (19 and 20) are called "causal" because we are connected with infinite possibility living " at cause" rather than just responding to what exists. Knowledge and Will are fused.

The Lotus, appearing at level 22 (the lowest sublevel of E4, the intuitional plane) contains a jewel at its very top. The jewel is the light of divine origination, called the Monad in esoteric literature. Lotus energy comes from above the head through the crown chakra in the silvery thread called the *antahkarana*. This thread is created when a reciprocal "dialogue" between the soul and refined mental thoughts directed toward the greater good of all life occurs.

E4 to E7 levels correspond to transpersonal realms that Elmer says are the planes where Divinity exists within us. At these levels, one identifies Self beyond the personal and experiences a sense of timelessness. One is no longer bounded by the belief in separation.

Although there are levels above and below E1 to E7 levels, they exist in such subtlety they are not included in the diagram.

The horizontal lines differentiate personal and transpersonal planes of awareness, both of which are also aspects of the planetary "field of mind."

Changes in Subtle Body Anatomy

One of the ways in which individual energy and information is exchanged with corresponding collective fields of consciousness is through the chakra system. Chakras are the primary conduits and transducers of energy and vibration, also called *prana* or *chi*, from the physical form to the various sheaths (as described in Miller's chart above) and from the sheaths to the form.

We might think of the sheaths as vibrational egg shapes layered around the body. The chakras, which will be discussed further in Chapter 13, extend out from the physical body and interpenetrate all of these sheaths, including the physical body. What applies to the individual field of consciousness simultaneously applies to the collective fields — "as above, so below AND as below, so above." What passes through the chakras takes on the subtle qualities or essence of both the internal and external. That is, an individual's thoughts affect the collective mental field, and the same is true for an individual's feelings and emotions as they correspond to the astral or emotional collective field. For example, fostering lofty thoughts creates resonant pathways between the individual mind and the collective mind. We also draw in or attract to ourselves the frequencies of that which we place our attention on and that which has resonance within us. The higher and most refined vibrations help lift lower vibrations. This is how we literally embody divinity. We are interpenetrated by it, and we and we give it form. Adyashanti says:

> "As the opening progresses, the body must readjust. When space opens up, it provides room for the body to re-harmonize and to return to its natural state. During this process some people's bodies experience a real shakedown. This can be quite dramatic because the energy that has been trapped on various levels — physical, mental, emotional and spiritual—is released." [10]

As individuals' throat chakras open, fuller expression and articulation occurs. The heart chakra expresses universal and unconditional love, and the third eye expands clairvoyance. Simultaneously, the internal process of *kundalini* rising up the spine centralizes the core alignment of the energetic body. This core becomes lighted, burning off karma. The rising of the *kundalini* provides integration of internal and external

326

experience. This also allows for the sphere of influence to be more expanded and to have a non-local impact that facilitates the awakening of latent possibilities.

As the central channel becomes more coherent, balanced and integrated, it actually creates a light in the head, which is both a transmitter and receiver of abstract thought. The mind receives lighted consciousness that the brain interprets to the best of its ability. We are constantly offered the opportunity to be inspired or impressed with information and energy of a higher frequency. The more coherent the vehicle of body, emotions and mind, the more enlightened one can become.

Life in the Body
Ruth Eichler

I've known for a long time that part of my journey this life time has been to embody Spirit, to eventually be the Soul-infused personality, to use Assagioli's words. I believe I've spent so many other lifetimes in search of Spirit in transcendent ways and so many lifetimes in which it literally wasn't safe to stay in the body. So the journey to truly live in the body and have Spirit pour through has been a long one. I had to learn that I am infinitely safe in order to stay present in the body. I repeatedly say, "Thank God I've lived this long!"

Mary Inside the Heart
Ruth Eichler

Eckhart Tolle says that body awareness anchors you in the present, a message consistent with the divine feminine — Mary and Sophia and their divine sisters by many other names. The divine resides in the body. I couldn't find that inner stillness for any length of time until I was able to gracefully stay in the body. Perhaps that was one of the reasons the book, The Secret Life of Bees, was so profoundly important. August laid her hand on Lilly's chest and told her to never forget that Mary was inside her heart—embodied. During the Sun-Moon Dance, I felt what seemed like August's hand on my chest for a long period of time saying the same words.

Journey into the Temple
Ruth Eichler

Is the body a temple as we've heard from so many traditions? That message even came from my Methodist upbringing and is present in the mystical Sufi tradition. For so long I didn't fully inhabit the body. Even in my twenties before awakening, I became vaguely aware that my consciousness felt slightly above and outside of my body — present enough to teach in ways that seemed compelling to the students but still not fully home. That semi-dissociation is one of my regrets with my daughters in not being fully present during their growing up years –- even if I never worked more than half-time during their young years. I understand that I didn't know how to do it differently and would have had I known, but nevertheless, I am sorry that I didn't know how and that my being "out" affected us all. It was how I coped with anxiety, fear, emotions and whatever.

Spirit Infusing Matter
Ruth Eichler

While attending Angela Farmer's yoga workshop in Yellow Springs, Ohio, I was reminded that Mary Oliver once crafted these words — "looking into the white fire of a Great Mystery"— into a poem. Through gentle coaching and repeatedly bringing attention to physical parts of the inner body, Angela nourished that white fire of the Mystery. She frequently reminded us students to speak gently with the body's tight or injured places, assuring these places that we would listen carefully and not force them or hurt them again. I've done so much gentle, tender care of inner parts of myself such as the inner child, but I've done much less to care for and to nourish parts of the inner body

When the L5-S1 disc in my back herniated years ago, it catalyzed a major turning point in my life. Long after the injury, the muscles in my hips and lower back continued to constrict in an attempt to protect. Twenty-nine years of bodywork, chiropractic and yoga have helped enormously, but a few muscles continue to need to be coaxed to unknot and loosen.

Sometimes I wonder if I'd remained in my old life if I'd even be able to walk by this time. Yoga especially has befriended my low back. On the last day of the yoga workshop, Victor Von Kooten, Angela's partner, assisted me in an asana by pulling one straight leg to the opposite side of the body in a strong twist. He is so skilled and present that I completely trusted what he was doing, even though my hip inwardly yelped. I began to cry as ancient holdings inside the hips let go. When he asked if I was OK, I groaned, "Yes, it's just a release." A woman behind me then covered me with a blanket as the waves of release continued from the hips down through the legs and out the feet. The white fire of the Great Mystery is working to assist Spirit coming into this body. The integrating of that experience continued in waves over the next three days after returning home. Perhaps for the first time, Spirit infusing matter is less a concept and more of a reality.

Presence

> *You speak as if you are here and the Self is elsewhere. The Self is here, now. You are always It.* — Ramana Maharshi

The conscious embodiment of Spirit requires Presence. Presence means the experience of pure Being. We let go of attachments and preconditions, accept what is, and experience alert awareness. In order to really be present to the moment, we let go of the mind's analyzing, projecting and reminiscing and tune into joy and peace that emanates from our being. As Joseph Campbell so famously said, "Follow your bliss." Our whole self and the world around us become available, and with alert stillness we can live in the "now." Angeles Arrien says that the spiritual warrior is one who "shows up and is fully present." [11] Presence is that experience of the divine within us, the imminence of the Sacred Feminine, which many texts refer to as the Presence of God.

We experience Presence as a state of awareness on several levels simultaneously. On the material level, it is complete attention and deep listening that uses all of the physical senses and the heart. Richard Miller reminds us that when we are in this state that we always know the right response to any given moment.[12] Presence in the subtle realms acts as both context and container for our relationship with ourselves, with the environment, and with others. Spiritual traditions have spoken of an abiding peace, of being at one with a higher aspect of a divine Presence or ourselves. The Sacred Feminine seems to permeate that abiding peace.

Daniel Siegel, neurobiology researcher and author, reminds us of the power of presence as follows:

"When we feel presence in others, we feel the spacious-ness of our being received by them. And when we reside in presence in ourselves, others and indeed the whole world are welcome into our being."[13]

Developing the capacity to be fully present is a requirement of the ascension process; otherwise, we cannot have a direct experience of wholeness and of our intimate interconnected-ness with all of life. Oneness, at best, remains only a concept unless integration of various aspects of the human condition has occurred. In order to be aware of the embodiment of the Divine, we have to have a vehicle (body, emotions and mind) that can hold that awareness as a felt reality.

Various traditions have given us a multitude of practices in accessing this state ranging from breath awareness, presence to the mantra or sound given as the bead is counted, or any practice that eliminates judging and analyzing. Mindfulness meditation also helps us access this place of being in the present moment.

The Dalai Lama repeatedly reminds people that if we want happiness, we must start with happiness. If we begin with suffering, we are more likely to go into a mental response that relates to the past. He calls the future the past, too, because both are in the "past," or are conjured up by something that is not in the moment. The brain can structure thoughts or constructs for both past and future that may simply further activate suffering. The heart or higher consciousness found in heart/mind has the opportunity to respond to the present moment without blinders from the past or future.

> *Patience is quite simple. It means a full
> and open connection to the moment, a
> connection that involves tremendous
> integrity.* — Sharon Salzburg [14]

Really, Really Seeing
Ruth Eichler

Perhaps now I wouldn't cry if I again heard Emily talk to her mother-in-law while both reposed in their life-after-death in the play, Our Town as I did in the seven or so times that I've seen that play. She asked, "Don't they ever really, really see?" She meant that people in ordinary life aren't really present. Truly that line has shaped my life. I longed to stay present enough to really, really to see as Emily implored. Tears of grief fall for all the times I haven't been present. I'm not perfect at this spaciousness and really seeing business. Who knows how many other sun-dazzled snow banks that I've missed or how many times I've missed a precious moment with my husband because I was rushing to something else?

The Present Moment
Ruth Eichler

Part of the Sun/Moon dance is just staying in the present moment. When you spend hours each of four days dancing or walking back and forth from the perimeter of the dance arbor to the pole in the center, you're not exactly going anywhere—just back and forth, back and forth. I was never quite able to capture into words that feeling of inner Being. I've called it humming or warming, but purring may be closer when I'm fully connected to the moment.

The Tin Box
Ruth Eichler

Vic and I once retreated at Shantivanam, my favorite retreat place in Kansas, and carried home a book by Father Ed Hays, the founder and director. Vic began to read a story as I drove down the highway about a couple who kept a tin box of treasures — I think they were photographs. The essence of the story was that after the old couple died, the tin box of treasured moments remained. We both began to cry, so much so that I had to pull off the road until my eyes cleared before I could again drive. Over the years, we've often remarked, "That's one for the tin box." The sun creating a pathway to heaven on Lake Michigan last weekend belongs in my tin box. I wonder how many moments in a lifetime go into the tin box? Presumably if one is really mindful, the box will need to be larger.

Preciousness of Each Moment
Sacred Beloved

"Walk through your day as a child of wonder with eyes open, ears open, all senses open for the next precious moment. At the same time, and even more importantly, be present in the preciousness of each moment, which is the miracle. When you have left your world of physical incarnation, you can say, "Yes, I did really see," unlike Emily in your favorite play, Our Town."

Gaining a Bigger Perspective
Sacred Beloved

"Note the sun on the horizon. This represents the new day dawning in which all things are made new. Pay attention to the preciousness of each moment. Allow a little spring in your step. Refurbish your physical form and stay tuned. Turn your eyes to the cosmos. Stars have exploded and universes have been born and died. In other words, the limited view of a grain of sand on the beach has been expanded to all of the beaches of the world. You gain perspective.

This Day
Sacred Beloved

"On this day be filled with gratitude for being alive and in a healthy body. Celebrate life. Celebrate the precious moments of beauty, of wonder and of joy. The joy you have so long sought is at hand. We smile with you."

Light of Christ
Sacred Beloved

"First feel our love. Inhale the light, for indeed it permeates the very air you breathe. Know the peace that passeth all understanding. Be here until you feel the shift in your heart."

Eyes of Habit and Being Fully Present
Sacred Beloved

"You ask what you do when eyes of habit often see through eyes preoccupied with thoughts. First, receive our love. Allow and feel the silence. Breathe into relaxation and be fully here. About the eyes of habit: be gentle with yourself. Continue to record the moments that dazzle consciousness, which reinforces mindfulness, and set your intentions. We are very happy to assist and are glad that you are calling upon us. You are breaking out of the trance of incarnation, that veil that is blanketed over humanity. Do not despair if you are not fully in the now 100 percent of the time. Again receive our love, allow the silence to expand, and be filled with grace."

The Brain and Consciousness

> "Really powerful thoughts are perceived as powerful because they simultaneously run multiple circuits of emotion and physiology. Thoughts that we would define as neutral are perceived as neutral because they are not stimulating complex circuitry. Paying attention to which array of circuits we are concurrently running provides us with tremendous insight into how our minds are fundamentally wired." – Jill Bolte Taylor [15]

In the past several years, much research has been done in the field of neurobiology, giving us a map to these various states of consciousness and some information about how to attend to various levels of integration. Most agree that the brain (which is not just in the skull but operating throughout the body as neurons fire) affects how the mind perceives and therefore our state of consciousness, but the mind is not limited to the brain or body. Daniel Siegel is one of several prominent researchers of neurobiology, and he outlines and explains nine levels of integration, eight that must precede what he calls the "transpirational" level, the level that we are addressing in this book, a level required for ascension. His dimensions of integration roughly correspond with the levels of consciousness, which we previously addressed and with the Yoga Nidra stages identified by Richard Miller listed above. Although each addresses a different facet of integration, they all point in the direction of developing a "vehicle" that has the capacity to deeply know that we are one with others and with the All.

Daniel Siegel says that the first level of integration requires that we become mindfully aware. Awareness then promotes integration of various dimensions of our being. The mindful brain helps us to develop more self-mastery rather than being governed by past conditioning. The state of mindfulness facilitates greater vitality, even joy, and appreciation of life, liberating us from past patterns. As we approach things from fresh perspectives, we invite integration. The next seven dimensions of integration can occur in any order.

The second level of integration according to Siegel, vertical, involves bringing information encoded in the brain stem and limbic area, normally held in the unconscious, into conscious awareness. Body wisdom is then accessed in the service of greater awareness, creating a greater capacity for choosing the response.

The third level is what Siegel call horizontal. Horizontal integration means that the left and right hemispheres of the brain cooperate so that both sides can be accessed. Jill Bolte Taylor who so beautifully wrote of her experience of recovering from a stroke shares what she learned about these hemispheres:

> "As a result (of my stroke), I have gained a clear delineation of the two very distinct characters cohabiting in my cranium. The two halves of my brain don't just perceive and think in different ways at a neurological level, but they demonstrate very different values based upon the types of information they perceive, and thus exhibit very different personalities." [16]

A stroke happened to be Taylor's pathway to integration of the left and right sides of the brain and to higher consciousness, but of course, there are many other methods that work with right/left hemisphere integration that are beyond the scope of this book.

Memory integration, the fourth level, does not mean that we have to remember everything that ever happened in our lives, but it does mean that unresolved grief and trauma can safely be brought into the light of conscious awareness and processed so that the doors where these memories have been stored can be unsealed. Memories held in the unconscious can be resolved, allowing a greater flow of energy and information within the body/mind.

The fifth level of narrative integration means that we have a sense of our own story and purpose in life rather than just being a passive participant in life whose story and culture and family programmed idea of self. This level of integration requires a witnessing or observing self that can be aware of and process past experiences, be aware of the present moment and to be the author of our own unfolding story.

> *Stories have to be told or they die, and when they die, we can't remember who we are or why we're here.* — August speaking to Lily in *Secret Life of Bees* [17]

The sixth level of state integration allows flexibility in moving from one role, skill or mode of being to another. We don't become over-identified with any way of being and can move to a more global view.

The seventh level, interpersonal integration, means that we retain our differentiated sense of self. At the same time we truly realize that relatedness is essential and necessary for wellbeing. We become aware of the needs of others, and we are able to balance the "me" in the context of "we."

Siegel says that temporal integration, the eighth level, includes embracing both the desire for certainty and the reality of uncertainty. We also develop the capacity to hold both the desire for permanence and the awareness that impermanence is a fact of life. Temporal integration also bridges the wish to live forever and the truth of mortality.

When some level of integration has occurred at these eight levels, then what Siegel has named "transpirational" integration can occur. The coined word literally means to breathe across, and as one "breathes across" physical body sensations, encoded memory, and other bodily processes, one feels a part of and deeply connected with the greater whole. Vertical and horizontal levels of integration are brought into one whole. The illusion of separation dissolves, and we feel connected to a larger reality that transcends space and time. Prior identifications and perceptions of self become irrelevant, and one emerges into a much larger identification with core Self. What might look like self-absorption actually becomes a pathway to a much deeper caring for ourselves, for others and for the world. We truly embody the Golden Rule of doing unto others, as we would have them do unto us — because we are one. Kindness becomes a way of life, and transpirational integration can become part of daily life. [18]

New Neural Pathways
Ruth Eichler

I attended an Imago workshop with Pat Love recently and am fascinated by her research. She correlated brain research with couples and relationships. Novelty is one way to create new brain cells and neural pathways that enhance connection and joy. She also said that brain cells are always looking for higher brain cells to come into resonance with, and higher brain cells could be equated with higher consciousness or as a soul standing ajar. Brain cells that fire together wire together, and if they don't fire together, a pathway doesn't exist. Therefore, if we haven't experienced something like kindness, we won't be able to take it in unless the soul has been ajar and a new pathway has been created. She gave the metaphor of rain on a pile of dirt. The first rain will go in rivulets everywhere, and the next rain will follow the little ruts, and the more the ruts are created, the harder it is for the water go down another path.

While the soul is standing ajar ready to welcome the ecstatic experience, the old brain vigilantly stands guard scanning for danger. I learned in new ways why criticism and blame are so devastating to a relationship and even to the person expressing them because they bring up cortisol levels when the old brain tries to defend. The higher cortisol levels cause a lowering of serotonin, so anxiety and depression increase, and a sense of connection decreases.

I was also struck by the information that the part of the brain that deals with loving-kindness controls the part of the brain that deals with anger. It is much easier to focus on loving kindness thoughts as a way to switch out of the anger than it is to try to stop angry thoughts. Thich Nat Hahn proved this truth when he facilitated a walking meditation workshop for Vietnamese people who were in the war and American veterans of the Vietnam War. Walking and thinking thoughts of loving-kindness for three days instead of hashing over grievances brought both sobbing and healing to the surface. Pat Love says that the angrier you get, the angrier you get, so ongoing venting is no help at all, and is actually destructive. One of the things I liked about Pat's workshop was the hope and promise for creating that which we long for.

ENDNOTES
Chapter 11: Embodiment

1. Adyashanti, *The Impact of Awakening,* (San Jose, CA: Open Gate Publishing, 2000, p. 64).

2. Ibid., p. 71.

3. Ibid.

4. Joseph Rael, *Being & Vibration*, (Tulsa, OK: Council Oak Books, 1993, p. 60).

5. Rowena Pattee Kryder, *Co-Creation Code Deck.*

6. Richard Miller, *Yoga Nidra: A Meditative Practice for Deep Relaxation and Healing*, (Boulder: Sounds True, 2010).

7. Ibid., p. 38.

8. Elmer Green, *The Ozawkie Book of the Dead, Part I,* (Los Angeles: The Philosophical Research Society, 2001, p. 43).

9. Ibid., p. 46.

10. Adyashanti, *The Impact of Awakening,* (San Jose, CA: Open Gate Publishing, 2000, p. 65-66).

11. Angeles Arrien, *The Four-Fold Way*, (San Francisco: Harper, 1993).

12. Richard Miller speaks about this in his iRest/Yoga Nidra trainings and uses this phrase in his audio CD's. See www. iRest.us.

13. Daniel Siegel, *The Mindful Brain*, (W. W. Norton and Company, 2007, p. 161).

14. Sharon Salsburg, *A Heart As Wide As the World* , (Shambhala, 1999).

15. Jill Bolte Taylor, *My Stroke of Insight* (NY: Penguin Group, 2006, p. 156).

16. Ibid., p.133.

17. Sue Monk Kidd, *The Secret Life of Bees,* (NY: Viking Penguin, 2002, p. 107).

18. The nine states of integration have been taken from Daniel Siegel's Audio Learning Course, *The Neurobiology of We: How Relationships, the Mind, and the Brain Interact to Shape Who We Are* produced by Sounds True, 2008, Track 6 of CD #6 and Tracks 2 & 7 of CD #7.

Chapter 12
The Will

The next urgent task of each of us as humanitarians and world servers is to put more will in our endeavors. — Roberto Assagioli [1]

What Is "The Will"?

Intimately connected with the Self and higher consciousness, the Will is a central force within us that is the key to true personal power and freedom. We are capitalizing the word Will to refer to the aspect of will that comes from the divine realms, differentiating it from the "little will" that the personality self exerts. Consciously cooperating with Higher Worlds, the Will brings spirit into matter with an ever-present light.

The Will provides a call to the "little self," a higher message that transcends the whims of the personality. We might call these messages "divine marching orders." The Will also gives us the power to answer with a sacred "yes" to that higher call. Elmer and Alyce Green, pioneers of biofeedback and consciousness research, once called the Will a meta-force, true intentionality or the ability to freely choose without being manipulated by external forces, including advertising or beliefs held by the collective.[2] Whether tuning into the inner stillness of Being or making changes in our lives and environment, we experience the power to choose with our Will. As we tune in to the rhythms of Universal Life, we willingly participate.

> *Will is a power, which initiates, directs and orients. Its highest expression is total surrender to Cosmic Will, the identification with the rhythm of the universe.* — Roberto Assagioli [3]

Sri Aurobindo, a yogi, writer and teacher from India, advised:

> "If we surrender our conscious will and allow it to be made one with the will of the Eternal, then and then only shall we attain to a true freedom. Living in the divine liberty, we shall no longer cling to this shackled, so-called free will, a puppet freedom, ignorant, illusory, relative, bound to the air of its own inadequate vital motives and mental figures." [4]

> *It is difficult to imagine discovering a deep sense of "Selfhood" without discovering the Will."* — Molly Young Brown [5]

This Will is quite different from willpower. We all have experienced trying to "strong-arm" ourselves into doing something — the "should's and ought's." Perhaps we have directly or indirectly tried to coerce someone else to bend to our wishes. The personality will can help us to succeed in making decisions and accomplishing goals that meet our personal needs and wishes, but the flavor is much different from having that higher force move through us. Ultimately we release our identification with the small self and identify with the Will as an expression of living Truth.

Willpower can be the forceful mind opening the bud impatiently, whereas, in time, you would be able to spread from inside out. — Victor van Kooten, [6]

In his beautiful chapter on the will, Piero Ferrucci [7] also gives an example that differentiates the will of the personality self from that of the higher Will. He suggests that if you are in a rowboat in the middle of a lake, it takes lots of muscle power to keep the boat moving and to get it back to the shore. Little will is like that — lots of effort and often struggle. Even if we achieve success, we may become worn out and stressed. As anyone knows who has tried to begin a diet or an exercise program "next Monday," willpower often flags after a certain period of time. Working only from the point of view of the "little will," we identify with action and effort. We often experience anguish, depression, resentment, and confusion if we fail at what we have tried to achieve or if Will seems elusive to us so that we never get around to doing what we desire.

Ferrucci reminds us that if we are in a sailboat rather than a rowboat, the wind, waves, currents and sail make the task of getting the boat to shore much easier. We can pray that whatever we are called to do will *feel* effortless and joyful, regardless of the amount of work involved. When we express the Will, we align with the decision, one that seems to easily flow through us. What a difference that makes!

The real function of the Will is to direct, not to impose. — Piero Ferrucci, [8]

Assagioli, who brought Psychosynthesis forward to the psychological community in the twentieth century until his death in 1974, articulated a continuum of ways in which the Will expresses between our personal self and the transpersonal. There are three kinds of will: personal, transpersonal and Universal.

Personal Will

Perhaps more than any other factor, the Will is central to the ascension process. First the Will begins to make itself known, even if only vaguely, as an integrating factor for the personality. We have to have a sturdy personality self before that little self can be transcended. The personal will can be utilized in various ways. It is used to develop a healthy individual ego, strengthen the awareness of an observing "I," and to assist in the integration of body, emotions and mind. Or, it can create disharmony and stress when distorted or misused. The personal will often becomes attached or identified with some aspect of the personality and distracted from the higher will. It can also assist us in our spiritual evolution by looking to higher guidance. The personal will can help or hinder.

Jean Guenther, a Psychosynthesis therapist, speaks about her own journey in understanding the will:

> "In my early life I sometimes confused my will with my many passionate desires, which I imagined as a herd of wild horses. In time I realized my will is more like the horse whisperer, the skillful trainer and rider who befriends, collaborates with, and liberates the best of what is possible in each horse, balancing bridled activities with time in nature to run free. — Jean Guenther [9]

We hold the paradox that the divine is inherent in humanity, and that opportunities are required in order for us to become skillful in living a life guided by Will. The heart holds this paradox and provides the stability to begin to incorporate the impulses of the Will. As we begin to become aware of the Will, that meta-force helps to bring integration and harmony to the individual self. Millions of people have been drawn to various practices to "grow the little self" into a more mature human being, to open and stabilize the chakra system, to develop greater mastery of the emotions, and to practice right relationship. As we have success in doing this, we gradually align with the deepest and most creative directions within us.

> *The realization of the self, or more exactly of being a self whose most intrinsic function is that of willing gives a sense of freedom, of power, of mastery, which is profoundly joyous.* — Roberto Assagioli [10]

Transpersonal Will

At the transpersonal level, the Soul or High Self is an inner source of wisdom and guidance imbued with Will. The more we express and live the higher call of the Will, the more we will be concerned about the welfare of others and the whole rather than just our own concerns and desires. We have moved beyond the personality self into the transpersonal that interfaces between individuality and universality. The personality and soul begin to integrate. Assagioli said the personality becomes "soul-infused." Will from this level lifts us from "either/or" to the inclusive perspective of "both/and." It moves us beyond "we and they" to "we are in this together." We open to Mystery and begin to express from a higher level of consciousness, even though we may not, at a personal level, always understand the direction we are being prompted to move.

*The Divine Will is not an alien power
or presence. It is intimate to us and we
ourselves are part of it: for it is our own
highest Self that possesses and supports
it.* — Sri Aurobindo [11]

Universal Will

So far we have been speaking of the Will as it is individually
expressed, for even the transpersonal is related to a particular
human being, albeit one who is now tuned to a greater Reality.
As we progress through levels of consciousness, the Will not
only continues to assist in personal evolution but also begins to
become more aware of a Universal Will. Universal Will is the
Great Creative Force, sometimes called the Will of God, The
Great Mystery, or Great Spirit.

Gradually, we bring our intuition, understanding and cooperation to receive the Universal Will and to surrender to it. Our
collective challenge is to know how to be quiescent enough to
realign, to re-calibrate, and to respond so that we can sustain,
hold steady and not be bowled over by the intensity of the light
from Universal Will. Like walking out of a movie theatre on a
bright, sunny afternoon, we might at first cringe. If, however,
we can awaken into the light, the brightness doesn't bother as
much, and we can collectively lean into it as an opportunity.

*Your free will is not born of hesita-
tion, but of irresistible awareness of
truth.* — Rowena Pattee Kryder [12]

Eventually at higher levels of awareness, or what we called
the "third initiation" in chapter 4, one becomes more and more
identified with the transcendent Reality even while retain-
ing unique individuality. The concerns at this level expand
far beyond the personal and become a group impulse. These

higher, more refined states are what are being made available to everyone at this time. As more of humanity moves to the third initiation, we become agents for the higher Will, co-creating with the Divine. The Will of God freely flows through human beings who are now working at a causal level, far beyond the mental level.

Group initiation is possible because of the uniting of wills at high levels, the unity of all who wish to serve humanity. We are moving into a greater reality than we have ever known, and even time is no longer considered a constraint because we have moved into a different dimension. Like the Phoenix, we are consumed in the fire of love and the Higher Will. That will becomes our own, and the prayer "Thy will be done" becomes our reality. Eventually we become absorbed into the greater Will, one with the all.

The Great Invocation, a prayer first recorded in books by Alice Ann Bailey and adapted in 2000 by the Lucis Trust, speaks to the Universal Will and requests that consciousness be brought into the hearts of humanity and the Earth. It is a prayer that speaks to these times of ascension:

The Great Invocation

From the point of Light within the Mind of God

Let light stream forth into human minds. Let light descend on Earth.

From the point of Love within the Heart of God Let love stream forth into human hearts. May the Coming One return to Earth.

From the centre where the Will of God is known Let purpose guide all little human wills— The purpose which the Masters know and serve.

From the centre which we call the human race Let the Plan of Love and Light work out And may it seal the door where evil dwells.

Let Light, and Love, and Power restore the Plan on Earth.

Different Ways in Which the Will Is Expressed

Personal will has three aspects: strong, skillful and good will. All are aspects of the over-arching Will, each of which can be trained in specific and appropriate ways. Generally, each of us has much more of an affinity for one of these aspects of the Will than another, the Will shining through our unique personalities. We can draw upon whichever aspect of will that best fits our particular personality and situation.

Strong Will

Strength is the most familiar aspect of the will, generally perceived as the primary component of the Will. Assagioli says,

> "In the strength of the will lies its power, its impetus, and its energy. In developing the strength of the will, we make sure that a willed act will contain enough intensity, enough 'fire,' to carry out its purpose." [13]

Power is the keyword for the Strong Will. When a person is aligned with the higher aspects of consciousness, the Strong Will shows up in the life as mastery, strength, courage and authority. It carries the qualities of determination, intensity and one-pointedness. Strong Will is neither passive nor intrusive. From this stance we prove to be effective, responsible, competent, capable, just, and fair. However, if this impulse is diverted through a part of the personality that misuses the Strong Will, we find people who are authoritarian, dominating, arrogant, overpowering, controlling and often quite stubborn.

When we develop greater maturity and mastery over this aspect of will, abuse and misuse transform into empowerment. Strength is then used for the highest good — not only of the individual — but also for all. Yet, power is only one aspect of the Will.

Skillful Will

Wisdom is the keyword for the Skillful Will, for the right use of discernment, understanding, and intelligence often get far better results with greater economy of energy than forcefully and directly accomplishing desires and goals. Effective strategies require that we have some understanding of our psychological world so that we can efficiently create inner and outer change. Assagioli said that an understanding of and ability to access the psychological elements of desire, sensation, feeling/emotion, thought, imagination, and intuition greatly enhance our ability to use the Skillful Will. [14]

> *The skillful aspect of the will consists of the ability to obtain desired results with the least possible expenditure of energy.*
> — Roberto Assagioli [15]

The Skillful Will brings us inspiration to bring about what we desire in a way that feels effortless. However, the misuse of Skillful Will just to meet one's own needs at the expense of others involves manipulation, behind-the-scenes scheming, cynicism, and at times cruel betrayals.

Good Will

The keyword for Good Will is love. It is the compassionate heart of the personal will. We live in a relational world, and the good will is essential in order to move beyond conflict into harmony and wellbeing, without which ascension cannot occur. As we learn to express unconditional love, we become more genuinely affectionate, loving, sensitive to the needs of others, empathic, peaceful, caring, accepting of ourselves and others, appreciative, and compassionate — the juice required for all relationships to flourish. We pay attention to what has heart and meaning.

> *It is necessary, both for the general welfare and for our own, that our will be good as well as strong and skillful.*
> — Roberto Assagioli [16]

When the good will becomes distorted, one can become codependent, self-pitying and too passive. Or, a person might express this less evolved aspect of love by becoming possessive, jealous and blind to the realities of what "is." Good Will ranges on a continuum of these kinds of distortions to the kind of love expressed by the Divine Mother.

Angeles Arrien articulates what it means to be a Warrior, one of the four archetypes she so beautifully writes of in *The Four-Fold Way: Walking the Paths of the Warrior, Teacher, Healer and Visionary* and in her teaching and retreats. The way of the Warrior incorporates all of the three above aspects of the will — strong, skillful and good. She says that when you are a Warrior:

Your "yes's" mean "yes" and your "no's" mean "no."

You say what you really mean.

You truly do what you say.

You are able to be firm yet yielding.

You bring your full presence to any situation; you "show up."

You are able to "look again" and to respect another.

You express your leadership skills in an honorable way.

You are aware of any of the shadow aspects of warrior and choose a higher path.

You are able to center and be in your own Will.

Transpersonal Will

Vivian King, a beloved Psychosynthesis teacher, called the Transpersonal Will the Joyful Will, and certainly joy can emanate from the Soul when the will is coming from that place. Soul is a life force animating the personality self, which includes body, emotions, and mind. When our personal will is strong, good, and skillful, and when it is in alignment with the Transpersonal Self or the good of the whole, then one naturally and effortlessly experiences joy. We are fulfilling our purpose, we find meaning in our actions and life, harmony exists between sensations, emotions, and thought, and we are connected to all those around us — to the whole.

> *Just as there is a personal will, so there is a Transpersonal Will, which is an expression of the Transpersonal Self and operates from the super-conscious levels of the psyche. It is its action, which is felt by the personal self, or "I," as a "pull" or "call.* — Roberto Assagioli [17]

353

Aziza Scott, a Sufi teacher and retreat leader, once said that we could experience joy and sorrow simultaneously. This paradox is explained because as the Transpersonal Will moves through the personality self with joy, the human being may at the same time experience painful emotions from life experiences. The Transpersonal Will does not obliterate the emotions of the little self, but it brings a different tone and perspective.

In *The Act of Will*, Assagioli retells an old story that illustrates different perspectives ranging from the mundane to the Transpersonal:

> "When a medieval cathedral was being built and three stone-cutters were asked in turn, 'What are you doing?' the first replied in an angry tone, 'As you can see, I am cutting stone.' The second answered, 'I am earning a life for myself and my family.' But the third said joyously, 'I am building a great cathedral!' All were doing exactly the same thing, but while the first had a sense of futility because of the dull and humble nature of his work, and the second found a small personal purpose in it, the third saw the real purpose of the stone cutting. He realized that without it the cathedral could not be built, and he was infused with the *joy* of his partnership in a meaningful goal." [18]

Alice Ann Bailey says that some know how to distribute good will but do not know how to use their will for good. Good Will means that one-pointed intention using the Will as a strong force of love. Now is the time when a shift is possible, and Will to good is essential in the ascension process and is also associated with the Sacred Feminine.

> *I emanated upon thee a force of love so that thou may be fashioned according to my glance.* — Qur'an

Energetic "Anatomy" of The Will

> *We are building the palace for the king, wherein the king must live.* — Hazrat Inayat Khan

Though entire books could be and have been written about each aspect of the energetic "anatomy" of the Will, we will only briefly touch on a few key aspects.

Antahkarana

Antahkarana is a Sanskrit word meaning "rainbow bridge" and is described as a thread or cord of consciousness and spiritual light that is developed over many lifetimes. This energetic connection is made by the interplay and dialogue between the Soul and the personality self and becomes the main conduit between the various levels of consciousness. The rainbow bridge is made up of rays or colors of various streams of energy that carry the impulse of various lifetimes. The Soul in its most refined form — sometimes called the Solar Angel — waits for our personal invitation or invocation before it enters our consciousness. Perhaps, like the chrysalis that is programmed to become a butterfly, we both yearn for the awakening and liberation and also may be concerned that the familiar is soon to end. Consciously meditating on the soul and eventually identifying as the soul, especially with the use of breath and visualization, helps to intentionally create the rainbow bridge.

Seed thoughts and questions originating from the personality can be projected into the *antahkarana* threads in meditation and returned as blessings and inspirations to the waiting mind and then interpreted by the brain. Thus, practice and desire on the part of the individual can invoke this relationship between personality and Soul, but only the higher spiritual vibrations can energize and vitalize this conduit. The *antahkarana* helps pave the way for readiness to identify as a soul rather than to identify as the personality self.

Some say that Jacob's ladder, a dream reported in both the biblical Old Testament Genesis and New Testament John, actually portrays the *antahkarana* — the bridge between heaven and earth. In Jacob's dream, angels of God ascend and descend on this ladder.

This rainbow bridge becomes a conduit for higher inspiration to enter through the crown chakra into the head. This soul light is reflected through the eyes and is likely the halo seen in artists' depictions of saints and holy beings such as Jesus.

The light moves from the higher mind into the brain, which is the *antahkarana's* recording agent. This stream of light then descends into the heart, one of the places where the *ida* and *pingala* meet, those solar and lunar energetic channels described earlier in the Sacred Feminine chapter. The *antahkarana* becomes an internal and external impulse for integration and coordination and leads to greater integration of the personality. The personality self then becomes "soul infused," thus allowing the Soul to be able to use the vehicle of the personality in a more integrated way. When integrated, the three aspects of will — love, power and wisdom — become available as needed.

As we strive to develop a relationship with the Soul, the light of the Soul creates awareness of our immanent and transcendent divinity. Noticing what creates bliss and makes our heart sing provides a clue as to what the Soul is revealing. When we identify trends or patterns that keep arising in our lives, both challenges and high points, we often find that the Soul is hinting at a focus for our attention.

During the process of developing the *antahkarana*, an "Earth Thread" is also developed which extends from the Soul to the core of the earth. The Will serves as a lightening rod that conducts the higher energies through the body to the ground, safely and constructively. This thread or energetic stream helps build a rainbow bridge with the entire planet and a connection with all that is.

The Shushumna

This Sanskrit word can be translated as "very kind and gracious" and also refers to a joyful mind. In practice, the *shushumna* is a stream of living energy that rises from the root chakra to the crown — thus an internal *antahkarana* — alongside the spine. It is also called the "central channel," and as it becomes resonant and energized, it coheres whatever is in the field, including thoughts and feelings. This is especially valuable with mental thought, as it brings greater clarity. The emotions also become less confusing and chaotic. All of the systems related to the physical body — organs, arteries and veins, major nerves, meridians, chakras — all energetically flow up and down this central channel. As we consciously breathe and visualize the *shushumna*, *prana* or vital energy is exchanged in all of those systems, bringing greater health, vitality, and maturity.

This energetic central channel also helps provide enough coherence and stability in order for the higher realms of light to be embodied. Love and light must be embodied before it is safe for the higher Will to be utilized by the personality self. Love and light qualify the personality and mental understanding. Only then can we implement the Will without misuse of power.

Kundalini energy

Kundalini, another Sanskrit word, is that energy that lies dormant at the base of the spine until it is activated and channeled upward through the chakras, accelerating our spiritual evolution. The root chakra responds to the development of our will, which can be seen as the directed, fundamental intentions inherent in our actions. When that will becomes aligned with the will of Soul, the *kundalini* energy is awakened and begins to rise through the subtle energy centers of the chakras. Aligning with our spiritual will leads to the transmutation of the serpent energy into a greater expression of love, intelligence and compassion.

The kundalini energies rise crisscrossing the spine, looking just like the caduceus symbol used by the medical profession. Ancient spiritual traditions call these two energies *ida* and *pingala* and say that they are masculine and feminine energies. The union or balancing of *ida* and *pingala* has been called the inner marriage. It is the wedding of sun and moon, night and day, masculine and feminine, and it implies a sacred union within all aspects of one's self.

If the energy of the *kundalini* is aroused prematurely, many physical, mental and emotional aberrations can arise. And the lower will also would be expressed in harmful ways.

How Do We Cultivate the Will?

In his seminal book, Assaagioli guides us in how to develop the Will. He says:

> "The experience of the will constitutes both a firm foundation and a strong incentive for starting the exacting but most rewarding task of its training. It occurs in three phases: the first is the recognition that the will exists;

the second concerns the realization of *having a will*. The third phase of the discovery, which renders it complete and effective, is that of *being a will*, which is different from 'having' a will." [19]

Phase 1 of Cultivating the Will: The Will Exists

The fullest realization of the personal will is not about doing but rather about our very being. Just being alive, personal will exists within us, even if we are initially oblivious to it. The Sacred Feminine has been immanent within us all along, and the power of the will is fundamentally rooted in being. The use of the personal will begins here. Tom Yeomans, another loved Psychosynthesis teacher, says that including Being as a stage in expressing the Will allows meditation and centering practices to be a means of developing and strengthening the will, for they in essence intensify being, essential for the eventual conscious use of will with integrity.

Through an act of will, we can bring presence to this state of pure being, often experienced as a deep, stable peace, joy and equanimity in the heart. The only action required is bringing attention to that which already exists, and gradually we become aware of the will, although we might not call it by that name. Gradually we discover that will has been hidden below the surface of consciousness. Sustained attention over time leads to intention, which would involve a more active expression of the will through doing, discussed below in "I have a will." Thus the will is awakened or aroused from within, not just built up.

> *Rather than breath controlled by effort, ride the breath, like a kite on the wind— dependent on each change in total awareness, non-doing.* —Victor van Kooten [20]

In this process of learning that the will exists, we become aware that our attitude matters. We soften to receive the breath; we soften to hear the deeper messages from the will. An attitude of gratitude can open us to new revelations of the Spirit and our own inner being. We let go of resistance and come to accept what is. An opening occurs, and we begin to embody wisdom, freeing us from fear, doubt and insecurity. We become receptive to the Higher Will.

> *Basically the Universe says it all in only one word: AUM. It is up to us to sit and listen to hear all the messages we need to know from this one vibration.*
> — Victor Van Kooten [21]

> *All harm and sorrow are my own doing. False perception of illusionary appearance is ignorance in my mind. When illusion dissolves, undeluded wisdom is simply present.* — Dilgo Khyentse [22]

Phase 2 of Cultivating the Will: I Have a Will

The second part of Roberto Assagioli's book, *The Act of Will,* contains six chapters on the stages of Willing, all of which are applicable to knowing that "I have a will." The stages he outlines are: 1) intention, 2) deliberation, 3) choice, 4) affirmation, 5) planning and 6) execution of action.

1) Intention/Purpose

The personal will can be pulled in different directions from both the inner and outer worlds, which can disconnect it from the higher impulses. Therefore, the central aspect of working with the will is first knowing what our purpose or goal is and being conscious of what we will do. Is it for a higher good

— for others, the planet, or us? Without an awareness of our intentions, life lacks meaning and direction. We ask ourselves what our present purpose is, whether that is just for one experience, an entire day or for a much longer cycle of life.

We can create an intention for any practice whether a session of yoga or the creation of any project. Intention is the first step in manifestation of anything. We generally receive what we intend, although this can be mitigated by conflicting unconscious forces within us. For example, if we are afraid of being in a relationship at the same time we are sending out an intention for a relationship, the will is divided, and generally the unconscious, personality will wins.

> *Without intention, the concept of free will and creativity, central to the experience of being human, would reduce us all to purposeless automatons.* — Dean Radin

Dean Radin, a senior scientist at the Institute of Noetic Sciences, reports two "willed intention" experiments conducted by IONS. One of the experiments involved a double blind, randomized, placebo-controlled protocol to see if chocolate that had been exposed to positive intentions from experienced meditators improved mood more than unexposed chocolate. Each person ate one-half ounce of chocolate each day for one week and recorded their mood on a standard questionnaire. By the third day, the average mood in the group receiving chocolate with good intentions had been enhanced significantly — a 67 percent increase — more than those in the control group. The odds of this occurring by chance are 25 to 1. [23] This is just one rather fun experiment pointing to the power of intention. Many other willed intention experiments have also strongly supported this power.

Sometimes the intention is not so explicit, and we can take a more feminine, receptive approach. For example, we could intend that we are open to the highest possibility, as occasionally we don't know what to specifically ask for. For example, when Lesley is working as a healer, she doesn't try to design the outcome but rather remains open to what is coming from that person's Soul into consciousness regarding the experience or illness.

Many find that saying a simple prayer in the morning helps set the day. If we asked a thousand people who consciously begin their day with a mundane or sacred intention, they might give a thousand different answers. We can choose prayers from various traditions that have resonance with our hearts to help us set our intentions. They help us to be present with gratitude and awareness of something larger than our own life and remind us to keep open to new ways of seeing and being. We agree to co-participate in an ordinary/non-ordinary life.

In *Enlightened Courage* Dilgo Khyentse says that the purpose of many Buddhists teachings is for us to realize that our thoughts, actions and lives can be directed not only to our own liberation but also to the good of all. When he uses the Sanskrit word, *"bodhicitta,"* he means the mind that strives toward awakening and having compassion for all sentient beings. A few quotations from his book speak of these intentions:

> "May all my virtuous acts bear fruit as others' happiness."

> "Consider that all your virtuous acts of body, speech, and mind are for the whole multitude of beings numerous as the sky is vast. Since beings are countless, the benefit of wishing them well is unlimited."

> "When in a painful event, we gain perspective by opening to others' suffering through saying 'wherever space

pervades there are beings suffering like this. I imagine that their illness is concentrated in my own heart.'"

"Throughout the whole day, I will remember b*odhicitta*."

2) Deliberation/ Priorities

We further invoke the will by deliberating on what our priorities are. Perhaps there are several desired ends, but the limitations inherent in life make it imperative to find what calls us most deeply. We often experience a struggle in the gradual awakening to what is deepest within us and letting go of attachment to what is less so.

Ten on a Ten-point Scale
Ruth Eichler

My Saturn return seems to say, "Are you remembering what is really important?" After September 11 many people commented on getting their real priorities straight. We shouldn't need a September 11 to reinforce this lesson.

A couple of years ago, I attended an Imago training with a magnificent, soul-infused teacher, Hedy Schleifer. I rather proudly told her that I was only putting on my life plate those things that were an eight or above on a ten-point scale. With a radiant and sincere smile, Hedy responded, "I only put ten's, and teaching these workshops is a ten." Hedy had a significant medical crisis a couple of years prior to the "ten" pronouncement. How could I ever again put anything but a ten?

3) Choice/Decision

The Patterns that we choose to have in our lives we must first become. — Greg Braden [24]

363

The will is thus not only strengthened through being, but also through choosing to do those things that align our personal behavior with the spiritual will. Making a firm decision is a critical component of activating the will in our lives. One of the significant steps in the Twelve Steps used in addictions recovery is the third step, "Made a *decision* to turn our will and our lives over to the care of God as we understood Him." In this case the little will of the personality is being surrendered to a Higher Power, but no action in the remaining steps can occur without this decision.

Similarly, Eric Schiffman, a yoga teacher, shares in his yoga workshops five assertions that he says each day about the decisions and choices that will be made that day. He says that this is his small mind talking to Big Mind:

a) Today I will make no decisions by myself.

b) I will make no decision by myself because it's no longer intelligent to do so.

c) Instead, I will make all my decisions in silent counsel with the Infinite.

d) I want to do what you would have me do.

e) What would you have me do?

This is how that light will be brought into the day — in thought and decision. My will yields to the higher Will. Erich advises that we ask what he calls Big Mind or the Infinite even the most mundane questions. By practicing on the smallest decisions, we gain skill in asking that the higher will be imbued into our every waking breath and into every aspect of our daily life. We invoke blessing into the mental field, making it receptive to the impressions coming from the higher and more refined consciousness and bringing it into the heart and then into the daily life.

> *The responsibility is to "Change our attitude and maintain it firmly" through mental choice.* — Dilgo Khyentse [25]

William James, father of modern psychology, once said, "Each of us literally chooses, by his way of attending to things, what sort of universe he shall appear to himself to inhabit."

Many versions of a story about either two wolves or two dogs have appeared in books, movies and Internet sites over the last several decades, and every version speaks to the importance of the choices that we make about our approach to life and how we handle our emotions. In some versions, an indigenous elder speaks, and in others someone else represents the wise one. All variations end with the same message. One popular version follows:

The Two Wolves

An old Cherokee Indian was speaking to his grandson:

> "A fight is going on inside me," he said to the boy. "It is a terrible fight, and it is between two wolves. One is evil — he is anger, envy, sorrow, regret, greed, arrogance, self-pity, guilt, resentment, inferiority, lies, false pride, superiority, and ego.
>
> The other is good — he is joy, peace, love, hope, serenity, humility, kindness, benevolence, empathy, generosity, truth, compassion, and faith. This same fight is going on inside you, and inside every other person, too."
>
> The grandson thought about it for a long minute and then asked his grandfather, "Which wolf will win?"

The old Cherokee simply replied, "The one we feed."

If the will is not used with hard, sometimes uncomfortable choices, Tom Yeomans reminds us that the "Soul remains un-grounded and unrealized, a deep sensitivity cut off from full embodiment and expression." [26] We are often confronted with many challenging choices: How do we respond to wrongdoing? How do we forgive others and ourselves? How do we live a life of meaning? How do we balance our many obligations in the world with the needs of the self? How do we find motivation to follow through when the going gets tough? These, of course, are but a tiny fraction of the choices we must make daily, each choice making a difference.

> *And after your death ... you will begin to see that your life here is almost nothing but the sum total of every choice you have made during every moment of your life. You will begin to realize that every word and every deed affects your life and has also touched thousands of lives.*– Elisabeth Kubler-Ross

Nobility of Spirit
Ruth Eichler

I have been fascinated by Quincy Jones' autobiography simply called "Q", my latest audio feast when commuting. His creative genius and profound musical talents inspire me as does his amazing spirit. But most of all, I am in-spired by how he transcended pain and suffering through his music and how he eventually navigated the waters of fame and fortune to still remember the essence of spirit in himself and in others.

When he was only five and his brother, Lloyd, was three, their mother developed schizophrenia and was hospitalized in a state mental institution. Torn by a swirling mixture of fear, compassion, humiliation and overwhelm, the brothers were plagued by their mother's angry outbursts and inability to express love throughout the next 55 years. They ran wild with gangs on the south side of Chicago while their beloved father worked. Then they endured misery with a hateful stepmother and six more siblings.

When Quincy Jones was only twelve or thirteen, he hung out where the musicians were, and on more than one occasion, he was able to get famous jazz musicians to teach him to play the horn or some other instrument. Quincy would come at 6:00 a.m. before school for a couple of hours of instruction. The musicians had played until four in the morning and yet were charmed enough by this kid to get up at 6:00 a.m. to teach him without pay. What kind of inner spirit would inspire enough sense of self-worth to muster up that kind of chutzpah? Why would many people in the same circumstances succumb to and die from drugs and alcohol? And why do others make a different choice?

I have a notebook called, "Inspirations and Revelations," where I have pasted stories and quotations of people who possess a nobility of spirit. Nobility of spirit remains the option, the choice, though most people do not recognize the choice because of the haze created by victim consciousness.

4) Affirmation

Our beliefs and actions either limit or free us, and our experience of the world is based upon what we choose to affirm. What we affirm creates a greater possibility of receiving that which we have affirmed. Affirmations are most effective when they are stated in first person, present-tense language. "I am peaceful." "I successfully complete my goals for the day." "I live from a place of joy and love." These words, as one of the stages of willing, give dynamic power to what is intended. These affirmations form a synthesis of faith and conviction, a combination of intuition and reason, and they are deeply connected to heart and soul.

Assagioli also used what he called "evocative words" as ways to elicit will in bringing about our desires. For example, we might choose a word such as "patience" or "kindness" or "empowered" as a way to evoke that quality within our being. We feel and experience ourselves as already embodying that quality, and if practiced over time, the quality becomes real within us. We act "as if" until it becomes a natural part of us. Our perception greatly affects our feelings, and our feelings impact our perception.

Visualization can be another powerful tool in the affirmation stage. Assagioli used several symbols or images that help to evoke the will itself such as a flaming torch, lance, scepter, crown, or tower. Feeling into and embodying an image through art or imagination, we can further mobilize our will. We might imagine a mountaintop illuminated by the rising sun, a charioteer holding the reins of three horses, a person at the helm of a boat, or an orchestra conductor conducting. Similar to evocative words, visualizations can also help us embody qualities such as strength or compassion. Many people meditate upon the image of a divine being, absorbing the qualities of that being.

> *In yoga poses, we use the powerful capacity of the mind to visualize and keep this vision until the body actually responds,* — Victor Van Kooten [27]

5) Planning/How To

In this stage, we search out and discover what can facilitate us in this task with the greatest ease and efficiency. Sometimes the planning takes only a moment — pick up the friend's birthday card on the way home from work or put on your coat and boots for a winter walk in the woods. Sometimes planning is an exciting part of creating something. Some of us have pads of paper by the bedside, expecting and receiving inspirations for the planned project in the middle of the night or in the wee hours of the morning. The mind seems to be quite creative during this time when all other distractions are at rest. Some use a method called Treasure Mapping in which images and words are put on a big piece of paper to facilitate visioning — incorporating intention and allowing the plan to emerge and unfold. Others prefer a project planner with goals, objectives and timelines clearly delineated. Many long-range plans unfold over years, such as when to have children, how to move forward in a career, or planning the necessary steps to retirement. In any case, planning the "how to" is a stage of willing.

6) Direction of or Execution of Action/the Doing

And finally, we bring into manifestation what we intended, having navigated the various stages of willing — whether instantaneously or slowly over time. In bringing forth the action, we also skillfully make use of thinking and imagination, perception and intuition, feelings and impulses. We consciously act, having faced obstacles along the way with firmness and intelligence. Hopefully, we are still having a good time with the actions feeling joyful and effortless. And, we can be flexible enough to let go of the outcome or to change plans when the need arises.

Believing is the second power: the first is Willing. The proverbial mountain which Faith moves is nothing in comparison with that which Will can do. — Victor Hugo

Performing acts of courage or doing something we've never done before exercises our will and moves us in new directions.

In her many workshops and books Jean Houston reminds us that at this juncture in history we now have the opportunity with global consciousness and technological interconnection to access practices from many different cultures and traditions around the globe. Many of these traditions have practices that relate to the activation of the will, and these many resources assist us in our journey home.

Phase 3 of Cultivating the Will: I Am a Will

When we have moved beyond "I have a will" to "I am a will," we have progressed to the "Holistic" level of consciousness spoken of in *Spiral Dynamics* or the third initiation. The development of the will can lead us to pure being when practices and strenuous concentration are no longer needed. We experience increased inner peace through voluntary blending with Spirit. Aligning as or with Higher Will is freedom earned because we no longer struggle with the assertions of the little self or ego. Just like the stages in a butterfly's metamorphosis, each stage in our evolution to ascension is necessary. The caterpillar eats voraciously, and then it dissolves in the chrysalis with a new identification. Yet another identification occurs when it emerges from the cocoon and flies.

In many regards, we have returned full circle to Being and "The Will exists," although now the Will is fully awakened and present. We now act as an agent of and are at one with the Higher Will, imbued with unconditional love, wisdom and power.

Choice is not born of looking this way or that, but is born of compelling intrinsic truth that flowers from the soul. Here is the transmutation of rhythms of life.
— Rowena Pattee Kryder [28]

Eventually the knowledge of the Divine takes possession of our consciousness on all its planes and the image of the Divine is formed in our human existence even as the old Vedic Sadhakas did it. For the integral Yoga, this is the most direct and powerful discipline. — Sri Aurobindo [29]

Right Use of Will

Right use of will, no matter which stage is involved, requires unconditional love. Also, the doer does not need to be identified with the action but rather directs it from a place of detachment and being. Right action springs from Being, which is the context for the doing.

Consciously working with our will brings our Soul into our daily lives, enhancing wellbeing, bringing joyful aliveness to our endeavors. We experience freedom through acting responsibly; we become the master of our own ship rather than being tossed by the waves; and we experience purpose and meaning in our lives.

One of the most calming and powerful actions you can do to intervene in a stormy world is to stand up and show your soul. Struggling souls catch light from other souls who are fully lit and willing to show it. — Clarissa Pinkola Estes

The act of will becomes spiritually alive coming from our very being, and we express what Angeles Arrien describes as our "original medicine," as follows:

> "Many indigenous societies believe that we all possess 'original medicine': personal power, duplicated nowhere else on the planet. No two individuals carry the same combination of talents or challenges. ... Not to be 'in our medicine' or bring our power into the world precludes healing from coming to Mother Nature and all her creatures." [30]

Sometimes our "original medicine" is expressed through action, imbued with one's being, and sometimes it is expressed through purposeful non-action and silence. We are guided on how to express the will.

Willing from a Self-Realized place gives us freedom, power and mastery, a profoundly joyous feeling. When the heart is right, the Universe arranges itself to bring us what we most desire because it is aligned with the Higher Will. Positivity and joy create a climate that brings more of the same. Synchronicities abound in the life, bringing delight and wonder as the inner life is mirrored in the outer life. In Angeles Arrien's retreats, she repeats:

> "What shows up at my gate? Three similar, external things mean that I need to pay attention and befriend what is at the gate."

And, Hazrat Inayat Khan, the Sufi mystic, reminds us that we must ask:

> "The heart is the gate of God; as soon as you knock upon it, the answer comes." [31]

The Sacred Feminine and the Will

Because of its one-pointedness and energetic vertical orientation, willing often appears to be masculine in nature. However, the receptive nature of the Sacred Feminine is also inherent in willing, especially from the point of view of just Being and that the will exists immanently. As we live and breathe, consciously participating with the will, it emanates from us, joyfully and lovingly guiding the dance of life.

Part of the training of the will is learning receptivity to impressions that come from higher realms. We are impressed upon with intuitions and inspirations, assisting us in discerning what actions to take. We might say that we invite in the higher will rather than invoking it directly, a subtle difference in tone.

As we learn to embody and express the Higher Will, we experience the sacred, inner marriage of masculine and feminine qualities. The strong, focused masculine images of the will such as the sword can be balanced by love and light. When the right and left hemispheres of the brain are balanced, we embrace subjective, intuitive insight, a feminine quality, and sharp, clear intellectual understanding in understanding and acting upon the Will impulse.

The practice of yoga is one of the many practices that help us embody and express the will in a balanced way, bringing wholeness to our lives. The breath integrates the physical form with the exterior world. As we develop flexibility, strength, balance, core strength, and open the spine and the hips, we cultivate the central energetic channel and ground, bringing heaven and earth together. We can live IN and through the body, not only expressing the will but also being the Will.

After we have created the desire and commitment to move in a particular way throughout the day, we express the will with one-pointedness and yet are very accessible and yielding to other people. A sacred space is created in every relationship so that there is a collaborative exchange that invites the highest outcome possible. These collaborative decisions are not entered into without an agreement to collectively create a particular state of awareness that invites the listening to, honoring of and acting out of what is from the Great Mind or Higher Will.

The most fundamental agreement in group work is to participate in alignment with the highest insight that the collective can hold and bring in together as an act of will. We live unwaveringly from a sense of Self and enter the sacred space within the group with openness to outcome. In this time of change, we often don't clearly know what the outcome will be, but we can know how to hold in that sacred space with integrity and alignment. The group, then, participates in deciding and carrying out what is collectively willed. The saying from the New Testament that "where two or more are gathered together" applies here. Collectively we can more safely receive and act upon the fiery energies of the Higher Will.

> *Ignite others by living your truth.*
> — Rowena Pattee Kryder [32]

Surrender

After we have learned to live from an integrated personality and have mastery over our emotions and mind, we learn that the personality self cannot will itself to become enlightened. It can only surrender to the movement of the Higher Will. Sri Aurobindo says that above and beyond the personality self is the Universal Mother who not only carries but is the Higher Will:

> "From Shakti, the universal Mother, the person can get all his inmost soul needs if only he has a true knowledge of her ways and a true surrender to the divine Will in her." [33]

ENDNOTES
Chapter 12: The Will

1. Excerpt from a lecture by Roberto Assagioli given in Sundial House, Tunbridge Wells, England, August 1967.

2. Roberto Assagioli, *The Act of Will*, (NY: Penguin Books, 1974).

3. Elmer and Alyce Green, *Beyond Biofeedback,* (Knoll Publishing Co., p. 230).

4. Sri Aurobindo, *The Synthesis of Yoga,* (Pondicherry, India: Sri Aurobindo Ashram Trust, 1976, p. 90).

5. Molly Young Brown, *Growing Whole*, (1993, p. 111).

6. Victor van Kooten, *From Inside Out: A Notebook from the Yoga Teachings of Angela and Victor, Book II* (1997-98)

7. Piero Ferrucci, *What We May Be,* (Los Angeles: J.P. Tarcher, Inc., 1982).

8. Ibid., p. 77.

9. Jean Guenther, *Reflections on the Will, Part II*, Vol. 3, (March 2002, p. 59).

10. Roberto Assagioli, *The Act of Will,* (NY: Penguin Books, 1974, p. 201).

11. Sri Aurobindo, *The Synthesis of Yoga*, (Pondicherry, India: Sri Aurobindo Ashram Trust, 1976, p. 90).

12. Rowena Pattee Kryder, *Co-Creation Code Deck*, (Crestone, CO: Golden Point Productions, 2003, p. 32).

13. Roberto Assagioli, *The Act of Will*, (NY: Penguin Books, 1974, p. 35).

14. IBid., p. 49.

15. Ibid., p. 15.

16. Ibid., p. 17.

17. Ibid., p. 113.

18. Ibid., p. 110.

19. Ibid., p. 7.

20. Victor van Kooten, *Inside Out, Living Breath: from the Teachings of Angela and Victor*, (2006).

21. Victor Van Kooten *From Inside Out: A Notebook from the yoga teachings of Angela and Victor, Book II* (1997-98).

22. Dilgo Khyentse, *Enlightened Courage.*

23. Dean Radin, "Intention and Reality, The Ghost in the Machine Returns." *Shift: At the Frontiers of Consciousness*, No. 15, June-August 2007, p 23.

24. Greg Braden, *Awakening to Zero Point.*

25. Dilgo Khyentse, *Enlightened Courage.*

26. From a paper on the will written by Tom Yeomans circulated to his students.

27. Victor Van Kooten, *Inside Out: A Notebook from the yoga teachings of Angela and Victor, Book II* (1997-98).

28. Rowena Pattee Kryder, *Co-Creation Code Deck*, p. 32.

29. Sri Aurobindo, *The Synthesis of Yoga*, p. 310.

30. Angeles Arrien, *The Four-Fold Way*, p. 21-22.

31. Hazrat Inayat Khan, *The Complete Sayings*, #208, p. 24.

32. Rowena Pattee Kryder, *Co-Creation Code Deck*, p. 32.

33. Sri Aurobindo, *The Synthesis of Yoga, p. 206.*

Chapter 13
Sound and Light

Knowledge is love and light and vision.
— Helen Keller

Part 1: Sound

The late Don Campbell, a twentieth century pioneer in bringing sound to the forefront as a means of accelerating wellbeing and accessing higher states of consciousness, has written:

> "To enter into the initiation of sound, vibration and mindfulness is to take a giant step toward consciously knowing the soul. ... Listening, learning, study and practice are important tools. But we need the courage to enter into ourselves with the great respect and mystery that combines the faith of a child, the abandon of a mystic, and the true wisdom of an old shaman." [1]

The power of sound to assist in adjusting to the increased frequency shifts is tremendous, for sound has a powerful affect on our physical, etheric and spiritual bodies.

Finding Our Own Soul Note

> *Each person has his note. It is a fact that each person has his sound, a sound that is akin to his particular evolution. ... The person who has found out the keynote of his own voice has the key to his whole life.*[2] —Hazrat Inayat Khan

As we learn to live more authentic lives, having peeled away layers of persona and dictums vibrating in the collective consciousness, we are able to hear and express that soul note more clearly. Indigenous peoples speak of living our "original medicine," meaning that we harmoniously live from a place of inner integrity and that we share our unique gifts with the world. If we do not play our true notes in the Great Symphony, not only do we suffer, so does the world. In this time of acceleration, the more we penetrate the mystery of sound — including the sound of our own soul — the more we are able to connect with the sound of the Whole. Hazrat Inayat Khan, a Sufi mystic, tells us that our soul was sound before it incarnated, and Rumi the beloved thirteenth-century Persian poet, advises us as follows:

> God picks up the reed-flute world and blows. Each note is a need coming through one of us, a passion, a longing-pain. Remember the lips where the wind-breath originated, and let your note be clear. Don't try to end it. BE Your Note. Sing out loud! — Rumi

Healing with Sound

Every object has its own natural frequency, that is, how fast it vibrates. Each part of our body — every liquid, cell, tissue and organ — has its own natural frequency. Our chakras and auras, while less dense than the physical body, also vibrate with their own unique frequencies. Together these frequencies form our own personal vibratory note.

Sound creates changes within all of these systems as has been demonstrated by the science of cymatics. Dr. Hans Jenny, a Swiss scientist, photographed thousands of images of inorganic matter exposed to sound of varying frequencies. Once exposed to sound waves, the blobs of inanimate material gradually changed form, creating beautiful, animated patterns. When the sounds subsided, the material returned to its original form. His work graphically shows how sound impacts matter, including every aspect of our physical and energetic bodies. The rhythms of our heartbeat, brainwaves and breath can be altered through sound. Even molecular structure can be changed with sound, and sound can create form.

Resonance is one of the factors that facilitates various aspects of ourselves coming into harmony. Resonance is the vibratory rate of an object, and sympathetic resonance occurs when one vibrating object causes another to match its vibration or to vibrate in harmony with it. The sound waves from one have reached out to touch the other. If two guitars face each other and we pluck the string of one, the sound waves from that guitar will cause a similar string on the second guitar to vibrate in resonance. Acoustic resonance means that something vibrates sympathetically with another vibration. If some part of us is not vibrating in its optimum frequency or is in disharmony with other parts, illness may occur. By using harmonious sound frequencies, resonance can bring about health and wellbeing. Jonathan Goldman, one of the modern-day pioneers of sound who teaches around the world says:

> "Let us conceive of the human body as a wonderful orchestra which is playing this marvelous symphony.

When we are in a state of health, the entire orchestra is playing together." [3]

Provided there is a sympathetic resonance with the person requesting healing, sound healers who incorporate knowledge of energy, intuition, intention, and sound can have profound affects on every level of being whether for self or another. Even the planet can be brought into wellbeing if there are enough beings sounding in sympathetic resonance with each other and with unified intentions.

The few examples that follow only hint at the amazing power of sound to heal. Mitchell Gaynor, M.D., author of *The Healing Power of Sound: Recovery from Life-Threatening Illness Using Sound, Voice and Music,* has worked extensively with critically ill patients and achieved remarkable results. Joseph Rael urges us to chant the vowel sounds of our name and/or the body part in need of healing. For example, he says if your hand is broken, you can chant the sound of "ah" for the vowel in hand. Don Campbell who personally experienced the remission of serious lung and bone problems through toning sounds, says:

> "By allowing sound to move into the body through the breath, the life force can activate, vibrate and restore balance within." [4]

Edgar Cayce, who died in 1945, predicted that sound would be the medicine of the future. Although still in its infancy as far as mainstream society and medicine is concerned, sound is becoming more known, and more practitioners are learning to use sound as a healing modality. For several decades, dozens of universities have included Music Therapy as both undergraduate and graduate degree programs. For example, the University of Kansas and Western Michigan University, among others, have offered degrees in music therapy since the 1950's. Others have come on board since. Helen Bonny, a music therapist, founded GIM (Guided Imagery and Music), and dozens of practitioners have been trained in this powerful, safe therapeutic tool. Many sound practices are available from other gifted teachers such as Joseph Rael, Jonathan Goldman, Hazrat Inayat Khan, Don Campbell, Chloe Goodchild, to name just a few.

The ancients and many indigenous peoples have used sound from drumming, chanting, toning, and singing for healing, calming and soothing. Egyptian medical treatises from 2,600 years ago refer to incantations for the curing of many ailments from infertility to insect bites. According to Old Testament reports, David's harp playing eased King Saul's depression. Today sound and music are returning to a wider audience to assist in creating health and wellbeing at all levels of being. It will be exciting to see how extensively sound healing is incorporated into mainstream healing practices in the next few years. Edgar Cayce's prophecy is being realized.

Vowel Sounds

Vowel sounds are of particular importance in both ancient and modern sound practices, for in most traditions, the vowels connect us with divine energies and the sacred names of the gods. In one of his trance states, Edgar Cayce, known as the "sleeping prophet," once said that the ancient Egyptians used different vowel sounds to activate different chakras.

Joseph Rael, who of necessity grew up speaking several languages, was interested in sound and vibration from the time he was a small child. While learning languages, he says:

> "As I vocalized the sounds and meditated on them, I came to the realization that sounds, especially vowel sounds are the vibrations of principal ideas encoded in

the human gene pool. Words made from these sounds will carry with them the principal ideas that are the same, no matter what language a person is speaking." [5]

One of the practices that we have so enjoyed at the EarthSong Peace Chamber involves what we call "vowel singing," inspired by Jeanne White Eagle, who with her husband, John Pehrson, traveled to many of the peace chambers around the world. Vowel singing means just that: singing vowel sounds. Each of us listens to our own heart for the vowel sounds that want to be sung, and we sing them together in community. Each vowel may be sounded on only one pitch or varied pitches, as we create a song that has never been sung before. One of our favorite stories concerns a group of Sound Mystery School students who were vowel singing when a hummingbird appeared above a skylight window. Suddenly, the hummingbird zipped into the open door and hovered inside the roof of the peace chamber until the last note sounded. It then flew out the door, an amazing witness to the power of sound.

> *When you create your own chant with the pure vowel sounds, the sounds will teach you.* — Joseph Rael [6]

Dedication of the EarthSong Peace Chamber
Ruth Eichler

One of the things Joseph Rael does with sound is to have people chant just the vowels of their names. He had all 39 people in our peace chamber chant the vowel sounds of first my name and then Vic's at the dedication. He had explained in his talk his interpretation of those sounds, as he also has done in his books. He says that "ooh" (as in Ruth) means carrying — in other words, I am someone who carries people, which is true. At first hearing that explanation,

I felt a little weighed down. Enough of this carrying! But in the chamber with people chanting in harmony the "ooh" sounds, I heard the sound of angels and the oneness of us all. I am totally supported, both in the visible and invisible worlds. Therefore, the carrying becomes effortless. The entire day flowed in that sense of timelessness and joy.

Toning and Chanting

Many traditions and individuals have used toning and chanting for eons, and the methods and sounds produced vary accordingly. Laurel Elizabeth Keys, who accidentally discovered toning and later published a book, *Toning: The Creative Power of the Voice* in 1973, described toning as letting the body speak whether that be through groans, screams, or long-held vowel sounds. She reported:

> "Each time that I toned, my body felt exhilarated, alive as it had never felt before; a feeling of wholeness and extreme wellbeing." [7]

Don Campbell, one of her students, defined toning as the conscious elongation of a sound by using the breath and voice. He assures us that these sounds "do not have to be interesting,

383

beautiful, or creatively organized for an audience." He further explains:

> "By sounding one's own body, it is possible to give it a tune-up. Singing is a good way to start, but most songs do not sustain a sound for a long enough time to reap its benefits. To tone for ten to fifteen minutes a day can greatly change the way the mind and body work together." [8]

While toning generally implies expressing some kind of sound with intention, chanting often connotes the singing of sacred words and meanings. The Sufi practice of dhikr repeats sacred messages such as "God is all there is," chanted in Arabic, over and over — usually at least 101 times. In Tibetan tantric chanting, repeating the name of a deity and invoking its presence allows the chanter to embody the energy of that being. In all cases, we go beyond the ordinary, and we become present in the Now. One chants or tones until one IS the sound. Teachers from various traditions suggest chanting or toning for ten or twenty minutes.

Mystery Schools, whether ancient or modern, know that sound can interface between spirit and matter and bring the unconscious into consciousness. We are nourished at all levels by sound. Joseph Rael says:

> "Chanting affects our bodies on a cellular level and it affects all the Earth and plants as well. It clears away blocks so that life energy can flow uninterrupted; it frees stuck energy in the physical world around us. Chanting also brings new energy from the heavens, from the realm of pure ideas, into the biosphere." [9]

Overtones/Harmonics

Many believe that the true power of sound is found in harmonics and that one of the most powerful healing tools available is overtone chant. All sound carries not just one tone but also multiple layers of sound and frequency. Sound vibrates in the form of waves and is measured in hertz (Hz), cycles per second. The lowest frequency in any given sound is called the fundamental, and all of the tones of higher frequency, called partials, are also overtones. For example if the note of C, which has a frequency of 256 Hz, is the lowest note in a particular harmonic, the note of G (392 Hz) is an overtone. Even in the audible range of sound, we generally only hear what we think of as one tone, but in reality there are many. As the universe is created from sound and vibration, harmonics exist everywhere — from electrons to galaxies.

Overtones are important in this discussion because opening to these multi-layered sounds speeds healing and integration at all levels of being. In the film *Requiem for a Faith*, the Tibetan scholar, Dr. Huston Smith, reported that overtones awaken numinous fields. While the fundamental apparently works on the physical body, the overtones affect the subtle, energetic bodies. Overtones can dissolve dissonant energies in the energetic field that are potentially harmful to the physical body.

Mongolian shamans, sometimes called Tuvan singers, have used overtoning in their healing for centuries. Tibetan monks have used overtoning to reach heightened spiritual states, and Australian Aboriginals have used overtoning, not through their voice, but through an instrument called the didgeridoo. Many other instruments can also be used to produce overtones such as Tibetan singing bowls, gongs, monochord and tempura. In recent years, teachers such as Jill Purce and others have taught thousands of people this skill. Much harmonic chanting is now available in audio formats such as those by David Hykes and the Harmonic Choir, Michael Vetter and Jonathan Goldman, among many others. Whether using the human voice or another instrument, the purity of intention carried by the energy of love is crucial. Overtones interface with many levels of consciousness, affecting change.

Jonathan Goldman, author of several books and many CD's of beautiful harmonics, speaks about the power of group sounding, which certainly creates overtones as follows:

> "Sounding in a group can create a morphic field resonance through a unified consciousness. Fields created through group sounding have potentials far greater than we've dreamed. On our own, we can consciously interface and affect our own vibratory levels. In groups, sacred sound can influence not only others and us, but can also adjust the planet to a new level of consciousness" [10]

Manifestation through Intention and Sound

Jonathan Goldman says that virtually anything can be accomplished through vibration and that miracles are possible. In all of his seminars and books he teaches that intention is crucial in working with sound. His formula is as follows:

Frequency + Intent = Healing

Vocalization + Visualization = Manifestation

No doubt we can benefit from beautiful sounds and music even if there is no specific intention, but coupling sounds with intention multiplies the effect. What is the purpose or consciousness behind the sound being created? Is our intention to harm or to heal? Even if we don't have harmful intentions, if we are angry, our sounds will carry the vibration of anger. Hazrat Inayat Khan cautions us:

386

"There is nothing man cannot accomplish by the power of dhikr (a Sufi chanting practice), if only he knows which dhikr, how to use it, and for what purpose. Just as there is creative power in sound, so is there also destructive power, as in the Scriptures the expression 'the blast of the last trumpet' signifies the destructive power of the sound." [11]

When we are aligned with our deepest, spiritual Self, we are in alignment with the Divine Will, which can mitigate lower aspects of ourselves that might be out of balance. When a group aligns with this Higher Note, then even more miracles are possible. Joseph Rael urges us to live from this higher aspect of ourselves:

"If we humans are going to continue to evolve, we now need to understand the vastness of who we are. We need to understand the vastness so that we can become that vastness, so that we can portray it by how we live, and live from that place of high potential. We live as aspects of the Higher mind." [12]

In the Beginning was Sound

The truth is this: Sound is the basis for all that is. Everything comes out of sound, and sound comes out of vibration. Really only one thing exists, and that is the breath of God in a state of movement creating the vibration of matter. [13] —Joseph Rael

In the beginning was the Word or sound, something that many cosmologies around the world hold as true. Hindus believe that when all was dark and quiet, Nada Brahma, the Sound God Creator, uttered the first sound of "Om." From that sound, movement occurred and the world was created. Similarly the Maori people of New Zealand believe that when there was only darkness and water that their Supreme God called Io created light, sky, and earth by speaking words. Hopi Indians revere Spider Woman, the earth goddess, and Tawa, the sun god, who brought inanimate forms to life by singing the song of creation. The Egyptian God Ptah is said to have created the world by his voice. Joseph Rael reports that his Picuris Pueblo people believe that in the beginning there was nothing and that this "nothingness" wanted to know itself. Wah-mah-chi, the Tiwa name for God, then created the world through breath and movement — that is, vibration. Most of the many creation stories hold that sound is core of creation itself — not just the creation of seas, mountains, animals, plants and human beings but also of ongoing creation.

Many cultures use sound as a way of communicating between the worlds. The Balinese use sound as a way of linking the worlds, saying that their king of gods invented the gong to summon other gods. Shamans of almost every tradition have used sonic means of gathering assistance and information from other realms — drums, rattles, the voice, and many other instruments.

Joseph Rael tells us that he has spent his life teaching the truth that sound is incredibly powerful. He goes on to say:

> "The true basis for Universal Intelligence is sound. If you go back to the original sound, it will awaken the archetypal vibrations in you. We are like the top of the carrot. We need to go back down to the root, the very tip. That is where the Circle of Light is." [14]

Sacred Sounds Embedded in Language

In the beginning was sound. Most ancient languages are also created from sacred sounds with embedded, layered meaning. Sanskrit, one of the earliest ancient languages, is probably the oldest living language of the world, one still used today in sacred texts and chants. Vibrations of the primordial sounds are used to positively impact consciousness. Each letter has its own vibration and is an aspect of the Absolute, God or creation. Just chanting the word "Om/Aum" is said to purify the emotions and mind, to relax the body and positively charge the surrounding environment. Mantras are words chanted that have specific effect on the mind and psyche, depending upon the meaning of the sounds or words chanted. They are sounded with the mouth, felt in the heart and sung into action in the life.

Whereas the sound of Om created the universe according to Sanskrit scholars, the letter Yod — point of origin — carries the primal vibration of the universe in the Hebrew alphabet that also comes from antiquity. Each Hebrew letter, a primordial sound, is connected to the creative forces of the universe and is alive, vibrating with the pulse of Divine intention. Each letter is infused with an eternal quality of life and contains hidden meaning. Some Jewish mystics say that the Hebrew alphabet contains a missing twenty-third letter that holds the energy of the feminine and has been prophesied to bring together masculine and feminine energy.

Ancient Egyptians used sophisticated hieroglyphic words to create vibratory fields to elicit whatever they wanted to call forth. Jean Houston, who wrote a beautiful book about Isis and Osiris, says:

> "We know that in the ancient Egyptian temple the human voice was used to summon archetypal realities. It was

389

the instrument par excellence of the priest and the en-
chanter, and there was both great art and great science
in the careful and specific use of tones, each of which
had a particular force." [15]

In each of these ancient languages, plus high Javanese, old
Chinese and many other indigenous ones, meaning was intimately connected with sound. In each of these cultures, the
art and science of using sound vibrations as a powerful force
was highly developed. Mystery schools existed in many places
such as Egypt, Rome, Greece, Tibet, India, and other places
of learning where an esoteric understanding of vibration as a
causative force in the universe was a refined science.

Joseph Rael often speaks in his books and in person about the
language of the land itself, and he encourages us to listen to
that vibration for meaning and life. In so doing, we regain the
original power embedded in the vibration of the land. He further explains:

> "There is a language of the land and it has the vibration
> of those original sounds that created us. When you hear
> the language of the land, you will know that language,
> because all humanity comes from sound. ... Indigenous
> languages that have been used for millennia by people
> living close to the land carry the original vibration of
> the language of the land." [16]

Reclaiming the knowledge of sound and its proper use, known
to the ancients and to mystics down through the ages, is essential to our process of acceleration.

Listening and Silence

When we go into the inner chamber and shut the door to every sound that comes from the life without, then will the voice of God speak to our soul and we will know the keynote of our life. — Hazrat Inayat Khan

Only when you drink from the river of silence shall you indeed sing. — Kahil Gibran

Silence poses a paradox: we need to experience silence, stilling the body and mind, in order to hear the multitude of sounds that exist at all times in a vibratory universe. The inner quiet can alter brain waves, slowing them, making true listening more possible. Joseph Rael frequently speaks about listening to the Infinite Self or the vast Self through everything — trees, birds, the wind blowing, spoken language, breath, the land, objects such as tables and bowls, and silence itself. He says it is the only way to become a "true human."

It is, therefore, simply through listening, and using that listening and paying attention, that one finds the guidance of the Great Mystery along the path of life. — Joseph Rael [17]

We become still and even the orchestra of internal rhythms of heartbeat, respiration, brainwaves and other systems can become known. In his book, *Healing Sounds: The Power of Harmonics*, Jonathan Goldman speaks about five levels of listening: 1) listening to audible sounds allowing ourselves to be a vehicle for sound currents; 2) listening to harmonics that were already present but often not "taken in"; 3) listening for imagination that is often generated by listening to certain kinds of music; 4) listening so that the sound takes one to alternate planes of reality; and 5) listening to silence itself, becoming aware of the inner and outer harmonics. (pp. 82-87)

The Vedic sages differentiated audible sound, which they called "*ahata*" in Sanskrit and inaudible sound, which is called "*anahata*." Sufis call inaudible, mystical sounds "*sawt-e-sarmad*." Generally, only advanced meditation practitioners hear these "inaudible" sounds. However, some people are born with synesthesia and have an innate ability to perceive colors of sound and to hear sounds beyond the usual human range. They intuitively know that everything is vibration. Perhaps as humanity accelerates, more people will experience this gift without spending years sitting on a meditation cushion.

Hazrat Inayat Khan says that the wider our horizon, the more that we are able to hear the music that is the source of all creation, the so-called music of the spheres: He says, "The music of the spheres is heard and enjoyed by those who touch the very depth of their own lives." [18]

Sacred Feminine and Sound

As we have spoken in an earlier chapter, the receptivity found in silence is an aspect of the Sacred Feminine. She is found in the space between the sounds or between the breaths. Joseph Rael says that in chanting, both masculine and feminine energies are involved. He says, "The feminine brings down from higher mind the sustenance of sound; and the male then expresses sound." [19]

The Sounding Mother of All
Ruth Eichler

Lately I have had several experiences with "sounded" containers of one kind or another. What do I mean by "sounded" containers? They have come in different images, so perhaps it is easiest to speak about each one.

Yesterday at the Sufi retreat while chanting words that mean "the veiled or hidden one" and "divine guidance," the image of a giant cave of the heart came in the center of my chest — a warm, velvety blackness illuminated from within. The cave was She, and the walls of the cave began to sound and sing a primordial, beautiful song. The cave is sound. At one point, the aspects of my personality self that sometimes resist came into the cave called by the sound, the warmth, and the sense of being Home. There seemed to be three of these "parts" of myself, and each almost immediately became partially integrated into the cave wall. Their images were still visible, but they were mostly melded into the sounding container, and they too were part of the sound.

When I was with my meditation group (we've been meeting every other Friday morning for 13 years) last week, I had a similar experience, only that time there was a giant container somewhat like a cylinder that held everyone in our group and was much larger than just the group. Angelic beings seemed to incorporate themselves into this container, and once again, the entire container began to sound heavenly sounds. Perhaps this is what is meant by the music of the heavenly spheres.

This morning I was chanting the words meaning "divine expansion" and "all embracing," which seemed to me to mean cosmic consciousness. The embracing quality seems feminine, and everything, everyone, every aspect of Earth was held in this divine embrace. This container, which at first seemed cylindrical, morphed into a giant sphere that held the entire Earth. The entire time, this divine container was sounding beautiful sounds — not like recognizable songs, but beautiful celestial, yet earthy, sounds. I am so grateful and feel so blessed!

Fine Tuning the Instrument
Sacred Beloved

You and we are fine-tuning the instrument, and you are becoming more conscious of the process. Therefore, you are becoming a more precise melody played from a tuned instrument. We are now able to co-create a concert together.

Sound Mystery School
Ruth Eichler

In June of 2002, Joseph Rael came to our peace chamber to dedicate EarthSong. Approximately 40 people came for the series of events that day, including a teaching on sound, language and healing. He spoke of many things, and as usual, his voice took people to another realm. Everyone sat mesmerized listening to him, and somewhere in that talk, he quietly announced, "They have a sound school here, you know." At the break, Kay Ferry ran up to me and excitedly asked, "Did you hear what he said?" Indeed I had and had laughed when he made that statement, for I felt that my next assignment was at my feet. We will never know whether he was playing trickster in handing out that assignment or whether he was simply speaking from a plane in which there is no time and just reporting what he saw. In any case, only four of us heard the message that we had a sound school, which didn't exist at that moment in time. For a time, all four of us convened and imagined Sound Mystery School into being. Two decided to not pursue the actual teaching, and Kay and I then created EarthSong Sound Mystery School, a yearlong program that included six weekends — one for each of the four directions, one a vision quest and one for closing. We were blessed to have so many wonderful people from near and afar who attended these programs for seven years. It would probably still be continuing except that I received my next "assignment" of this book and couldn't devote time to both in addition to my usual work. A community has grown out of these Mystery Schools that nourishes all of us.

Sound School and Divine Assignments
Ruth Eichler

This past weekend, Kay, Shirley, and I slept in the peace chamber sort of like an adult slumber party. I've never spent the night in the peace chamber before, and I was surprised that I slept much better than anticipated. We had decided to do a mini retreat to provide further midwife experience for the emerging EarthSong Sound Mystery School.

Then we spent the day in the cabin writing vision and mission statements and brainstorming goals and curriculum seeds. Kay has dreamed of creating a Sound School for years. She currently works with individuals in private sessions with sound. I took the initial set of six lessons with her several months ago and was intrigued. My father's death and life in general intervened, and I didn't do another round of sessions.

In the beginning, I thought my role was to call together the troops to prepare for the birth. I'm intrigued with sound but have not studied it for years as Kay has. I've been waiting for my next teaching assignment, and knew I wasn't allowed to, nor did I want to, create something to teach just because I've been teaching forever. Here it is.

Synchronicities
Ruth Eichler

Our EarthSong Sound Mystery School is now in utero, and we are her midwives and creators. Actually I don't take much credit at all as creator, because I think we actually are instruments for this unfolding and have huge amounts of help and support.

I'm still learning as we go what a Sound Mystery School is, and yet I feel delighted at the exploration and unfolding. I was thrilled how easily the twelve goals emerged yesterday, and I know that I just need to keep showing up and doing my part, and the rest will emerge as we go. We are all part of a richly hued, multi-colored tapestry, one weaving yet with our individual threads.

The Call of the Drum
Sacred Beloved

You have heard the call of the drum. Yes you will study sound. Certainly sound is a healing tool and you are all reaching into to new level of consciousness, and you are on the forefront of the crest of that wave. And sound is a peacemaking tool. If you break the sound barrier of consciousness, you will see the light and hear the heavenly spheres. As with anything, it is possible to misuse the powers of sound, but those who are emerging into new consciousness through their exploration and learning with sound will be changed beings. You begin to experience the oneness of all and that we are all part of the same vibration echoing throughout the Universe. Yes, my beloved friend, the drum has called you. Some were called long ago, as many of you know. Legions of us are here to assist in this work.

Mystery School Chalice
Sacred Beloved

R: I'd like to hear more about the vastness that I have felt and the effects of the Sound Mystery School.

SB: Yes, we are happy that you answered the call, and you are correct: what you have entered is beyond measure and comprehension at this time. For one thing, you have evoked the container of Mystery School that carries vibrations that have been amplified for thousands of years. The container radiates golden, magnetic energy, and you all experienced this chalice. You are part of a living chalice. In addition, as you already know, this school is associated with the peace/sound chamber that is part of a powerful, vibrating grid of energy, so it is as if you have just plugged into a vast current of electricity. The hollow tube that you experienced throughout the weekend and beyond is partly due to plugging into these two overlapping energy fields. In addition, as you also know, legions of us are here to assist in this work. As the Christ said, where two or more are gathered in my name, there shall I also be. You have been called in part to carry the Christ energetic forward. You were correct in knowing that initiation is to be a significant part of this process for people, for they are each to become more a vessel for the Christos consciousness. Some will go through the initiation of having the personality self or the ego being sublimated to and infused by the High Self/Soul. The fear is temporary, as you know. We lovingly hold your hand. You will not drown as you fall into the stream. Indeed you will breathe easily in the stream of light.

R: Is there anything that I can do to assist in this process?

SB: (Laughter) Just to be willing. We see that you are, Dear Sister, and it is natural for the small self to feel some trembling and holding onto the one standing foot. The Great Mother, whom you love, is greatly happy to hold you in her arms just as she has been seen to hold the Babe in her arms throughout the ages and cultures. We welcome you home, Dear One.

Part 2: Light

And God said, let there be light: and there was light. — Genesis 1:3

Your life is something opaque, not transparent, as long as you look at it in an ordinary human way. But if you hold it up against the light of God's goodness, it shines and turns transparent, radiant and bright. And then you ask yourself in amazement: Is this really my own life I see before me? — Albert Schweitzer [20]

The Pervasiveness of Light

Just as with sound, light in all of its manifestations has intrigued, inspired and mystified human beings since the dawning of time. Almost all scriptures of the world speak of light, and most identify a Supreme Being with light that gifts life on earth with its nourishing potential. Peoples from antiquity throughout every region of the globe honored a Sun God or Goddess at some time: for the Egyptians it was Ra or Re; for the Greeks Apollo; for Hindus Surya; and a goddess named Amaterasu reined in Japan, to name a few. The ancients knew what we know today — that without the light from the sun, there would be no life on earth. In modern times, we might speak of divine light or the light of God.

> *On a cosmic level, we begin to experience the power of the goddess (Nut) to birth the sun as the creation of all life in the universe, a celebration of the joy and pain of the Big Bang.* —Normandi Ellis [21]

How significantly we are impacted by light is reflected in our language, whether we consciously realize it or not. Expressions such as "light hearted," "light touch," "you light up my life," "being enlightened," a "flash of insight," "seeing the light," or "light of the soul shining through the eyes" abound in our speech. We've all had moments when light has touched our very being and "brightened" our spirit such as moments of awe while watching a beautiful sunrise, sunlight sparkling on water, or a radiant rainbow arched across the sky. Some of us might even remember singing with gusto and joy, "This little light of mine — I'm going to let it shine."

> *When we see with the eye of the soul, all is light. We can see the interconnectedness of all the lives that surround us.* — Thich Nhat Hanh

The Science of Light

At the end of his life, Einstein who had spent much of his career trying to understand the nature of light remained with more questions than answers. Scientists will continue to deepen their understanding of light. But, what does all of this science

399

have to do with acceleration at this time? Matter absorbs light, and the two interact causing changes in both. Atoms receiving higher energetic particles of light can get "excited," increasing the energy available and then emitting energy. In this time of acceleration light is not just about consciousness or a metaphor but is also literal within our gross and subtle bodies.

Just as sound waves (i.e., frequency of vibrations) come in a range of speeds, so do waves of light. Light waves appear in a spectrum of frequencies, the frequency depending upon the number of cycles that pass through a point in space during a certain amount of time — usually defined as cycles per second. Just as with sound, light waves are measured in hertz (Hz), a measure of cycles per second. Visible light that can be seen as color ranges from 430 trillion Hz (red) to 750 trillion Hz (violet) per second and represents only a tiny part of the entire spectrum. The full spectrum ranges from 3 billion cycles per second for radio waves to 100 quintillion Hz in gamma rays.

Scientists have shown us that light has a dual nature and is both a wave and a particle. Quantum physicists say that a light wave, which comes in various lengths, "collapses" into a small point. It becomes a tiny discrete particle or packet called a photon, a small bundle of energy that carries electromagnetic radiation. Light, then, is a collection of one or more photons moving through space as electromagnetic waves. The faster the frequency of light, the more energy it contains; the slower the frequency, the less energy it contains. Despite varying degrees of frequency, light travels at the same rate of speed in a vacuum — 186,282 miles per second. David Bohm, a renowned physicist, said that, "All matter is frozen light." What we see as visible light are zillions of photons that are produced by light sources and reflected off objects.

Donna Mitchell Montiek, a teacher of meditation and esoteric studies, says:

> "Photons are the particle nature of light itself. We are light, our molecules and every atom in everything in existence is, at essence, photons. All is light, and in this increased cycle of cosmic light we shall see and feel Light. It is calling forth the truth of our being." [22]

Rudoph Steiner, the Austrian mystic, said that the awakening of consciousness is like "the lighting up of an inner sun" and added that he meant this literally, not just metaphorically. Jacob Liberman, a modern writer on light, says:

> "The distinctions we have between science, spirituality and healthcare are dissolving — and each is being traced back to light. Mystics, scientists and healers agree, on their respective terms, that light holds the secrets of human awakening and transformation." [23]

Body as Receiver and Transmitter of Light

> *The Truth/Light — Force is working through us, and we shall know it, not only as the recipients, channels, and instruments, but by becoming part of it in a supreme uplifted abiding experience.*
> — Sri Aurobindo

In *Light: Medicine of the Future,* Jacob Liberman suggests that, "If our receptivity to certain aspects of vibration experience has been reduced, then the sieve becomes clogged, impeding the flow of energy through the body and preventing the reawakening of the original experience that caused that portion of our being to close down." He goes on to say that our "state of mind determines energy assimilation, which, over time, alters brain circuitry patterns and eventually determines the state of our health." Liberman's experiences with treatments with color is that they rebalance the vibratory rhythms in the body.[24]

All living cells of plants, animals and human beings emit bio-photons, weak electromagnetic waves — also known as light — not observable to the human eye. Sophisticated, sensitive instruments developed by scientific researchers over the last few decades can now measure this light. Fritz-Albert Popp, a German researcher, proved the existence of biophotons in 1974, their origin from DNA and later their coherence or laser-like nature. He also discovered that healthy cells emitted biopho-tons differently from unhealthy cells. In 1996 he founded the International Institute of Biophysics in Neuss, Germany, a net-work of scientists from 13 countries, all involved in biophoton research and the study of coherence systems in biology.

According to the biophoton theory developed by Popp and other researchers, biophoton light is stored in the DNA molecules of cell's nuclei, which constantly absorb and release light. This web of light connects cell organelles, cells, tissues, and organs within the body — a vast communication system and a regula-tor for all life processes.

Popp and other researchers have now discovered through instrumentation that light communication systems are present in the grid of acupuncture points and meridians covering the body and at the chakra locations along the front and back of the spine. The following comes from a review of Marco Bischof's 1995 book, *Biophotons: The Light in Our Cells:*

> "The holographic biophoton field of the brain and the ner-vous system, and maybe even that of the whole organism, may also be the basis of memory and other phenomena of consciousness, as postulated by neurophysiologist

Karl Pribram and others. The consciousness-like coherence properties of the biophoton field ... indicate its possible role as an interface to the non-physical realms of mind, psyche and consciousness." [25]

Some researchers have claimed that biophotons may be associated with the subtle energies variously known as qi, chi, or prana, and some regard them as the light of consciousness. This exciting research provides vast implications in fields ranging from cancer research to holistic medicine to biotechnology to consciousness itself. The research is certainly relevant to our understanding of the acceleration process.

Our Subtle, Energetic Light Bodies

That each of us has a subtle body woven of the fabric of light is no whimsical fantasy or illusory trick of the mind. – Pir Vilayat [26]

Our essential nature is Light. Each unique energy field, including the physical etheric, emotional, mental and causal, is composed of distinct vibrational frequency patterns of light, each increasing in frequency the subtler it is. For example, the causal level vibrates at a higher frequency than the physical. As humanity's consciousness accelerates, more people will be resonating with the higher frequency levels. Throughout history, as at present, some individuals have been able to perceive energy fields with the physical eyes or other senses. Many people have reported perceiving angelic, light beings. This is most likely so because as the vibrational frequency increases for human beings, our "substance" in the form of subtle energies becomes more resonant with the vibrational frequency of the angelic realm.

Human consciousness has the capacity to heal the world and to bring inspired visions into material expression. Just as the halos of saints and enlightened beings that put their attention on transcendent, illuminated states demonstrated a light body of high magnitude, more of humanity can also now live as integrated beings with luminous light bodies, also called holographic or biomagnetic bodies.

The auric field that circulates around the outside of the body is shaped like an egg and is also referred to as the light body. It contains various layers, each increasing in frequency as it moves outward from the body. These embedded layers of light interface mind and matter. Each layer corresponds with universal planes of energy. The energetic bands for an individual correspond with bands that extend into the universal. For example, the emotional field band of the individual corresponds with the universal emotional field or plane of consciousness. Each band within the auric field is ever changing as it exchanges energy and information throughout the entire egg.

This etheric field around the body reflects the overall state of the chakras' health and integration between them. The chakra system conducts energy between internal and external fields and acts as a dynamic dialogue with the external environment. Like a permeable cocoon surrounding our body, the auric egg responds to both — our internal states and the outer world. When the fields that make up the aura's egg are depleted or over- stimulated, illness can occur. In spite of stressful personal situations or environmental demands on our immune system, we can manage the health of our auric field through conscious choices in all aspects of how we live. According to Oriental medicine, we can greatly influence the health of these fields through regulating thoughts and attitudes, paying attention to healthy food choices, breathing fresh air, meditating and exercising, all of which strengthen the integrity of the auric egg. Unhealthy life choices alter the balance of the field, allowing it to become less vital and less able to repulse external influences.

In a state of wellbeing and heightened awareness, we can literally "glow." The greater the inner illumination, the more this radiance can be seen by the naked eyes. This glow is often depicted by artists as halos around the heads of saints and enlightened beings.

Oriental medicine assesses the quality of life by looking at the human being as one whole system with each "part" interacting and influencing the whole. Practitioners of this art do not just look at individual organs like livers, or emotions, or family stress. They look at a unified system.

A Korean Acupuncture Clinic
Lesley Carmack

When I trained in an acupuncture clinic in Seoul, Korea, I was not able, nor was I encouraged to speak or understand the Korean language. Patients arrived with varying concerns, and I was never told the nature of the complaint, whether it was a sprained arm, breast cancer, or a bad dream.

We primarily used pulse diagnosis and subtle energy field observations for diagnosis and needle placement. Pulse diagnosis assesses the rhythms within twelve different pulses that coordinate with energy meridians and body regions. In Oriental medicine, the pitch, tone and volume of the spoken words as well as the pulse readings, color of pigmentation, and changes in facial expression are all "listened to" for diagnostic purposes.

Another common practice used in diagnosis was to show patients colored fabrics and ask them to respond to what they liked and did not find pleasing. Their attraction or aversion to color indicated where blocks might be located in their subtle energy field. After treatment, the color testing might be repeated. The vibrational rhythms are rebalanced after receiving the acupuncture treatment. Healing occurs when we become comfortable with those aspects that previously resistant and disturbed.

One understanding of enlightenment is to bring light to areas that were previously dark. Whether bringing light for personal reasons or for others, we can illuminate and brighten awareness by expanding imagination and creativity. We can provide support for emotional wellbeing and brighten others' awareness; we can give unconditional love and help enhance abstract thinking and reasoning. Reclaiming this ancient view of wholeness is surfacing into our Western culture, consistent with the rising of the Sacred Feminine that also is holistic.

Every energy field affects every other at some level. Each individual's subtle bodies interact with the subtle bodies of larger and larger systems. Our energy fields interact and interpenetrate the energy fields of others, and we also connect with and mutually influence everything from trees to animals to mountains. We are part of one synergistic world — one orchestra with many instruments playing. In 1999, Bill Tiller, a well-known professor of physics at Stanford University, said, "For now, subtle energies can be defined as all those energies beyond those presently acknowledged in physics." He concluded, "Evolution moves on, in spite of prevailing paradigms." [27]

In the intervening years since Dr. Tiller's comment, more people have become aware of the "light body," whether intuitively sensed, seen, or known. The auric field is also known as the light body. The light body is a biomagnetic field that surrounds the physical body and contains information from each organ and bodily tissue within its subtle energy field. This field can now be mapped with the SQUID –Superconducting Quantum Interference Device — an extremely sensitive magnetometer. In her book, *The Subtle Body: An Encyclopedia of Your Energetic Anatomy*, Cyndi Dale reports about the SQUID. [28] The MEG (magnetoencepalograph), another sensitive biomagnetic device, also produces images of magnetic fields produced by the brain. Because such instrumentation is now available, perhaps the study of subtle energy systems will be more easily understood and accepted by more Westerners, eventually becoming part of mainstream approaches to health and wellbeing.

> *The recollection of the heavenly state is so powerful it will transfigure our aura causing it to flower into great beauty. ... Awakening to one's true nature restores wholeness and happiness.* [29]
> — Pir Vilayat

The Illumined Mind, Heart and Soul

Indeed, the Soul itself is light. As light, the Soul is humanity's direct ink with the subtle realms and is a manifestation of a divine life force that literally enlivens all of creation. Alice Ann Bailey, esotericist, reports:

> "The light in the head is no fiction or figment of wishful thinking or of a hallucinated imagination, but is definitely brought about by the function or fusion of the light inherent in substance itself and the light of the soul." [30]

Light is especially important to our spiritual unfolding — both as a means of infusing the personality with Soul light and as a bridge between matter and the subtle realms beyond perception. A soul-infused personality means that the substance of light has infused the subtle bodies and has changed the quality of light within all the subtle forms — emotional, mental and causal bodies. The personality and mind become a "vehicle" for the expression of higher consciousness. This is a gradual process of transformation of the total system, invited by and made possible by the integration of Soul and personality. As an expanded consciousness, we re-identify as the Soul rather than the personality, and we experience the oneness of all life.

In some meditative traditions such as those given by "The Tibetan" who communicated with Alice Ann Bailey, cultivating inner light for the development of spiritual insight first appears as "a light in the head." This light is said to be experienced in three stages: first as diffused light within the head and then as a light that surrounds the head (often seen as a halo). As this light intensifies, it consolidates and becomes an inner, radiant sun. Finally a small disc of dark blue or indigo appears at the center of the sun. [31]

*When the soul does not drink light it
begins to dry up. Loneliness and separation are the results of the soul's lacking
nurturing, so there must be a continuous
process to connect a soul to this flow of
light or love.* — Joseph Rael [32]

Pir Vilayat Inayat Khan poses a profound question that significantly relates to the theme of this book:

"How would the world be different if all of us were to
reclaim our inheritance as members in a 'tribe of light'
who vow to bring enlightenment to all creation?" [33]

In the ancient wisdom traditions, subtle energy light moves into
the three primary colors and when blended through love, will
and activity create actual substance. This subtle substance then
"clothes" the earlier impression of the original, spiritual subtle
light contained within. This contained light is the "consciousness within the form" and is liberated when we realize that
the light within and the light without any form are in essence
the same thing. When this awareness occurs, the light releases
sound, and the original "sound" is allowed expression. Thus,
as has often been stated, "In the beginning was the Word."
When Joseph Campbell said, "The privilege of a lifetime is
being who you are," he may have been referring to the capacity
to "sound forth" this joyful sound of our essential nature.

Many spiritual traditions speak of the light of the heart and use
practices that cultivate and radiate this luminosity. In a carefully
controlled study at the University of Kassel in Witzenhausen,
Germany, Puran Bair, co-founder of the Institute for Applied
Meditation, became a research subject. The experiment involved Bair being in a sealed, dark chamber while imagining
sending light from his heart to someone in need of healing, a

practice he calls Heart Rhythm Meditation. The light emitted was measured by a photomultiplier three feet away which recorded 100,000 photons per second when Bair was meditating with a heart focus, but only 20 photons per second when the meditation stopped. The light emitted during the Heart Rhythm Meditation was two orders of magnitude greater than what is required to be visible. [34]

> *Beauty is not in the face; beauty is a light in the heart.* — Kahlil Gibran

Thoughts and intentions are expressions of light energy that "live" in the subtle energetic realm prior to manifesting in matter. The process of receiving illumined thought, highly refined light, is a descent of energy from the higher mind into the brain, allowing us to know in a new kind of way and to expand our frame of reference. We experience "revelation" from this incoming light, which actually replaces old, energetic thought forms. Sometimes we consciously receive the illumined revelations and sometimes they remain hidden from view but nevertheless impact our life.

Though the physical eyes are conditioned to focus on a small slice of the total spectrum of electromagnetic frequency, our inner senses can perceive beyond the visible in three-dimensional reality. Clairvoyants and shamans have known this since the beginning of time. Many traditions teach that as we become more aware of inner light that we open to greater multidimensional awareness. Pir Vilayat urges us to remember our true home where we are linked to heavenly beings of light when he says:

> "The first step in reclaiming our Divine heritage is to question those conventional conceptions of reality that

close our eyes to the luminosity interlacing all of creation." [35]

I saw myself through the light that things carry in their essence—not through any extraneous light. — Ibn 'Arabi

Near Death Experiences and Light

Many people who have had near death experiences report seeing light so radiant that it illuminates everything. Although specific details of these experiences vary, light is very frequently present. The lives of most people who have had these experiences are profoundly changed.

They report that they know beyond any doubt that an afterlife exists and that love is the essence of the universe. Eben Alexander, M.D., used to believe that these NDE's, as they are called, were a result of hard wiring in the brain. He then slipped into a coma after contracting bacterial meningitis, which is often fatal. In his near death experience, he was taken on the wings of a butterfly to an immense void that was both totally black and brimming with light that emanated from an orb that spoke for an all-loving God. He recounts his experiences in his interesting and popular book, *Proof of Heaven: a Neurosurgeon's Journey into the Afterlife* (2012).

If we have experienced great luminosity through meditation or other practices during our life on earth, we will most likely not be afraid or retreat when encountering such immense light at the time of death or beyond. Many traditions have light practices, whether or not for the purpose of facing the afterlife. Buddhists have special practices just for the purpose of preparing one for the after death journey such as those reported in the ancient text, *The Tibetan Book of the Dead* or Sogyal

Rimpoche's highly regarded book, *The Tibetan Book of Living and Dying* (1992).

Although we don't know what Pir Vilayat experienced at his death in 2004, we can only imagine that his years of meditating upon light in general and his connection with the stars made his journey easier. He reports that throughout his life, he regularly connected with the stars:

> "Closing my eyes, I would reach right out into the lacy-bright nebulae, and seeing my body as a fragment within the vastness of infinitely revolving worlds of light." [36]

Health, Wellbeing, and Light

> *Just contemplating the idea of light during conversation has an instantaneous effect, as it awakens within another his own nature as a being of light.*
> — Pir Vilayat [37]

Although healers perceive and distribute energy in a variety of ways, all are using some form of light. Light profoundly affects the healing process. Light is both the substance and the bridge to the highest Source of wisdom and love, and it is through light itself that the healer receives energetic force and information. The angelic, as higher light beings, assist in healing by helping infuse light into places of imbalance that cause illness. When Lesley prepares for long distance healing sessions, she listens to Gregorian chants or some other kind of inspiring music to help lift her own vibrations to a higher resonance. Individuals exponentially enhance each other, and like finely tuned instruments, one will seek and resonate with the higher vibration.

Every person has a very subtle energetic light signature. Cells emit electromagnetic radiation at different wavelengths of very low frequency. This vibrational information can be used both for diagnosis and eliciting a healing response. When the healer introduces coherent and harmonious vibrational "information" that matches the patient's natural signature, the lower frequencies of the person in need of healing become coherent and balanced. Hands on healing (also called magnetic healing), and radiatory or distant healing, direct and reorient a subtle energy force. Distant healing demonstrates our interconnectedness and that our thoughts feelings and emotions affect the collective planetary field.

> *There is no reality in separation. The planetary etheric body is a Whole, unbroken and continuous.*[38] – Alice Ann Bailey

Some healing practices focus on specific areas such as the immune system or organs, while other practitioners seek to enhance the entire field of the client. In the latter case the healer seeks to refine and quicken the entire aura of the recipient through invoking and awakening the recipient's innate body wisdom and spiritual will.

The use of physical light in healing has a long tradition that has been vastly expanded today by technology. Physicians use full spectrum and bright light therapy for seasonal affective disorders, cold lasers for relief of pain, and UV light therapy for dermatitis and psoriasis. Leonard Wisneski, M.D., reports:

> "Integrative doctors use instrumentation to listen to the bio-orchestra with electrical devices, such as Gas Discharge Visualization instruments, for out-of-tune symphonies and reestablish harmony and cadence using

EM generating devices, such as lasers, to deliver light as electrical magnetic radiation to cells, tissues and organs to reestablish balance." [39]

In his groundbreaking book, *Light: Medicine of the Future* (1990), Jacob Liberman, O.D., Ph.D., reports on the differences in the effects of various forms of artificial lighting. Typically florescent light produces a rather distorted and limited spectrum of light. On the other hand, full spectrum lighting and spending time in the sunshine has been proven to have a positive effect on the body. Liberman also points out that morning light is from the red end of the spectrum and evening light is from the blue end of the spectrum.[40] Sunglasses with yellow or pink tints brighten or stimulate, and blue or brown lenses dull or depress things. Gray colors reduce the wavelengths of light in a more balanced manner.

Exposure to sunlight will produce decreases in resting heart rate, blood pressure, respiratory rate, blood sugar and lactic acid. It also produces increases in energy, strength and tolerance to stress. When children experience both sunlight and full spectrum lighting, they show significant decreases in visual problems, chronic infections, and chronic fatigue.

The Egyptians, Romans, Chinese, Greeks and others used light and color in healing. Eastern healers from China, India, and other Asian countries have used color and light for centuries and continue to do so today, along with many others around the world who have been trained in recent decades in various modalities. Practitioners correlate intuited color, heat, heaviness, and speed and flow of vibrations in the auric fields to determine excess or depletion of chi or vital energy surrounding the patient's layered "bodies." The quality, color and frequency of light influence our brains as well as the subtle energy fields.

The White Tara healing meditation, a Buddhist practice, uses color and mantra. The visualization includes radiating light successively in the colors of white, yellow, red, blue and finally green for stabilization. These lights fill the "bodies" surrounding the person, healing, rejuvenating and cohering the auric field around the body. [41]

Light and color also affect moods and behavior. Christopher Wolfgang Alexander, an architect noted for his theories about design and more than 200 building projects around the world, reports that if given a choice people gravitate to rooms which have light on two sides and avoid the room with light only on one side. The perception of color is the intrinsic property of the eye and brain to process electromagnetic energy. Color frequency and intensity open up pathways into specific brain structures such as the limbic system and cause us to identify light with safety and emotional security.

Whether or not scientifically measured, inner and outer light brings illumination to our body, mind and spirit. Our very health and wellbeing and the acceleration of consciousness are dependent upon light.

Light, Everywhere Light
Ruth Eichler

Clarissa Pinkola Estes says that, "Struggling souls catch light from other souls who are fully lit and willing to show it." In the scientific concept of super-radiance, molecules of water transmit light like super conductors, even bringing discordant energy into coherence. Water molecules imprinted with certain intentions transmit light that reflects those intentions. Like homeopathy, even if none of the actual molecules remain, the frequency remains and works. How fascinating.

415

With our bodies so highly filled with water, we are a perfect medium for transmitting light when activated. Vic and I went to see Father Bede Griffith shortly before he died. Though his body was frail, he was luminescent as if a lamp were glowing from within, shining through his thin, translucent skin. When Pir Vilayat initiated me as a cheraga only a couple of years before his death, he too emanated light.

Light is our divine inheritance. I want to be more conscious of and present to the quantum possibilities of light — of infusing the water I drink and the things I eat with light. I once heard a story about Edgar Cayce eating a steak in a restaurant. In his trance readings, he frequently cautioned against eating meat. When asked, he said that if his consciousness couldn't rise above the vibration of meat, then something was wrong with him.

One of my peak moments occurred many years ago while driving down the Kansas turnpike. I suddenly looked to the right and saw the sun scintillating, dancing, and shimmering on the surface of a small lake. I was so in awe that I had to pull off the side of the road just to watch. Thousands and thousands of dancing particles of light remind me of the light that exists within everything, and that reminds me that I have barely, barely opened to the potential that is ever-present, omnipresent of our divine inheritance.

ENDNOTES
Chapter 13 Sound and Light

1.   Don Campbell, *The Roar of Silence*, (Quest Books, 1989, p. 12-13).

2.   Hazrat Inayat Khan, *The Mysticism of Sound and Music: The Sufi Teaching of Hazrat Inayat Khan, Revised Edition* (Boston: Shambhala, 1996, pp. 41 and 84).

3. Jonathan Goldman, *Healing sounds: The Power of Harmonics*, (Rochester, VT: Healing Arts Press, 2002, p. 13).

4. Don Campbell, *The Roar of Silence*, (Quest Books, 1989, p. 66).

5. Joseph Rael, *Sound: Native Teaching + Visionary Art*, (San Francisco: Council Oak Books, 2009, p. 15).

6. Ibid., p. 16.

7. Laurel Elizabeth Keyes, *Toning: The Creative Power of the Voice*, (Devorss, 1973, p. 12).

8. Don Campbell, *The Roar of Silence*, (Quest Books, 1989, p. 66).

9. Joseph Rael, *Sound: Native Teaching + Visionary Art*, (San Francisco: Council Oak Books, 2009, p. 141).

10. Jonathan Goldman, *Healing sounds: The Power of Harmonics*, (Rochester, VT: HealingArts Press, 2002, p. viii).

11. Hazrat Inayat Khan, *The Mysticism of Sound and Music: The Sufi Teaching of Hazrat Inayat Khan, Revised Edition* (Boston: Shambhala, 1996, p. 20).

12. Joseph Rael, *Sound: Native Teaching + Visionary Art*, (San Francisco: Council Oak Books, p. 180).

13. Ibid., p. 11 & 19.

14. Ibid., p. 11.

15. Jean Houston, *The Passion of Isis and Osiris: a Gateway to Transcendent Love*, (NY: Ballantine/Wellspring, 1995, p. 117).

16. Joseph Rael, *Sound: Native Teaching + Visionary Art*, (San Francisco: Council Oak Books, p. 12).

17. Joseph Rael, *Being and Vibration*, (Tulsa, OK: Council Oak Books, 1993, p. 34).

18. Hazrat Inayat Khan, *The Mysticism of Sound and Music: The Sufi Teaching of Hazrat Inayat Khan, Revised Edition*, (Boston: Shambhala, 1996. p. 20).

19. Joseph Rael, *Being and Vibration*, (Tulsa, OK: Council Oak Books, 1993, p. 121).

20. Albert Schweitzer, Translated By: Reginald H. Fuller, Edited By: Ulrich Neuenschwander, *Reverence for Life*, (Harper & Row, 1969).

21. Normandi Ellis, *Feasts of Light: Celebrations for the Seasons of Life Based on the Egyptian Goddess Mysteries*, (Wheaton, Il: Quest Books, 1999, p. x).

22. Donna Mitchell Montiek, www.blazinglight.net, "The Suns of Humanity."

23. Jacob Liberman, www.jacobliberman.org.

24. Jacob Liberman, *Light: Medicine of the Future: How We Can Use It to Heal Ourselves NOW*, (Rochester, VT: Bear & Company, 1990, p. 177).

25. This review appeared on the website www.transpersonal.de.

26. Pir Vilayat, *Awakening: a Sufi Experience*, (NY: Jeremy Tarcher/Putnam, 1999, p. 100).

27. William Tiller, Ph.D., "Alternative Medicine: Subtle Energies" in the May/June 1999 *Science and Medicine* (vol. 6, no. 3).

28. Cyndi Dale, *The Subtle Body: An Encyclopedia of Your Energetic Anatomy*, (Boulder, CO: Sounds True, 2009, p. 7).

29. Pir Vilayat, *Awakening: a Sufi Experience*, (NY: Jeremy Tarcher/ Putnam, 1999, p. 110).

30. Alice Ann Bailey, *Rays and Initiation*, (p. 143).

31. Alice Ann Bailey, *Ancient Wisdom Teachings*.

32. Joseph Rael, *Sound: Native Teaching + Visionary Art*, (San Francisco: Council Oak Books, p. 27).

33. Pir Vilayat, *Awakening: a Sufi Experience*, (NY: Jeremy Tarcher/ Putnam, 1999, p. 103).

34. Reported at this website: www.appliedmeditation.org.

35. Pir Vilayat, *Awakening: a Sufi Experience*, (NY: Jeremy Tarcher/ Putnam, 1999, p. 100).

36. Ibid., p. 94.

37. Ibid.

38. Alice Ann Bailey, *Esoteric Healing*, p. 645.

39. Leonard Wisneski, MD, and Lucy Anderson, *The Scientific Basis of Integrative Medicine (2nd edition)*, (CRC Press, 2009, p. 306).

40. Jacob Liberman, *Light: Medicine of the Future: How We Can Use It to Heal Ourselves NOW*, (Rochester, VT: Bear & Company, 1990, p. 176).

41. Glenn H. Mullin with Jeff J. Watt, *Female Buddhas: Women of Enlightenment in Tibetan Mystical Art*, p. 102.

Index

I

T

Biographies

Ruth Eichler

Ruth Eichler, M.Ed., MSW, is a psychotherapist in private practice and has developed and facilitated hundreds of groups and programs for personal and spiritual growth throughout the United States, Germany and Russia. A visionary and community builder, she has guided the development of retreat centers and a holistic healing center and formed councils that share leadership through consensus, empowering all who participate.

Ruth has a lifelong passion for finding ways to nurture both depth and zest for life. She integrates insights, skills and wisdom in her life and in her work incorporated from Psychosynthesis, Imago Relationship Therapy, yoga, astrology, Sufism and Native American spirituality. Believing that all of life – cellular to planetary – moves toward wholeness, she has devoted her energies to bring healing, balance and integration for the wellbeing of individuals, groups and Planet Earth.

Her previous book, *Twelve Songs of the Soul,* is an integration of heart-centered astrology with Psychosynthesis.

She lives with her husband in Michigan where they have created a nature sanctuary and retreat, a Peace/Sound chamber for community ceremony and celebration of spirit, and classes leading to healing and wholeness.

www.12-songs.com; www.earthsongpeace.com

439

Lesley Carmack

Lesley Carmack, M.S., offers an integrative, multicultural orientation and esoteric insight to her focus of serving the impulse of emergent possibility of our collective future. She blends concepts and tools from conventional science, metaphysics, transpersonal psychology, ancient wisdom practices, and Vipassana meditation.

Lesley has worked for more than four decades as consultant, group facilitator, bioenergy healer and therapist, integrating diverse traditions and ideologies. She combines her training in counseling psychology, oriental medicine and acupuncture with her clairvoyant abilities to accelerate change and promote healing. Her intuitive and healing work has been validated as effective in documented, scientific research studies.

She has co-authored texts with her husband Jim on group dynamics, problem solving and creative thinking for the government and corporations. She travels internationally, teaching and presenting seminars that promote global, heart-centered awareness.

www.AwakeningHeartMind.com

60736524R00267

Made in the USA
Middletown, DE
03 January 2018